THE

TRUE SYSTEM

OF

RELIGIOUS PHILOSOPHY,

IN

LETTERS TO A MAN OF THE WORLD

DISPOSED TO BELIEVE.

BY

J. E. LE BOYS DES GUAYS,

EDITOR OF "LA NOUVELLE JERUSALEM."

TRANSLATED FROM THE FRENCH,

BY

JOHN MURDOCK.

THIRD EDITION,

REVISED AND CORRECTED BY

GEORGE BUSH,

PROFESSOR OF HEBREW IN THE UNIVERSITY OF NEW YORK.

FIRST AND SECOND SERIES.

BOSTON:

OTIS CLAPP, 23 SCHOOL STREET.

LONDON: J. S. HODSON AND WILLIAM NEWBERY.

1850.

PREFACE

TO THE SECOND EDITION.

The first edition of this work having been exhausted some months since, it has been deemed desirable to issue it in a new and improved form. With this view it has been subjected to a rigid revisal, and now makes its appearance in a style of execution in some degree worthy of its invaluable contents. It would not be easy to point to any single work illustrative of the conjoint philosophy and theology of Swedenborg, more happily adapted to its end. Taking the disturbed but meditative skeptic in the crisis of his mental conflicts, he leads him gently onward, from certain rudimentary principles of belief, through a series of well compacted and consecutive reasonings to the grand conclusions embodied in the faith of the New Church. The evolution of the argument is so skillfully conducted —one step of the demonstration rises so naturally from another— every difficulty proposed is so luminously cleared up—that admission after admission is forced from the doubter, till at length the momentous result is seen to be inevitable—man is immortal; there is a heaven and a hell; he lives as perfect a man after death as before; he dwells in a spiritual body, in a spiritual world; that world is replete with objective scenery suited to the senses which take cognizance of it; his destiny there is the necessary product of his life and character here; and every conclusion reached on the subject by the fairest reason goes to confirm the truth of Revelation.

Considering the profound and abstruse nature of the subjects treated, the work will be seen to be extremely felicitous in the clearness of its expositions, and a certain attractive simplicity in the style relieves the mind from that latent oppression which it sometimes experiences under the continuous influx of new ideas.

It will be seen, in the concluding letter, that a second series is promised, relating mainly to the principles on which the inspired Word is constructed, and by which it is to be interpreted. We are happy to announce, that in the present edition of the work, this series of Letters, as far as published, has been added to the preceding. This may perhaps enhance somewhat the price of the volume, but no reader of the first we presume would willingly dispense with the second. The whole will be found to contain a most able and beautiful expose of the leading disclosures of Swedenborg, relative to the philosophy of the universe and the constitution of the Divine Word.

New York, April 1, 1848. G. B.

CONTENTS.

PART I.

PART II.

LETTERS

TO A MAN OF THE WORLD.

LETTER I.

Like yourself, sir, I have been a prey to that moral malady, that spiritual stupor, which has resulted from the philosophy of the last age. All that you say, therefore, respecting the state of mind you are in, does not surprise me. I know by experience, how painful, how insupportable is doubt. I have experienced all the intellectual phases through which you have passed. In vain we have recourse to the sciences, the arts, or to high philosophy; in vain we throw ourselves into the vortex of business, or give ourselves up to the pleasures of the world; all this will not remove doubts from the mind of a man who is disposed to serious meditation. This state, you say, is very painful: certainly it is, for such doubt, like the vexation mentioned by the poet, incessantly rides behind its victim. Happy, however, are they, who in this age of religious indifference feel the agonies of doubt. The necessity of being relieved from such a state of mind excites them to enquiry: and whoever perseveres in such an enquiry, will be satisfied in the end. Your state is that of a sick man who knows his disease, and feels all its attacks, but who, on that account, can be restored to health. Would you not be more deserving of pity if, like the greater part of your associates, you were in a state of complete indifference? You would then resemble a paralytic who feels no pain, but for whom there is no hope of recovery while this fatal insensibility continues.

You are disposed to become a believer, without however, as you add, being compelled to renounce your understanding. I accept very willingly this restriction; it accords so much with my own views, that I should have proposed the reservation to you, if you had not mentioned it yourself. When I discuss any subject of religious philosophy with an unbeliever, I am careful not to say to him, "Lay aside your understanding and and believe blindly;" for this would certainly either break off the discussion, or render it altogether useless. I induce him, on the contrary, to make all objections which the subject allows of. I go so far even as to point out those which do not occur to him, in order that new doubts may not afterwards arise in his mind; for experience proves that a man does not arrive at a real conviction, on a controverted subject, only so far as he examines it in all its bearings, in the full exercise of his liberty and rationality. Truths can only enter the mind of man gradually, and in proportion as opposing errors are removed; and errors can only be removed so far as man acknowledges freely and rationally that what he believed to be true is false.

Thus so far from wishing to trammel our future discussion, I give it, as you see, the greatest latitude. And now, let us define, as far as possible, our positions respectively. I see from your letter, that you acknowledge a God distinct from nature, and that there is no doubt in your mind on this important point. You are in this, much farther advanced than most persons that are met with in society; for though it is not any longer the fashion publicly to deny the being of a God, yet how numerous are they, especially in the learned world, who make no distinction between God and nature! Question them on this subject, and they will at once declare that they admit the existence of God, but if they are pressed with questions, it will easily be perceived that in their minds they confound this God with nature. When it is a principle with a person not to admit anything as existing but what he apprehends with his corporeal senses, he is driven to this lamentable result. You do not find yourself very happy in this sad position, which I have likened to the state of a paralytic who feels not his malady. If you suffer, it is because your belief is limited to the acknowledgment that there is a God, the Creator of nature, and that, on all the other questions, you remain in a distressing uncertainty. For instance, relative to the immortality of the soul, you have nothing but probabilities; you have no certainty. The arguments of philosophy, and those of Roman Catholicism, in which religion you were born, are far from being satisfactory to your mind. You are desirous of believing that you live after death, because you feel in yourself something which tells you that the existence of man cannot be limited to the miserable life he leads upon this earth; but when your attention has been directed to all that has been told you on the subject of the human soul, you find the hypotheses of philosophers, and the ideas of theologians so vague, so incoherent, and so little in agreement with interior sentiments, that you are obliged to reject both.

With respect to the interior sentiment, or interior views and perceptions, let me here make an observation: it is, that theology and science, in putting forth fine treatises on the immortality of the soul, without previously giving any clear idea on the soul itself, have obscured the question rather than thrown light upon it; and that upon this subject, the ideas of a little child that has lost its mother, or those of an honest peasant who laments the loss of his companion, approach much nearer to the truth, as you will hereafter acknowledge, than those of a learned doctor of Sorbonne, or of a profound philosopher. I should not then be astonished at the little advantage you have derived from perusing these treatises.

Your wish to become a believer, without giving up the use

of your reason, shows me clearly why you have addressed yourself to a member of the New Jerusalem, rather than to a theologian of the Old Church. You have thought, no doubt, that a religion appearing in this age of rationalism, ought not to exclude reason from its religious philosophy, and in that you are not mistaken; but if you should think that the members of the New Jerusalem, like those innovators we see rising up on all sides, reject the Christian religion, you would be seriously mistaken. The New Jerusalem rests on Christianity, as Christianity rests on the Law and the Prophets. It does not abolish, but repairs and completes. We are, therefore, Christians; we are Christians in the broadest sense of the term—as you will be convinced when you understand the principles of the Lord's New Church.

Now that it is established that you are an *unbeliever disposed to believe*, provided you are not required to make a sacrifice of your reason, and that I am a Christian in the fullest acceptation of the term, that is to say, admitting, from the sincerest conviction of its truth, all that the New Jerusalem teaches, our respective positions are sufficiently defined for the present. The discussion now to follow can alone show to you what the name of Christian fully implies in the New Church.

We might now enter upon the subject, but before doing so, it will be well for us to understand each other on certain points relating to the argumentation. I shall point out in this first letter, such as appear to me the most important.

You wish to be convinced by reason; to your reason then, I must address myself. Now, in a subject so elevated, where we have to treat of God and his attributes, of the soul and its immortality, and in general of a world invisible to our natural or material eyes, your reason tells you that you cannot require natural or material proofs, or in other words, proofs which strike the senses of your earthly body. As for the rest, I do not think that your reason will refuse to admit the arguments which I shall offer. I will not depart from the rules of good logic, and I shall follow, as much as possible, the method of geometricians. Like them, I shall go from the known to the unknown; and like them, I shall have recourse to proofs from analogy. Now this kind of demonstration, it being admitted in the exact sciences, you cannot decline to accept. Lastly, when I shall speak to you of the spiritual world, I shall require you to abstract time and space, as in geometry they must abstract one or many dimensions of bodies, or as in mechanics, they must abstract movement, resistance of the air, friction, &c.

If this manner of treating rationally, and, so to speak, mathematically, the great question of religious philosophy, should excite your astonishment by its novelty, I would say to you: If a divorce has taken place between religion and reason, it is men alone who have caused it. God has never reproved reason because it was reason; but from the moment when man himself had perverted his noble faculty which he derived from God, things spiritual and celestial could no longer gain access to his corrupted reason. And as to the method of the geometricians, how could it be opposed to divine science? Do we not say, speaking of God, that he is the great Geometrician, that is, the Architect of the universe? Is not God the Architect of those globes which turn above our heads, according to laws mathematically established? Besides, have not the sciences also their metaphysical part? Ask the metaphysicians, who have entered into the depths of infinitesimal calculation, and they will confess that many among them, struck with the results to which they were conducted, have from materialists, which they were before, become spiritualists.

You see, moreover, that in all this, we have only to do with high questions of religious philosophy. As to those which relate to doctrine, properly so called, it would be quite out of place to mention them now. We must wait till the philosphical errors which would oppose themselves to their admission have been dispelled from your mind, and the spiritual truths which shall gain an entrance with you, have disposed you to receive them favorably. In a word, it is necessary that your convictions be well established on the questions to which our attention is to be first directed; but be it well remembered, that however strong this conviction may be, nevertheless it will not be faith; but it will conduct you to the faith which God alone gives to man when man is prepared to receive it.

Before closing this letter, I must make another observation: Though the New Jerusalem Church is in possession of truths of a very elevated order, and can by their means, resolve many questions which had hitherto remained without solution, she is, notwithstanding, far from pretending to explain everything. The intelligence of the creature, be he man or angel, will never be so far elevated as to comprehend the Creator. To comprehend God in his infinite Essence, it is necessary to be God himself. Accept, &c.

LETTER II.

The conditions which I proposed to you, relative to the mode of discussion, were so conformable to the reasoning spirit of our age, that I was convinced you would accept them; and I would in my first letter have introduced the subject, had I not been prevented by a motive altogether personal to yourself. When an author undertakes a treatise *ex professo*, he can arrange his plan himself, and treat it as he pleases; but such is not my task at present. What I have undertaken is to produce in you a religious and philosophical conviction; and I should regard myself as departing from my design, if I did not leave you full liberty to direct the discussion yourself. I therefore waited for your answer, in the intimate conviction that you would infallibly put questions to me on the points which had engaged your mind the most. Your letter proves that I was not mistaken; it embraces several questions which clearly show to me the present state of your mind; and I think I enter fully into your intentions, by considering the following question, which is more important than all the others, in the commencement.

"How," say you, "can we reconcile the *existence of evil* in the universe, with the idea of a God *essentially good and all-powerful?*"

You are aware, sir, that this first question presents the greatest of philosophical difficulties; but we may as well enter on them now as afterwards; only be good enough not to be astonished if I am obliged to make a long preparatory digression. To prove that this existence of evil presents nothing incompatible with the infinite goodness of God, nor with his omnipotence, it is necessary to have correct ideas, not only concerning God and his attributes, but also concerning man and the universe. You see that from the very beginning of the discussion, we have entered upon subjects, which for three thousand years have thrown philosophy into despair, and given birth to a crowd of systems, so little conclusive, that the friends of truth are still waiting for a satisfactory solution. Still it is not the fault of Philosophy, but of philosophers, who have wished to sound its depths without being enlightened from the torch of religion, and who have not called in the aid of religion, until religion itself had lost the true light. However, this is not the time to prove this propositiou; but you will often, in the sequel, have occasion to acknowledge the justice of it.

It is evident that our material world, in its whole and in its parts, subsists by the sun which is shining above our heads: without its presence, the globe which we inhabit, and all those which compose the planetary system, would infallibly fall into chaos. It is further evident, that all the effects produced by the sun, are owing to the heat and light which flow from it. Heat and light then are the two principles which cause our planet to subsist materially. But there are not only natural heat and light in our world, but also spiritual heat and light. When a man is moved by an affection, does he not interiorly experience heat? When a thought strikes him, is it not an internal light to him? This is so true, that in all languages, we cannot speak of an affection, without using terms which are suitable to heat, nor of a thought, without using terms which have relation to light. If we speak of love, we say that it inflames; of truth, we say that it enlightens. If we wish to describe an affection, we say that it is lively or ardent; or a thought, that it is brilliant or luminous. What other conclusion can be drawn from this, than that the affection of man is a spiritual heat, and his thought a spiritual light?

But whence do this heat and light proceed which affect us interiorly? Can it be from the sun which is visible to the eye of our earthly bodies? No one would venture to maintain this. This sun, because it is visible, is material. Now that which is material cannot produce what is spiritual. In vain would the materialist make use of the scalpel; he would never find in material organs the principles of affection or thought. In vain, would he analyse an affection or thought; he would never succeed in discovering in it the least particle of imponderous matter. To know whence proceed this heat and this light, recourse must be had to analogy, from which the following conclusion will be drawn, namely: that if natural heat and light come from the natural sun, which cannot be denied, spiritual heat and light must proceed from a spiritual sun, invisible, like them, to our material eyes. You will see hereafter how advantageous the knowledge of this simple truth will be, in studying the part of the universe which is inaccessible to the senses of our earthly bodies, and which we call the spiritual world.

We learn also from analogy, that the material world subsists from its sun, and, as incontestably, the spiritual world must also subsist from its sun; and the examination which we are now enabled to make upon ourselves goes to confirm the analogy. Indeed, if by our bodies we live in the natural world, by our spirits we belong to the spiritual world, and as spiritual being is but a compound of affections and thoughts, it is evident that it can only subsist by means of the spiritual centre, whence emanate spiritual heat and light, or affections and thoughts. Now if we who are yet invested with matter, cannot live without this spiritual centre, with much stronger reason, beings purely spiritual who constitute the other world could not subsist without it.

Now that we know there exists a spiritual sun, and that the invisible part of the universe subsists from this sun, let us enquire what can be the nature of such a luminary. All the affections of man belong to his will, and all his thoughts to his understanding; and these two faculties, will and understanding, constitute the life of man; for it has been said long ago, man is man because of willing and thinking; it follows that spiritual heat and light, which are in their essence love and wisdom, constitute life itself, and as this heat and this light emanate from the spiritual sun, it hence results again, that life resides in this sun, and that it is this sun which distributes life throughout the universe.

Although life itself resides in this spiritual sun, this sun is not life itself, but is only the first recipient of it. Life itself is God; and as real life with man is composed of love and wisdom, God, being Life itself, is consequently Love itself, and Wisdom itself. Love is his *Esse*, his substance; and Wisdom his *Existere*, his manifestation. All his other attributes are consequences of Love itself and Wisdom itself, as all the faculties of man are consequences of his will, the seat of his affections, and of his understanding, the seat of his thoughts.

If, in this argumentation, I have begun with the investigation of man in order to arrive at God, instead of beginning with God in order to descend to man, the fault belongs to those who have surrounded these subjects with such thick darkness, that we are, in this our day, compelled to appeal to the reason of man, before we can address his heart.

Love as it manifests itself in the creature is far from giving us a just idea of that Love which is the Essence of the Creator. However pure we might conceive human love to be, there will always be, between it and the divine Love, the inappreciable distance which always exists between the finite and the infinite. Nevertheless, in reasoning from what we are able to know of true love, we shall see cleared away, successively, the greatest difficulties of religious pbilosophy.

It is the essence of love to communicate itself: it must have an object to love out of itself; for to love one's self is not true love. God, then, who is Love itself, required an object, that is to say, creatures whom he might love. Hence the creation of the universe.

I will not here enter into particulars respecting God's work. If you would wish to know them, you will find them in one of the treatises of Swedenborg (Angelic Wisdom concerning the Divine Love.) I will only say, that to have a correct idea, you must throw aside the hypotheses hitherto adopted. That of chaos would only throw obscurity on the subject; that of the old theology is not even susceptible of examination. To pretend that God created the universe out of nothing, is going against the axiom, "*out of nothing nothing can be produced;*" now God, who is Truth itself, cannot make self-evident truth an untruth. The Divine Omnipotence, as you will see at the close of this letter, never opposes itself to the truth.

The design of God in creating this vast universe, being to

pour out his love upon objects out of himself, and fit to receive it, let us first survey the immensity of creation, and seek among so many created objects, to discover those which have been especially destined to satisfy the ardent love of the Creator, by an intimate conjunction with Him. Our eye at first discovers myriads of sparkling globes, and analogy, supported by the knowledge we have of the planetary system, shows us millions of other globes, which gravitate round the first; but our understanding also teaches us that bodies passively submitted to the invariable laws of gravitation, have none of the qualities adapted to fulfil the final end of the Divinity. These innumerable suns, and these earths still more innumerable, have then only been launched into the immensity of space for the use of more noble creatures. If, now, we descend to our earth, what do we discover in this multitude of varied objects which nature spreads daily before our eyes? I see there minerals, vegetables, animals, and, at the summit of this scale of beings, man. Does not a single examination of this chain show us at once, that the mineral kingdom was created for the use of the two superior kingdoms? that the vegetable kingdom is indispensable to the animal kingdom? and that the animals themselves, deprived of the moral sentiment, have only been to the Creator *means*, to the end that the only creature capable of reciprocating his love might exist on the earths of his immense domain, and there make use of all these objects of his divine munificence? It is then for man and man alone, that the whole universe has been created.

After having presented to you God, as Love itself and Wisdom itself; after having shown you that the universe, the expansion of his love, has been formed by his wisdom, and that all has been created by him alone, I am at length in a position to discuss your proposition. You might, however, believe that, far from having rendered the solution easier, I have increased the difficulties of it, in representing God as

Love itself and Wisdom itself—a definition which seems to embrace more than yours, which is, "God essentially good;" for it is always impossible, you think, to deny the existence of evil upon this earth, where everything attests the miserable state of man, where all nature presents but a permanent antagonism between all beings. I am quite of your opinion respecting this impossibility; but you will soon acknowledge that I have followed the course traced out for me by the very nature of things, and I hope to prove to you that evil proceeds not from God, and that, nevertheless, it is a consequence of the definition which I have just given.

Everything proceeded pure from the hands of the Creator. It is useless, I conceive, to insist on this proposition, which enters completely into our ideas. Love itself acting according to the laws of Wisdom, could produce nothing but good. From what source then is evil? and how could this evil wrestle with Love itself, in which resides Omnipotence? An attentive examination of the very nature of love, will remove these difficulties, which appear insurmountable.

If love, as we have acknowledged, is in its essence communicative—if it must have an object out of itself to love—it also requires that the object loved shall return love for love. To be convinced of this truth, it is only necessary to have once loved. Reciprocality being essential to love, God, in creating man with a view to shed down his love upon him, must have given him all the faculties necessary in order for him to reflect back to his Creator the love which he received from him. And observe well, that it was not sufficient that the love of man should return to the Creator; but it was still necessary that this love should include in it the condition indispensable to all true love; it was necessary, in a word, that the love of man should be in everything worthy of the love of God. Now, such a love could not exist with man, except so far as man should have the full and entire liberty to love God or not;

for without liberty there could be no love. How can any one believe himself still to be loved, if he discovers that the object he cherishes is *forced* to love him? If feeble beings who possess but a particle of love, disdain to be loved from compulsion, how could it be supposed that God, who is Love itself, had mistaken one of the essential principles of love, by constraining man to love him? With such a supposition, the end of creation has failed: God has worked in vain: his essence induced him to create beings capable of loving him, and he has formed only automatons—instruments purely passive, to be moved with wires. Would not this be to degrade, and even outrage the majesty of God, and compare him to a child playing with puppets?

No: God created man free; and he could not create him otherwise, because he is Love itself, and because liberty is an essential principle of love.

It is besides, upon this principle of liberty on the part of man, that all that there is most sacred in the world reposes—religion, morality, law. Without this liberty, religious rites become superstition—rules of morality become deception—and the punishments of law, atrocious injustice. Without this liberty, there is no longer, after this life, either happiness for the good man, or misery for the wicked; or God is a tyrant, only consulting his caprice in issuing his favors or maledictions.

Created free to love God or not to love him, that is to say, free to conform to the laws of divine order, or to transgress them, man lived at first conformably to these laws. All was then orderly in the universe—nothing disturbed its native purity; everything in its spiritual part was good and true; everything in its material part was good and beautiful The other beings of our globe followed the order of their nature respectively. Deprived of the principle of liberty, they had not the power to disturb the established order. Man alone could re-act against God, and so long as he did not use this liberty, the primitive order was maintained; but from the time when he began, by virtue of this liberty, to swerve from the laws of order, he introduced by this act a spiritual antagonism. Opposition to good produced evil—opposition to truth gave birth to the false or to falsity; then this spiritual antagonism produced one in the material creation: by degrees, the substance of things natural, perverted by evil, from good became bad, and the form of these things, changed by what was false, from beautiful became deformed.

Do not think, however, that the evil and the false, the bad and the deformed, which were introduced into the universe in these early times of the creation, were like the evil and the false, the bad and the deformed, which we see in it now. The evil and the false were then but a slight deviation from the good and the true. It was only by an increasing series of alterations and deviations, that human nature at length fell into those states of fierceness and barbarity, which history presents to us.

You see that the existence of evil is easily reconcilable with the existence of a God essentially good, since it is the act of man alone, and that it results from human liberty which is an essential principle of the love of the creature for his Creator. It remains for me to prove to you, that this *existence of evil*, can also be perfectly reconciled with the idea of an *omnipotent God*.

The custom of judging of the attributes of the Divinity by those with which royalty is surrounded, has been the cause of many errors. When a king, abusing his high station, has placed himself above the law, and governed his people according to his caprice, undoing to-day what he did yesterday, he has been said to be *all-powerful;* and as the greater part of despots have pretended to hold their power from God, it has been inferred that the divine Omnipotence, being superior to human power, could go so far as to do what is absolutely impossible. From this error proceeded all superstitions; for with these words, *everything is possible with God*, interpreted in the sense which I have just described, there are no absurdities which may not be admitted.

If God could do everything, according to the common understanding of the divine Omnipotence, he would not be God. This will doubtless appear to you a paradox, but it is nevertheless a truth, and a little reflection will convince you of it. Man, subject to error, can perfect his work only on the condition of revising and correcting it. If he be a legislator, he will only form his code after a long meditation, and having promulgated it, his laws will still remain subject to the changes which experience shall introduce. But can it be the same with God, who is Wisdom itself and Foreknowledge itself? When God created the universe, he said, Be it, and it was. Yes, by the word of Jehovah was the universe constituted, with all the laws which govern it; that is to say, with all the laws which could then be manifested, with all those which have since been successively manifested, and with all those which will be manifested throughout all time. All these laws constitute the Divine Order, and are called the laws of order.

You now see that there is no paradox in saying, that if God could do everything, according to the common acceptation of the divine Omnipotence, he would not be God. If God were to change a law of his divine order, would not this be declaring that he had been mistaken? and what would then become of one of his principal attributes, his divine Foreknowledge? Oh, let us beware of debasing the Divinity to the rank of a capricious tyrant; let us not compare him even to the best of kings; let us regard him only as a Father, whose love for all his children, as much surpasses that of the tenderest of earthly fathers, as the infinite surpasses everything finite.

The liberty of man being one of the essential laws of divine order, the divine Omnipotence consists in not destroying, but maintaining it. The existence of evil then, is perfectly reconcilable with the idea of an all-powerful God. We do not say that evil will therefore always exist; it will disappear from the earth, but having entered into the universe by the liberty of man, it is necessary that it should be removed by the same liberty. Accept, &c.

LETTER III.

You say that the theory which I explained to you in my second letter is ingenious: you acknowledge the logical connection of the propositions which served to establish it; but you meet with so many new ideas in these propositions that you are confused, and you justly consider that it would be precipitate in you to adopt the theory without having maturely examined it, and seriously digested it. This is well: you enter entirely into my views, and your hesitation gives me more pleasure than would an entire acquiescence. I willingly excuse the ephithet *ingenious*, which you apply to this theory, because you show a disposition to study it. Consider it attentively, and you will soon come to acknowledge that it is the only one your reason can adopt. Moreover you already admit—and that should satisfy me for the present—that it is much to be preferred to anything that has been taught up to this time, on so grave a subject; that it removes great philosophical difficulties, and gives much more elevated and sound ideas concerning the Divine Being than any that have been hitherto presented.

You add that you wish to make some objections, ask explanations, and submit reflections to me; but in your present position, not knowing our manner of resolving the other difficulties of high philosophy, you prefer to wait for a more suitable time; meanwhile, you request me to *give you some elucidations on the human soul, which may convince you of its immortality.*

You are perfectly right, sir, in wishing to arrive at a certainty that your soul is immortal, for this is the principal point. If so many men at this day are indifferent as to all that concerns religious matters, it is chiefly because they have not had anything but mere probabilities presented to them respecting their immortal existence, or their state after death. Our philosophers and theologians have made the question so intricate, that among men of the world, there is at least a half who deny this immortality, if not with their lips, yet with their hearts, while the other half believe it only upon simple probabilities. But to believe upon probabilities, when everything in this world leads us to indulge our selfish propensities; is this quite sufficient to give us a firmer resolution to resist evil? Does not everything that passes daily before us prove to the contrary? But let a man who has hitherto had but a vague idea of his immortality, become certain of it, and very soon he will not be the same man; a happy change will soon be wrought in him.

Suppose, that instead of speaking to men in vague terms respecting their existence after death, that existence should be demonstrated to them, by showing them in what it consists, and by answering all the questions which each should honestly make on the subject, with a view to acquire a complete conviction; would not the most salutary of revolutions be the result—a revolution far superior to those which have produced the most good, since it would be made without commotion? Induced by their new conviction to come out of that religious indifference which is the bane of our modern societies, men would seek to be instructed in true religious principles; they would cast far from them all the falsities which arise from scepticism and superstition; they would joyfully adopt a doctrine full of devotedness, full of love. Firmly convinced that their present life is but a state preparatory to entering fully upon a life which shall never end; and intimately persuaded that their state in eternity depends entirely on the short pilgrimage which they shall make upon this earth, they would live in the peaceful enjoyment of all the blessings which the Creator spreads daily and abundantly around them. Instead of regarding their fellow men as so many rivals, they would look upon them only as brothers; devotedness would take the place of selfishness, and feelings of envy and hatred would insensibly disappear, to make room for charity and love. Nevertheless, I am far from saying that man would be exempt from faults, that he would always live in conformity with principles of true doctrine; but at least, man would then learn by this doctrine of charity and love, to distinguish good from evil, and the true from the false; he would consequently know when he did evil; and his relapses, by producing in him repentance and the desire for renovation, would help to make him progress in the way of goodness.

What man is there then, who would be so inconsistent as not to regret having done evil, and not to resolve on doing good, if he were fully convinced of the immortality of his soul? What! I must be intimately convinced that I shall live eternally! My reason would tell me daily that the longest life on this earth, is not, in relation to eternity, so much as a grain of sand to the widest desert, or as a drop of water to the immensity of the ocean. I should know that my eternal existence depends on the manner in which I shall have fulfilled my duties towards my country, my fellow citizens, my family, and myself. Everything proves that man's conduct depends on the principles which he has adopted. See how ardently those who believe in this terrestrial life, follow the consequences of their false principles; and judge by this what it would be, if men were intimately convinced of their eternal existence. The certainty of this existence is then the most important point for man, and the most certain means of leading him to religious principles.

This certainty, however, is not obtained immediately. Man is plunged into such thick darkness on the subject of whatever relates to spiritual things, that he can only perceive the light of truth in the degree that he removes the clouds, or the falses which intercept it. Though there may be little good will and perseverance in him, he succeeds in disengaging himself from his prejudices; then his conviction is gradually established, and afterwards becomes so firm, that every reflection and observation on his part concur in confirming him more and more. I do not then pretend to convince you at once; but from the favorable disposition you are in, I feel certain that after a mature examination, you will admit the different propositions which I shall submit to you, however strange they may seem at first; and that the whole will result in producing a complete conviction of your eternal existence.

Your desire to be enlightened on this important point induces me to postpone to another period the developments which I wished to give you, in order to complete the question relative to the origin of evil; they will naturally find their place when we come to doctrinal subjects, and when I shall explain to you the nature of the fall. I must also before commencing, say that I shall consider as established, the propositions which have already been treated of, and that I shall continue to support myself by them, so long as you have not positively refused to admit them ; for this is a right which I hold from the very nature of our argument.

The design of God, in creating the universe, having been to pour out his love upon objects out of himself, and at the same time capable of reflecting back this love, I have shown you that if man were not created free, the end of creation has failed. I will now add, supporting myself always on the essence of God, which is love itself, that if man had not to live after his natural death, the end of creation would also have failed. Behold, you will say, a solution which I was far from expecting. You promised me new arguments, and you decide the question after the manner of theologians and philosophers; for many of them have supported themselves on the goodness of God, to conclude from it that man will live after death.

Be good enough, I pray, to wait a moment. You would certainly have a right to exclaim in this way if theologians and philosophers, before bringing forward the goodness of God, to deduce from it the existence of another life, had given you clear and precise ideas of that goodness; but have they ever presented, upon what they call the goodness of the Creator, anything but common-place ideas, almost always in manifest contradiction to the other attributes which they give to the Divine Being? What is, indeed, this God of theologians? He is a being always angry, who has only consented to pardon the human race for the disobedience of the first man, on condition that his own Son (innocent of this fault,) should suffer, in order to repair it, the most frightful torments; and who, not content with this, is only appeased so far as his Son supplicates him for pardon, and makes mention continually of his sufferings, and the blood he shed for the redemption of men. When they set forth the Creator under such gloomy aspects, they certainly cannot be permitted to support themselves upon, or to adduce his goodness, that they may conclude from it that man will live after death. And on the other hand, what is the God of philosophers? A being purely metaphysical, of whom they cannot form the least idea; consequently he is to them simply a compound of abstractions, having a mere word for their subject. When the Divinity is thus reduced to a mere word, however imposing this word may be, they cannot be allowed to adduce the goodness of such a being in proof of a new existence of man.

It is not thus that the new Christians, or the members of the New Jerusalem Church, represent the God of the universe. They lay it down as a principle that Love itself is his *Esse*, (being) and that Wisdom itself is his *Existere*, and that all his attributes are consequences of this divine Love, and of this divine Wisdom. You will see hereafter—for I should be departing too far from my subject to demonstrate it now—that the divine Love is Substance itself, and the first substance (*substance-type*) whence proceed all substances; and that the divine Wisdom is Form itself, and the *form-type*, whence all forms are derived; hence the Divinity, far from being what is called a metaphysical being, is Being itself—possessing in the most elevated degree, what constitutes a real being—namely, substance and form. Strong in this principle, the members of the New Church draw from it all possible deductions, and all, without any exception, come afterwards to corroborate and confirm it; and what further shows, in a manner not to be disputed, that this principle is the very truth is, that true philosophy and true theology are always found to harmonize with it; also, that the doctrine, all of charity and love, which flows from this principle, is in all points, conformable to the Biblical Writings, and perfectly reconciles all the apparent contradictions which these writings contain; also, that the historical events which have furnished the strongest arguments against the divine Providence, become, on the contrary, evident proofs of the inexhaustible love of the Creator for all his creatures. I should be drawn too far from my subject, if I now entered into explanations on these diffent points, which besides, are of a nature not to be treated incidentally; but farther on, I shall have occasion to develope them. Now that I have, as I believe, sufficiently answered the objection which I myself anticipated, it will be easy for you to comprehend, by the miserable life which man leads upon this earth, that the design of the Creator, or the design of Love itself, would completely have failed if man's existence terminated with his earthly life. This proposition is so self-evident that it is useless to insist upon it further.

Do not think, however, that by this I consider the question of the existence of man after his natural death as entirely decided. If I had only had this argument to present to you, I should not have undertaken to convince you. I have only used it to show you what new strength it acquires, when, instead of considering the divine Being as theologians and philosophers do, he is represented as being essentially Love itself, and above all, when we are well convinced that in creating the universe for man, God had no other end than to satisfy his inexhaustible love. Nevertheless, this argument would be enough to prove to man the existence of a future state, if his mind for a long time tossed about by the subtilties of philosophers, and the errors of theologians, had not come to lose the most simple notions relative to his interior being, and the part of the universe which is purely spiritual. It is true that philosophical spiritualists speak to him respecting the immortality of his soul, but they give him no information what this soul is, for they know nothing about it, and their ideas on this matter are far below those of a simple peasant. They speak to him of a future life but it would greatly embarrass them to tell him in what it consists. Theologians are also silent whenever it is a question to define the human soul; and if they sometimes endeavor to give an idea of the other life, their description only serves to frighten children.

Therefore, as I have told you already, so long as man, to convince him of his immortality, shall only have the commonplace views dealt out to him for so many ages, by poets and moralists, by philosophers of every shade, and theologians of every sect, he will remain in that uncertainty which to you has become so insupportable; for it is not by simple probabilities, that a conviction can be formed. But if, instead of having had represented to him the soul as a breath, as an unknown aerial something, man had had clear and precise ideas given to him respecting the interior being which animates him, which is himself, and which must survive his natural body; if, moreover, instead of the vague ideas which have been hitherto presented to him relative to what is commonly called the other world, the existence of that world were demonstrated to him; if he were made to know in what it consists; if the topography, so to speak, of that world were presented to him; if the continual relations which exist between this spiritual world (where he must live eternally), and the natural world (where he sojourns for a little while), were shown to him in such a way that he could himself daily and hourly verify the reality of a great number of these relations—oh then! you must allow that man by means of these knowledges, would easily succeed in forming the firm conviction that he will exist after laying aside his natural body; say if this conviction would not make him a truly religious man—if this belief become general, would it not effect, without any commotion, the most glorious of revolutions!

Well, sir, it is thus, and not by common-place ideas that I hope to establish in you a solid conviction. Yes, it gives me pleasure to repeat, you will ere long admit and acknowledge all the truths which I have explained to you. I am certain of this, because you are moved by a sincere desire to know the truth, and this desire will keep up your attention, and give you all the perseverance which is needed. If you had only been directed by a vain curiosity, I should have answered your questions by a few brief explanations; but I should have regarded it as useless to undertake seriously your conversion, for my endeavors would have been vain, and my reasonings futile. We can only convince those who desire to be convinced.

I will in my next letter begin the exposition of these important truths. Accept, &c.

LETTER IV.

In your eagerness to see the exposition which I promised you in my last letter, there is nothing, I assure you, to astonish me; and I am truly ashamed to receive from you apologies which ought to come from me, for having,by premeditation, postponed to the present letter the commencement of this exposition. I will not conceal from you, that in acting thus, I felt certain of increasing your desire to know our ideas respecting the soul of man, and respecting that world into which we all go when we leave this earth. Indeed, a man must be sunk into the lowest degree of sensualism, if the noblest faculties of his being remain inactive in the presence of such important questions. If, however, there are very few persons who interest themselves now-a-days about spiritual things, it is not, you may rely, because the generality of men have fallen into this gross sensualism; but only because the wants of natural life, the perplexities of business, and the propensity to worldly pleasures divert their minds continually from them. But let some event happen which may throw back the attention of the man of the world upon this grave subject, and you immediately see him willing to devote himself to the serious meditations which the subject demands. If persons usually keep in this frame of mind but a very short time, it is because the efforts are vain which the understanding makes to adopt the noblest aspirations of the heart; it is because the understanding, led astray by the lucubrations of philosophers, or the errors of theologians, offers nothing satisfactory to the reason; then, wearied with wandering in the labyrinths of so many ideas which have no ground to rest upon, men hasten to enter again into what they very improperly call the realities of life.

Allow me to make another observation: How can we help being astonished to see philosophers always moralizing, and theologians always dogmatizing, when it is so evident that the writings of both classes—because of the false ground they go upon—are themselves the principal causes of the moral and religious disorders against which they strongly declaim? I willingly admit that they are sincere—that their intentions are pure, and their labors conscientious—but yet can this excuse them, when past and present experience is sufficient to show them clearly that they are pursuing a false course? Do they not know that for ages their predecessors have moralized and dogmatized without meeting with any success? Do they not see that they themselves are moralizing and dogmatizing without making men any better? After so many deceptions which follow one another continually, can they without being chargeable with want of foresight, expect to be more successful than their predecessors, especially when they continually adopt the same errors? But why do they continue to wander in the same crooked paths in which people have been misled so long? Why do they not enter the new way which is open to every one who seeks the truth from a pure love of truth? Why is this? The answer is easy. It is because they are like the abbot of Vertot, *their seat is made.* For them the truth has no more attractions than it had for this historian. Their seat is indeed made. Can it be believed, for example, that they are the men to forget all they have learned and begin their studies anew? Can it be believed that they have self-denial enough to acknowledge that the writings to which they owe their reputation are contrary to the truth? If the abbot of Vertot, who then had only his indolence to overcome, was unable to conquer it, how can they do otherwise than yield, who have to struggle against all the exigencies of self-love?

This reflection is not out of place here; it presents on your part the following objection which has often been made: "Why do not the celebrated men of the day adopt the principles of high religious philosophy which are held in the New Jerusalem Church? Is not the silence they maintain on this subject a strong presumption that these principles, while they seem very brilliant and solid, do not bear the test of a profound examination?" This is an objection which has long been brought against us; but you may now see what this presumption amounts to, which I confess may appear very strong at first sight. Far from furnishing an argument against our principles, this silence, on the contrary, is altogether in their favor; nevertheless, it certainly is prejudicial for a time, to the propagation of our doctrines, because we have not always an opportunity of making known the true cause of it. There is, indeed, a great number of persons simple enough to judge men according to their writings, and to believe that those who establish themselves as instructors of the people, are beings separate from, and superior to the greater part of human weaknesses; but experience proves every day that the learned more than all other men, are in general governed by a passion which produces in them most fatal results. This passion is the love of their own intelligence; it is this which even when they know it not, directs them in almost all their actions. This constrains them, as it involves their reputation, to say nothing whatever respecting Swedenborg's writings on the subject of religion; and this they do, because these writings contain true principles, both of philosophy and religion, and a complete refutation of the vain systems of philosophers and theologians.

I ask pardon, my dear sir, for this digression, and I ask it also, for those which will follow, because it will often happen that I shall make excursions here and there; but you may rest assured that I shall not lose sight of the propositions which are to be the subjects of this discussion; and, after any deviations, will always return to them. Your own proposition prescribes this course to me. It would be difficult, for instance, to make myself well understood by you, if I confined myself simply to declaring the preparatory propositions which I shall be obliged to employ, and did not stop occasionally to dwell upon those which, as they are not familiar to men of the world, can only be admitted by them in proportion as they perceive them rationally. Hence the necessity of my digressing sometimes from the principal subject. Some of the truths which I shall develope may excite your surprise, as much by their appearance of novelty as by their contrast with the ideas prevailing in the world; but do not let this stop you, only give me a little continued attention, and it will not be long before they become familiar to you. Besides, these truths have not always been strangers on this earth; they were known and believed in ancient times, and their disappearance is only due to the depravity into which the human race fell, by the bad use they made of their free will.

I come at length to the exposition which I promised you. It divides itself into two parts: the first comprising the questions relating to the soul and its immortality, and the second those relating to the spiritual world; but as these questions are connected together, and illustrate each other, I would have you to wait until this exposition, which will, no doubt, take up several letters, is entirely concluded, before you form a definite judgment on the propositions which, at first sight, may appear strange, or to have need of further developements.

Men are generally agreed in the acknowledgement that what lives in man is his soul or spirit; only the materialists affirm that what is called the soul ceases to exist when the body can no longer perform its functions, while the spiritualists pretend that the soul or spirit survives the decomposition of the body. I may, then, assume as a principle, that the soul or spirit of man is that which lives within him.

But what is it that lives within man? or what is it, properly speaking, that constitutes his living principle, or the *esse* of his life? It is evidently his affection or his love, which has for its seat the voluntary faculty. However, if there was in man only affection or love, without any manifestation, man would not exist: to exist really an *esse* must have a manifestation. Consequently the affection or love of man manifests itself by his thoughts, which has the intellectual faculty for its seat. Although *esse* and *existere* are inseparable, and only make one, since an *esse* is an *esse* only so far as it *exists*, still they can be separated in thought; thus we can say that the love or the affection of man is the *esse* of his life, and that his intelligence or thought is the *existere*, or the manifestation of his love and affection. Hence, I have already told you, that in God, Love itself is his *esse*, his substance, and that Wisdom itself is the *existere*, or the manifestation of his Love.

If it is evident that man lives, it is also evident that he does not live of himself: man does not produce life, but only receives it. And whence does he receive it? I answer, from God—from God alone—who is life itself. Life is *one*, as God is *one*. God transmits life throughout the universe, and yet, no created object has life in itself; for it would be a continuity of God, which is impossible. Every one is a recipient of life or of God, not by *continuity*, but by *contiguity;* and thus it is that life is in everything, according to the nature of the object which receives it, and that nevertheless, no being has life in itself. The father does not give life to his children; for to give it to them, it would require him to have it as his own, and he is only the recipient of it. From the father proceed only germs adapted to become, like himself, recipients of the life which emanates from God alone. It is thus that men receiving life from God alone, are brothers—not only all those who inhabit this earth, no matter what may be their diversity of color—but those also who people all the earths throughout the immensity of space. They are all brothers, inasmuch as they all have but one only real Father, who is the sole God of the universe. The learned may dispute as long as they please, whether the different races that inhabit our earth have proceeded from one man or from many men: their debates are of no importance to us. The brotherhood of man is established in our doctrine upon too solid a basis ever to be shaken by science.

I know that for eighteen centuries it has been repeated in the Christian world that we are all children of God: I know that this proposition is at the head of all the catechisms; but alas! it is with this truth as it is with the human soul which we are now considering. These two truths, because of not having been put forward and understood rationally have been considered as propositions very good to figure in sermons and moral essays; but too obscure and uncertain to deserve to be taken into consideration in the practical affairs of life. Oh! if men were generally convinced that man does not live of himself—that he does not receive life from his father—that he does not give it to his children—that there is but one only Life—that this sole Life is God himself—that God is essential Love—that his Love causes him to diffuse life continually into all the objects of creation according as every object is adapted for its reception—that of all creatures, man alone, by virtue of his organization, receives this life in the highest degree, by not opposing himself either to the entrance of the divine Love into his will, or to the entrance of the divine Wisdom into his understanding—if, I say, men were generally persuaded of these sublime truths—the "fraternity of men" would no longer be a vain term! Far from being weakened, the love of the son for the father, and of the father for the son, would be increased. The son would regard his father as the true representative of God upon the earth; the father, impressed with the goodness of the Creator to all his children, and with the importance of the functions that are entrusted to him, would strive to perform them worthily; and then God, being better known by men would be loved by them, as his love has so long invited and called upon them to love him.

By considering in a former letter the nature of man, we were led to a knowledge of God: and now, as we have acknowledged that man receives his life from God alone, the knowledge of God, will be a means of drawing us to the nature itself of the soul or spirit of man. But before commencing this enquiry, I have to offer some remarks to you on the subject of spiritual substance.

Among modern spiritualists, there are some who willingly admit that there are forms in what they call the other world. This no doubt arises from having been accustomed from their childhood to these forms, the existence of which is acknowledged by the Greek and Roman mythologists. Now, it is these very philosophers who are the most offended when they hear mention made of spiritual substances, as if a world composed of forms only could be anything but an imaginary world, or as if a being without substance and form were not an imaginary entity, which in itself is nothing. And observe what strange ideas prevail in the present age. Men are not at all shocked when such puerile notions are seriously put forth, and yet they cry out if a single word is said about spiritual substance. It is easy, however, to perceive that there can no more be really any form without substance than substance without form. Nothing real can exist without substance and form; for substance and form are two things which may, it is true, be separated in thought but not in reality

When I said to you that far from being merely an ideal being, which in itself is nothing, God is Being itself (*Esse*), possesing in the supreme degree what constitutes a real being, namely, substance and form; it was saying to you implicitly that his divine Wisdom envelopes and contains his divine Love; and thus God has really a form which envelopes and contains a substance, Love being the true substance and Wisdom the true form. If you now enquire what is the form of the Divinity, I will answer, that the universe being an emanation of the divine Love, or of the first Substance—an emanation put in order by the divine Wisdom, or First Form (*Form-Type*) this universe must present in the forms of objects of which it is composed, images of this First Form, and I will add that as the form of man is the most perfect of all forms, it becomes evident that God is in the human form.

God, then, is VERY MAN. Yes, my dear sir, with all deference to the philosophers of all schools, and to theologians of all sects; God, the Infinite being, the Jehovah of the Bible, the Eternal Father of Christians, the One God in three Attributes or Essentials (and not in three persons) of the New Jerusalem Church, the Creator, Saviour and preserver of the universe—this God who is Life itself, and by whom we exist and subsist—this God is VERY MAN. And it is because he is the Human Type (*Homme-Type*), the Perfect Man, that we his creatures, we who live and subsist by him, have in his image and his likeness the human form.

This important truth is so different from the ideas of the age respecting the Creator, that it will be difficult at first for you to admit it. But when you shall have considered it; when in the course of discussion you shall have acknowledged that it is the fundamental basis of true philosophy and true theology; when you shall have seen that by it the greatest difficulties are removed, and that it provides us with the means of carrying our rational investigations into the spiritual world, and the internal of man, so far at least as it is possible for a finite being to reason on such profound subjects—then you will receive it with so much the more joy, because you will be convinced that it would be impossible for you without it, to form an exact idea of the true God. Although I do not pretend to convince you at once that God is VERY MAN, I will, notwithstanding, offer you some arguments in favor of this truth.

It is, in the first place, absolutely impossible to represent to yourself a being without form. Philosophy has invented a God without form, in order to explain to itself a God as Creator and everywhere present; but by abstracting space, this fiction can be dispensed with. When you shall have accustomed your mind to make this abstraction, and shall have some ideas of the spiritual world, and the relations which exist between that world and ours, you will conceive that a God who is VERY MAN, can have created the universe, and be perpetually present in all his work.

A just idea of God is more important than is generally believed. How, indeed, can we love God, if it is impossible for us to form an idea of him? That a philosopher may be seized with an admiration for the Creator of the universe, when he beholds the rising sun, or the face of nature smiling and flourishing, or the starry vault in a beautiful night, I can easily enough conceive. He yields to the emotion of enthusiasm; he ceases then to *reason* concerning the Author of so many wonders, for he admires him; and I am convinced that if he endeavored to discover what was the inmost of his thought during this momentary rapture, he would acknowledge that the Creator was truly to him then, a real Being, and not a purely metaphysical one — that is to say, deprived of substance and form. But if this philosopher should tell me that he loves the Creator, I could not conceive it possible. To love, there must necessarily be an object; it is also necessary that this object be really present, or at least present to the thought of him who loves; and in this last case it is necessary that the presence in thought should be very manifest. Now the God of philosophers could not be thus present to their thought, since he is an incomprehensible Being, of whom they cannot, by reasoning, form to themselves any idea —and is it not the same with theologians? Can they form to themselves the least idea of their God? I speak, however, only of the first Person of their Trinity. It is true that the Roman Catholics, in their temples, represent God the Creator under a human form, but in their writings and at the head of their catechisms, they declare positively that he is a pure Spirit, and from the idea they have of spirit, it is plain they do not give to him definitively either substance or form. Now as the real end of religion is to establish relations between God and man, and to lead man, by the knowledge of God, to love this God with all his heart, and to love also his fellow men because of God, it becomes evident that any religion which presents the Creator deprived of substance and form, (without which he is no longer conceivable in thought), thus takes away from man all means of conceiving of this God the Creator and consequently of loving him, and by this shows manifestly that it is not the true religion.

The belief in God-man has, from the most remote time, been admitted by the generality of men, in preference to the vapory idea of the philosophers. The more you go back into antiquity the more you find this belief prevailing. This arises from the circumstance that the simple and unsophisticated man is generally much nearer the truth than the learned man who is spoiled by his systems, and inflated by the love of his own intelligence; for the former follows the impulses of his heart, while the latter gives himself up to the foolish conceits of his understanding. The belief, however, in a God-man has been charged by philosophers with pride: they have said that man had made God after his own image. If this assertion were true, we should see the simple minded generally adopting the God of the philosophers, and men proud of their intelligence, believing in God-man; but experience proves the contrary. Besides this reproach of pride cannot apply to the New Jerusalem Church; for to say that God is VERY MAN, when the principle is established that God is Life itself, and that all men derive their life from God, is not this implicitly saying, that it is the human race which is conformable to the Type itself of life, to God the Creator of all things?

Finally, if it be evident that it is absolutely necessary for God to be a substance and form, in order to be a real being, and also that he may be apprehended by the thought of man, and be loved by him, it is also evident that if God were not substance and form, the end of creation would have failed; for we have acknowledged that the universe was created with a view to man, in order that this creature, the only one endowed with liberty, might return to the Creator the love which he received from him.

But is it indispensable that the Divinity should have the human form? May he not have some other? I have already said that the universe, in the forms of the objects which compose it, should offer images of the first Form (*Forme-Type*); and that of all forms, the form of man approaches the nearest to perfection. These assertions are proved by the observations of science. When we examine the chain of beings, do we not find that man is the first link, and that all the succeeding links are no more than successive alterations of the first? You are doubtless acquainted with that series of pictures which presents scarcely a perceptible difference between them, when one of them is compared with that which precedes or that which follows, and yet the first represents the Apollo of Belvidere, and the last a frog. What the painter has done for a frog, he could have done for any other animal, whether by increasing or diminishing the number of his pictures. The type of man, then, is found in every animal, in whatever state of degradation it may be; and it is thus, because every creature is an image, more or less imperfect, of the Prototype (*Type-Createur*). This successive degradation of the human form in the chain of beings, is sufficient then to resolve the question. It would moreover, be absurd, after having recognised this successive degradation, to suppose that the form of God the Creator, was that of any one of the inferior beings of this chain, rather than that of the being who constitutes its first link, and to whom all the rest are subject. If some nations have given an animal or vegetable form to the Divinity, this proves the necessity of representing him under a form; and it shows the state of spiritual degradation into which those nations had fallen.

As this great question of God-man has been incidentally treated upon as being necessary to the subject which engages our attention, I will not enter here into further developements; but I shall often have occasion to return to it either in answering objections which it will give rise to in your mind, or in treating on several points connected with it. It is important, moreover, in order to understand it well, that you should accustom yourself to abstract space and time; and I propose to submit to you shortly our ideas on the subject of this abstraction.

I now return to our discussion relative to the soul or spirit. We have seen on the one hand, that God is Life itself; that his Life consists in Love and Wisdom; that his Love is the first Substance, and his Wisdom the first Form (*Form-Type*);

that from the Divine Love, as the first Substance proceed all substances, and that from the Divine Wisdom, the first Form, proceed all forms; that God has the human Form; that he is VERY MAN, or the Human Type (*l'Homme-Meme ou l'Homme Type*); and finally that everything in the universe presents an image which more or less approaches to the form of the Creator.

We have seen on the other hand, that the life of man is his soul or his spirit; that this life consists in will and understanding, or in affections and thoughts; that the human will is a recipient of the Divine Love, and that the human understanding is a recipient of the Divine Wisdom. If, now, we recollect that man does not live of himself, and that he derives his life from God alone, who is Life itself, it will only be necessary to connect these different propositions, one with another, in order to arrive at the following conclusions:

1st. Life itself, or God, being substance and form, the life of man, that is, his soul or spirit, is also substance and form.

2d. God having the human form, the soul or spirit of man has also the human form.

3d. The Divine Love being the first Substance, all things which, in the soul or spirit of man, belong to his will, that is to say, all the affections, are spiritual substances.

4th. The Divine Wisdom being the first Form (*Form-Type*), all things which, in the soul or spirit of man, belong to his understanding, that is to say, all his thoughts, are spiritual forms.

And as there cannot be any substance without form, there is not a single affection in the soul or spirit of man without at the same time a thought which corresponds to it, so that every spiritual substance is always clothed with a spiritual form. It is thus that everything constituting the soul or spirit of man is endowed with a real existence.

It results, then, from all that precedes, that the soul or spirit of man is a substantial being, having the human form; or, in other words, that the soul or spirit of man is a real being having a spiritual body, endowed with all the organs which constitute the material body with which it is clothed. Thus the spirit alone receives life, and if the material body seems to live, it is because the spirit lives in all the parts which constitute this body—the spirit is the man; the material body is but a garment with which the Creator has covered it, according to the laws of order, that it may perform its functions in the natural world

Thus the human form belongs to the spirit, and the body has this form only because it receives it from the spirit.

These truths, my dear sir, will excite your astonishment; but it will be easy for me forthwith to make you understand, that the material body of man can only derive its sensibility and form from this spiritual body, whose existence has just been established; and I think it will be sufficient for this, to prove to you: 1st, that of itself the material body is insensible; 2d, that of itself it has no form properly its own.

1st. *The material body is of itself insensible.* Chemists divide matter into inorganic and organic. It is evident at once that inorganic matter is insensible; with respect to organic matter, M. Dumas has lately shown, in his lectures on chemistry, that of elementary bodies there are not more than ten or twelve at most from which general physiology borrows materials; and that of these ten or twelve bodies there are only four, viz., oxygen, hydrogen, carbon, and azote, which constitute nearly the whole of the composition of living beings. The material body of man is, then, of itself insensible, since it is only composed of oxygen, hydrogen, carbon, and azote, elementary bodies evidently insensible. If, then, it appears sensible, it is because each of the innumerable parts which compose it is the envelope of the same corresponding part of the spiritual body, the only body which can be gifted with sensibility.

2d. ***The material body has not of itself any form which is properly its own.*** This results from the fact that matter has not, *of itself*, any particular form. This proposition may seem to you paradoxical, for matter always offers itself to our eyes under a form which seems properly its own; but observe, that I have said *of itself*. Life never ceasing for a moment to exist in all creation, and this life impressing a form upon all bodies according to the present state of their substances, matter presents itself, and should always present itself to us, clothed with a form which seems properly its own; consequently, to have an idea of what matter can be *of itself*, we must recollect what mathematicians have done when they have treated of the motion of bodies: they have laid it down, as a principle, that a body which has received an impulse must always proceed in a straight line, and never stop. This proposition is, like ours, in manifest opposition to facts: and yet nobody has ever disputed it, because mathematicians would have replied: Abstract for a moment the resistance of the air, and of the friction which results from it, and you will see that our proposition is not to be disputed. Well I will say to you, in like manner: Abstract life for a moment, and you will acknowledge that matter cannot of itself have any particular form. The four elementary bodies, of which our material body is composed, would not have been combined together, so as to present a human form, if they did not cover a spiritual body which has itself this form.

This letter is very long; but I wished not to conclude it, without having given you at least some idea of what the soul or spirit of man really is. I will give you in my next letter, the continuation of this exposition. Accept &c.

LETTER V.

I presumed rightly, my dear sir that you would press me with questions; but I am far from reproaching you for it, because the kind of impatience which you show is easily explained, and is not, to speak favorably, anything more than an ardent desire to be released from your painful situation. You would like to grasp at once the whole of these theories, which surprise you by their novelty, and still more by their elevated ideas. Lost for a long time in the midst of the dark labyrinth of modern philosophy, you have eagerly laid hold of the thread which I have presented to you; but this thread, which should guide your reason, as yet consists for you only in the sequence of the logical deductions which I present to you; but if it should be broken—if the numerous propositions which are yet to be examined, and which engage your mind, should not all form a logical connection with those which precede—if, in a word, there should afterwards be found a want of continuity in the whole system—how would you escape from the labyrinth? Would you not run the risk of being drawn back the more into its dark windings, in proportion to the nearness of your approach to the half enlightened part which borders on its outlet? The flashes of lightning in the midst of night serve only to make it afterwards more dark. Here is your fear; and you express it with so much sincerity, that I should hasten to satisfy you. No: be well assured you have nothing to fear; the thread will not break; follow it with confidence and yon will come out of your labyrinth. All I ask of you is perseverance, and you will find that all the other theories will come in groups around those which I have already presented to you, and constitute in their harmonious whole, the true system of religious philosophy. You will see then, that far from dreading the examination of historical facts, this philosophy will itself be able to urge it; for all those facts which have furnished to scepticism its strongest arguments against the divine Providence, can, on the contrary, *with it*, prove very evidently how much this Providence is always admirable in all its ends.

I had at first intended to answer, in this letter, the questions which you address to me; but after having considered that the greater part of them will be explained in the course of the exposition which I have commenced, it has appeared to me more convenient to continue it. As to those for which there is not room in it, they will be treated of before we go to another subject.

I shall not resume the course of our discussion, without saying a few words to you relative to the simultaneous use which I have hitherto made of the two expressions *Soul* and *Spirit*. My only object was to render myself more intelligible, in making use at once, both of the word commonly received and of that which we ordinarily use; for we mean more particularly by the word *Spirit*, the man who is disengaged from his material covering; and sometimes even to avoid the mistakes which might result from the different acceptations of this word, we make use of the expression *man-spirit*. Thus the man-spirit or *spirit* being with us the man existing in an immaterial world, just as *soul* is to men of the world the principle which survives the decomposition of the body, I shall not any longer use the two expressions simultaneously, but shall more particularly make use of that which we are accustomed to employ. I return now to the principal subject.

It results very evidently from all that I have said to you in my last letter, that man is not annihilated by that so much dreaded event which is called *death*.

You have seen, in fact, that he continues to exist, not as a breath or vapor without substance, not as a fleeting and impalpable shadow, not as a thought without an organic subject, not by transmission of one body into another but indeed, as a true man, with this same organised spiritual body, from which he derived, in the natural world, his sensibility and his form, thus preserving all his identity, taking away with him all that causes him to be man, and only leaving on the earth the external covering by the aid of which he had been in communication with our world, and with the objects included in it. This is what we call a *man-spirit* or in a word, a *spirit*.

Man then does not cease to exist when his material body is no longer in a state to perform the uses for which it was destined; he lives, but on another theatre; he lives, but with a life then much more active, and much more complete than that which he had on this earth; for his spiritual body is no longer encased in a gross covering, as in this world.

This being demonstrated—Does man live in the spiritual world eternally?

This last question must necessarily be settled before we shall be able to conclude that man is immortal; for it is not enough to prove that he lives after his natural death; it is necessary still to show that his existence beyond the grave will be prolonged to eternity.

You will observe however that at the point where we have arrived, the difficulties which the question of the soul's immortality presented are quite removed. Indeed, that which is necessary above all to prove to the men of our age is, that they will live after the dissolution of their bodies. Let man be convinced of this truth, and if there should still remain with him any doubts about the eternity of his spiritual existence, it would be easy to have them removed. If, on the other hand, very great difficulties are experienced in convincing him that he will live after death, it is because being deprived of the most important spiritual truths, he has generally habituated himself to reason only from the illusions of his senses. He is accustomed only to admit with entire conviction, what he sees with the eyes of his body; now, he sees every day the scythe of death cutting down men indiscriminately, and he has never seen one of his victims reappear. He does not know that if everything in the material world presents to us this picture of the successive decomposition of beings, it is because matter of itself is dead, and only receives from the spiritual world the life with which it seems to be animated. He is thence induced to believe that man, like all other beings which dwell with him on the earth, is annihilated by natural death. It is then very difficult when man has fallen into such a state, to convince him with only the common views of philosophy, or even with the arguments of the old theology, that he is excepted from the general law, and that he is destined by his Creator to live eternally. But when it is proved to him that the soul is a substantial being, having the human form—when he has understood that man after his natural death, lives in a spiritual body, that is to say, in a body not subjected to the laws of matter—when he knows that he dwells with this body in a world where all must be life, since matter does not exist there—then he can no longer experience any great difficulties in admitting that man, when become a spirit, lives eternally in a spiritual world.

To demonstrate to you the eternity of this spiritual existence, I will satisfy myself in giving you only two proofs: one of them I will base on the Essence itself of God, or on his divine Love; the other shall be founded on his divine Wisdom in the work of Creation. The first of these proofs, which might alone establish a complete conviction, is that which I derive from the Essence itself of God. You have most readily acknowledged that God is in his Essence Love itself. This definition has pleased you, because it satisfied both your heart and your reason : it is besides, so conformable to the sound idea which ought to be formed of God, that no one, I believe, would venture openly to dispute it. If then, God in his Essence is Love itself, he must necessarily be constant in his love, since *constancy* is one of the essential qualities of love. Now, would not God give the most manifest proofs of *inconstancy* if, after creating human beings that he might love them, and himself be loved by them in return, he should annihilate them? Let us conclude then, that the spirit that has responded to the love of the Creator while living in the material body, will live eternally in the spiritual world. When I have shown you in what consists the existence of the spirit, you will see that God, who never infringes the immutable laws of his divine order, permits him also to subsist eternally who has rejected his love.

My second proof, founded upon the Wisdom of God in the Creation, requires that I should previously give you some ideas upon the nature of the beings that are designated in general by the name of Angels. If I am obliged to speak to you of Angels, on the subject of the immortality of the soul, before showing you in what that which is called Heaven consists, it is because all great questions have numerous points of contact; and it would be impossible thoroughly to treat one without approaching others. Besides, it must be thus in a true system; for in order that its different parts.may form an harmonious whole they should be connected with each other.

Those who believe in the existence of angels, generally think that they are beings created before man and of a superior nature. This opinion, besides resting upon no foundation, is an error. All intelligent beings who exist in the immaterial world, whatsoever other denomination is given to them, are men, and all have lived upon earths before living in the immaterial world. These are two truths which it will be easy to prove.

First: *All the Angels are men.* To admit this proposition as an incontestable truth, it is enough to know what we are to understand by man. God being VERY MAN, and the human-type (*l'homme-type*) the name of man must belong to every creature who is formed in the image or according to the likeness of God, that is to say, who is fit to receive freely his love and wisdom. *Man* then is every being endowed with a *will* fit to receive *freely* the divine love, and with an *understanding* fit to receive *freely* the divine wisdom. And as liberty is an inherent quality of man, it results thence that every man by virtue of his free will appropriates or rejects, in different degrees, this love and this wisdom, which are always in the effort to enter into him. From this it is that the difference proceeds which is observed between all men, and which causes each to be himself, and impossible to be confounded with another. But whatsoever may be the diversity which exists between intelligent beings, whether Hottentots, Laplanders, Chinese, or Europeans; whether black, copper-colored, or white; whether they inhabit this earth or the planets of our solar system, or even those of other systems; in a word, whatsoever may be the character, stature, and color of a being, provided he has a cerebellum and cerebrum, formed in such a manner as to be able to receive the divine love and the divine wisdom, this being is a *man*.

Now, according to this definition of man, a definition which is but a consequence of principles already explained, you see that there cannot exist intermediate beings between God and man, and that thus angels are, properly speaking, men. If, however, from a recollection of instruction received in your childhood, there remains yet a propensity to consider angels as beings of a nature superior to man, I would suggest to you, that in these same instructions you learned also that God had created man in his image, and according to his likeness. Now if an angel, who is also a creature of God, was of a nature superior to that of man, pray, tell me, what could that nature be? Use all the efforts of your imagination, and see if it would be possible to conceive of a nature superior to that which is in the image and according to the likeness of God. Those who held this language to you contradicted themselves. No, I repeat it, there are not and there cannot be beings intermediate between God and men, or of a nature superior to that of man, and this, because God is VERY MAN; and besides, all beings to whom are given the name of angels, have the human form, because the first form (*Form-Type*) is the human form. All angels then are men.

Second: *All Angels have lived upon earths before living in the immaterial world.* It is very evident that it is only in a preparatory world, that is to say, in the natural world, that intelli gent creatures are enabled to use free will, or choose between good and evil, between the true and the false. If the inhabitants of heaven could become guilty or rebellious, none would be certain of remaining there, whence heaven would be no longer heaven, for the single idea of the possibility of being driven thence would destroy that happiness which makes heaven to be what it is. You will see presently when we treat upon the mode of the existence of Spirits, that there is no choice to make in the spiritual World, because choice has been made in the natural world; you will see that every one then enjoys, not free will, but *liberty*, which in the good consists in doing good *freely*, without fearing evil, and in the wicked, in freely doing evil without experiencing remorse; so that the liberty of one is true liberty, with all the enjoyments which result from it, and that of the other genuine slavery, the slavery of evil, with all the torments which it produces. If then, there is no enjoyment of free will but in the natural world, from all necessity it results that angels have first lived upon earths, or that they have been created without being endowed with free will. Now, in this second hypothesis, far from being superior to man, the angels would be much inferior to him, for they would be no more than automatons, destitute of the principle of reciprocality, and thence unworthy of the love of God. In fact, from the principles which have been set forth in my second letter, a being created perfect would be but an instrument purely passive, or a machine. It thence evidently results that angels are men, who during their life in the natural world have been rendered worthy to receive afterwards the divine Love and the divine Wisdom in a very high degree.

Thus is confirmed anew this proposition, already advanced, that man was the sole end of Creation; for since there are no intermediate beings between God and man, it results necessarily that all that exists, as well in the natural as in the spiritual world, has been created with a view to man, who is the only being capable, by his constitution, of returning to his Creator the love which he receives from him. The spiritual or immaterial universe being thus found to be peopled only with men who have lived originally upon the earths, if these men who are spirits or angels are not to live eternally, it follows either that they would successively cease to exist, as in our world, or that they would cease to exist all at once. There are no other suppositions to make; now these suppositions are both inadmissible.

To suppose the *successive* ceasing of the inhabitants of the spiritual world, to make way for others, would be to suppose that the immaterial world might be no longer capable of containing all the beings who are daily leaving the earths; this would be as a consequence to assimilate the spiritual to the material, or to compare life to death; for it is life which constitutes the spiritual world, and you know that matter of itself is dead or deprived of life; it would be, in a word, to materialize affection and thought. Now, if affection and thought can be exempt from the laws of space even in this world (of which you may easily convince yourself, since your affection and thought know no distance), how could it be supposed that they would be subjected to these laws when man is no longer imprisoned in matter? The first hypothesis is then inadmissible.

To suppose that the inhabitants of the spiritual world should cease to exist *at one time* would be supposing that that world might be annihilated, for what would a spiritual world be totally deprived of intelligent beings? And as the material world is of itself dead, and has life only from the spiritual world, this would be to suppose the annihilation of all that has been created. Now, if the whole creation were annihilated, God who is Love itself, could no longer diffuse his love, the essence of which is to be communicative; and his divine Wisdom which is Foresight itself, would be imperfect, since in creating the universe that the divine Love might might be satisfied, it would not have been able to accomplish this end. Such a supposition, which would accuse the divine Wisdom of want of foresight, is then likewise inadmissible. Thence results the second proof of the eternity of the spirit in the immaterial world.

Now let us recapitulate what has been said on the immortality of man. I have shown you in my last letter, that man does not cease to exist at the time which is very improperly called death; that he continues to live in the spiritual world, with a body organized like the one he had in the natural world —that this body, of a nature wholly spiritual, is not given to him at the time of his passage from one world into another—that he has had this spiritual body in the natural world—that it is truly by it that he experienced sensations in this world, and that it has had the human form, his material body having been but a simple covering, with which the Creator had invested him that he might perform his functions in the natural world. Lastly, in this letter, to establish the certainty that the spirit, or the man divested of his material covering, must live eternally in the spiritual world, I have demonstrated that if he should cease to exist, God, who is love itself, would contravene one of the essential conditions of love, by exhibiting himself as inconstant, which cannot for a moment be supposed; and moreover, that the end of creation would not be attained, which could not be admitted, without accusing the divine Wisdom of want of foresight. From all this results rationally the complete proof of the immortality of the soul.

Do not believe, however, that I rest upon the reasonings which I have presented to you. Strange would be my illusion, if I thought I had established in you a firm conviction. because I had proved to you, by a logical train of arguments, that you were to live eternally. No, my dear sir, should you even say: I am altogether convinced, I could not believe it; not that I would doubt the sincerity of your avowal, but because in the actual state of your present ideas, a firm convictiou on such a subject could not be formed but by a long series of meditations. I will grant you then all the time necessary, and will furnish you, in each of my letters, means for meditating on the eternity of your existence; for of all theories which are yet to be examined, there is not one which does not bring new confirmative proofs of this important truth.

As that which is the most difficult to admit in this discussion, is the existence of the spirit in the human form, with a spiritual organised body, I cannot too much insist upon this point. To the proofs then already given, I shall add some others drawn from the observation of certain facts which may be easily verified. These new proofs will be so much the more to your taste, as it is generally required, at this day, that theories should be confirmed by facts.

Towards the conclusion of my last letter, I proved to you that the material body of man is of itself insensible, and has no form properly its own. These two truths, drawn from modern science, already evidently confirm the existence, with man, of a spiritual organized body; for if the material body has of itself neither sensibility nor form, it is necessary that both of these should be derived from the spiritual body. It remains now to confirm, by the observation of facts, that this spiritual body has the same organization as the material body which covers it.

When a man receives a wound, he suffers. Why does he suffer? Because the separation of continuity which exists in the wounded part disturbs the organization of his body. But what is it that suffers in him? is it matter? No: since it is of itself insensible. Is it his soul? Yes, since his soul, or his spirit, that is, his life, is the man himself. Now, how could you, from the ideas of philosophers, conceive that the soul, the spirit, or the life, could suffer from an act purely material? Hitherto it has been absolutely impossible to account for it; in vain explanations have been sought; the physiologists in their researches have not been more fortunate than the psychologists; neither the one nor the other have as yet presented anything satisfactory. But if recourse is had to our theories, and a spiritual body is admitted, organised like the material body, all is easily explained. We invite you to the test.

Life is composed of affections and thoughts; the affections being spiritual substances, and the thoughts spiritual forms, the life peculiar to every being is always organised, by means of these substances and forms, by reason of the affections and thoughts or instincts of which this being has been created susceptible. Now man having been created such that he could receive the divine love in his will and the divine wisdom in his understanding, it results from this, that in him life is in a complete state; that it is an image of Life itself or of God; and that consequently it is, in the whole, a substance having the form of God, that is to say, the human. Observe at the same time, that man cannot act in the material world but by an intermediation of matter; that it is for this reason that all the parts of his spiritual body have been covered with material substances which constitute his natural body, and it will be easy to comprehend why man suffers when his material body receives a wound.

Indeed, when the material body is in its integrity, the spiritual body is able to act freely according to internal impulses; but if the material body is hurt, whether by contusion, by incision, or in any other manner, the action of the spiritual body not being able to put itself forth freely, there is pain, suffering. If, for example, there is separation of continuity in a part of the material body, there is not, in truth, on that account separation of continuity in the corresponding part of the spiritual body, but this body being no longer able to act in our world by the injured part of the material body, there is pain so much the more acute, so much the more severe, as the disturbance is great; and this pain may even affect the whole organization of the spiritual body, if the injury is of a nature to disturb its general action. If, moreover, the injured part is an organ indispensable to the general action of the spiritual body, such as the heart, for example, or such as the lungs, the material body, not being of any further use to the spiritual body for acting in our world, it is impossible that the two bodies should remain longer united. Then the separation takes place; the material body being then nothing more than a corpse, and the spiritual body disengaged from the bonds which confined it in the natural world, at once exists without the need of translation, in the spiritual world.

Let me support what has been said by a phenomenon which has often been produced. You have no doubt conversed with soldiers who have suffered amputation of their limbs; our late wars have unhappily but too much increased their number. Have you not often heard these brave men complain of severe pains which they experienced in the heel or the toe, though their leg has been left many years since in the field of Austerlitz or the plains of Leipsic? Has it not sometimes happened to you to see them even—so strong is the impression—suddenly carry the hand to the part affected, with the intention of compressing there the pain, and have you not then perceived their disappointment when, for the hundredth time perhaps, they seized nothing but a piece of insensible wood? If you have never witnessed such facts, ask the first person who has suffered the loss of a limb, and he will confirm you in the reality of it. If afterwards, struck with this extraordinary phenomenon, you would desire to know the cause, would you inquire of science? You would receive no satisfactory answer. Should you be more fortunate in consulting philosophy? Philosophy would be dumb. But have recourse to the principles which I have explained, and you will easily obtain an explanation which will satisfy your reason.

The amputation of a leg or of any other member of the material body, cannot deprive the spiritual body of this member. The person who has lost a limb preserves then his spiritual body in its integrity; if the spiritual limb is not visible to the eyes of our material body, it is because the material is not capable of seeing anything but what is material. It is not, it is true, the material eye which sees; it is the spiritual eye; but as in general the spiritual eye cannot see in our world but by the medium of the material covering, for this reason I say that the material can see nothing but what is material. Now, since the spiritual leg of the person amputated always exists, though invisible to the eyes of our body, it is not astonishing that this leg, or even its extremity, should be affected with a pain of which the amputated person will experience the sensation; it is the spiritual body which suffers in him, and not the material. Besides, as there are circumstances where, with those who enjoy their material limbs, a pain in the superior parts extends even to the heel or the toe, and becomes even more severe in these extreme parts, it may clearly be seen that it should be the same in like circumstances, though the material leg no longer exists.

According to the same principle of the integrity of the spiritual body, notwithstanding the mutilation of the material body, the man who has been deprived of his material eyes, preserves his spiritual eyes entire, he is only blind as to that which concerns the objects of this world. He does not see these objects, because the spiritual eye, as I have told you, cannot see in the material world but by the medium of the material organ of vision, and this organ failing, the phenomenon of natural vision ceases immediately. In like manner, the deaf man does not hear, because the spiritual ear cannot perceive the sounds of the natural world but by the intermediation of the material organ of hearing, and if this organ is hurt, deafness ensues; but the deaf man preserves entire the spiritual organ of hearing.

If during sleep the blind man has had a dream and retains the recollection of his dream, he then acknowledges that he saw objects which were presented to him as distinctly as he saw natural objects when he had the use of his eyes. The deaf man acknowledges also, when he retains the recollection of his dream, that he then perceived sounds as distinctly as he perceived natural sounds before his state of deafness. How are we to explain these facts? It will be said without doubt that they are the effects of the imagination; but then what is this imagination? It would be very difficult to answer the question. The imagination is often suggested as a reason: it is a word which the philosophy of the day highly esteems, for it serves to withdraw it from embarrassments when it is pushed to its last entrenchments; but it is very evident that to attribute such facts to the imagination, would be evading the question, and not resolving it. To explain now to you the theory of dreams, would be digressing too far from my subject; we will examine it together hereafter; I will only say that generally in dreams, it is the spiritual body of man which is alone active, and this is sufficient to give an explanation of the facts respecting the sight of the blind and hearing of the deaf.

The blind man sees then with his spiritual eyes, and the deaf man hears with his spiritual ears.

It would be easy to multiply confirmative proofs of the existence in man of an organized spiritual body, by explaining the extraordinary facts which some new branches of science reveal; but I should be drawn into too long a digression, for these new branches of science being yet for the most part devoid of theories, and presenting, to say the least, as many inconveniences as disadvantages, I could not speak of them without specifically pointing them out, which would cause you to lose sight of the exposition which now engages our attention. Nevertheless, when you become acquainted with the order of the spiritual world, and the mode of existence of its inhabitants, you will always find me disposed to reply to the questions which you may think proper to ask on the subject of these new discoveries, and I will take care to put you on your guard against the dangers which they may present.

Accept, &c.

LETTER VI.

Although you have acknowledged the force and stability of the proofs which I have given you concerning the immortality of the soul, yet I could not hope to establish an unshaken conviction on this point, if there were not in reserve some other means of strengthening that which you confess begins to be formed within you. Of what use would it have been to have proved to you that your material body is only an envelope, and to have shown you that this envelope, though necessary to your present existence, is not indispensable to constitute the real life, of which the life of this world is but the first link? Of what use would it have been to have convinced you that there exists in you a spiritual body—that this body is absolutely organized like your body of flesh, and that it is as indestructible as everything else which is of a spiritual nature? Of what use would these truths be, if I were not to make you acquainted with the spiritual world, of which it is yet impossible for you to form an idea?—if I were not to place before your eyes this new theatre upon which your man-spirit must exercise to all eternity the functions of his immaterial nature? Without a knowledge of that world, how could you combat in yourself the objections of every kind which would come in crowds to assail your first conviction? One day you would believe, the next deny.

Far from having brought relief to your position, I should only have rendered it the more intolerable, by exciting in you a desire to believe, without presenting to you all that is necessary to establish and confirm your faith. You would have had a right to say to me: "This breath, or this vapory being of philosophers and theologians, I thought little about, since it is impossible to form a clear idea of it; I thought no more about angels, whom they represent in human form, for the wings which they give to them show plainly enough that they are but pure fictions. However, I might have been able in some degree by an effort of the imagination, to represent to myself, in the midst of the immensity of the etherial regions, souls wandering here and there, and angels flapping or poising their wings to support their bodies. But your men-spirits, and your angels in a perfect human form, what idea can I form of their existence? Philosophers and theologians place but little stress on their lucubrations relative to the nature of the soul; almost all confess that they are far from relying with certainty upon what they advance, while you on the contrary, appear to have not the least doubt of your assertions

Hasten, then, to draw me from this position, or else, while wishing to relieve me of my doubts, you will but have increased them."

With great propriety would you thus address me, if I should delay satisfying the desire you must have to know something of this spiritual world: therefore I am anxious to give you some ideas which will enable you at once to comprehend the the whole. You will see then that the spirit, disengaged from the matter with which it is here covered, possesses all that which is necessary for its existence; and that the life which it enjoys is much more complete than that which it had upon this earth.

It would, without doubt, be easier to present to you these views, if you were acquainted with our theory of degrees, and our manner of regarding space and time; but in your present state, it is necessary to proceed at once to the subject; I shall, therefore, enter upon it without any preliminary remarks.

The knowledge which we have of the man-spirit will conduct us directly to that of the spiritual world. In this, it will be sufficient to follow the law of analogy, for there must exist, between the spiritual and the material worlds, relations analogous to those which exist between the spirit and the material body. Now if the spirit is a real man, if the form of the material body belongs to the spirit, and these are two truths which we have acknowledged, we must thence conclude that the spiritual world is a real world, and that the form of the material world belongs to the spiritual world.

Indeed, from this alone, that you have acknowledged the truths which concern the man-spirit, you are forced to admit the correlative truths which apply to the spiritual world. If, as the discoveries of modern science prove, the matter of which our body is composed, is of itself insensible, and has of itself no particular form, with much stronger reason must it be the same with inorganic matter. If the material body does not live of itself, how can the other objects of nature have existence of themselves, and how can nature, in the complex, exist of itself? If the matter which composes our bodies has not form of itself, how can that which constitutes the other bodies of nature, of itself present to us the indefinite variety of forms which charm our sight, and how can the whole of nature have a form? All the objects which exist in our world receive, then, their form from objects similar, or properly *corresponding*, which are in the spiritual world. I say *corresponding*, for though the things in the spiritual world appear like those which are in ours, it is to be observed, however, that they differ from them in this, that they have in them life, because they exist and subsist from the spiritual sun, in the interior of which resides the Divinity; while the things of the natural world, existing and subsisting from the material sun, have no life in them, but what they receive by the intermediation of the spiritual world.

Since, according to this, there cannot be in our world a single object which is not the *correspondent* of an object existing in the spiritual world, in reality, that is to say, in substance and form, the strict consequence which we must thence draw is, that there is in that world, as in ours, stars which appear fixed in an azure vault, a horizon with its zenith, atmospheres with their meteors, countries watered by rivers, seas confined to their limits by coasts, the three kingdoms with all that constitutes them, and the indefinite variety of all the objects of art, which result from the labors of man. Thus, my dear sir, if until this moment, as I have supposed at the commencement of this letter, you had not been able to form in yourself an idea of the existence of men-spirits; if you had not known where to place these spiritual bodies, organized like our material bodies, you see now, that by means of these objects, which are all of an immaterial nature, men-spirits enjoy a real existence, which it is no longer impossible to comprehend. You see, also, that far from being lost in a vapory immensity, they exist upon a solid earth, and are surrounded with real objects, for the earth upon which they walk, the houses which they inhabit, the air which they breathe, and all the objects in general which are before their eyes, or which they touch, are then for them as real as our earth, our habitations, the air, and all that which surrounds us is now real for us.

You will, without doubt, be as much astonished in learning these things, as you were when I announced to you that your soul or your spirit is a real man, having a spiritual organization, like that of your terrestrial body. Nevertheless, the first truth must have served to prepare you for the second; for these are, as I have told you, two correlative truths, and the admission of the one, necessarily draws after it that of the other. Your astonishment would be still greater, if I should at once make you acquainted with this spiritual world in all its details; but before presenting you with the details, I must endeavor to convince you of the reality of the whole.

As you read that which precedes, your mind, it seems to me, will be greatly excited to know where this spiritual world can be situated. This desire appears to me so much the more natural on your part, as from your quality as a man of the world, you cannot yet think of spiritual things, but from ideas of space and time. Yet the spiritual world, from its very nature, is entirely freed from the trammels of space and time; for space and time are accidents inherent in matter, and can only exist in reality in the natural world. I will return soon to these truths, which I now merely announce, for it is important that I should present to you at once, some general considerations upon the relations which exist between God, the spiritual world, and the natural world. This subject being of an abstract nature, I claim for a moment all your attention.

When you do a work you are directed by a motive, and you have an object in view. This object is, philosophically speaking, the *end;* the motive which directs you, is the *cause;* the work which you do is the *effect.* These are three things which are connected together by relations which it is important well to determine.

With very little reflection upon that which passes in your mind when you act, you will easily see the difference which exists between the end and the cause, in acknowledging that the *end* or the aim, is an affection which resides in your will, whilst the *cause* is a thought which has for its seat your understanding. But that you may be better able to comprehend this difference, and follow this discussion without any effort, I shall support what I have said by an example.

When a sculptor wishes to make a statue from a block of marble, he is evidently moved to satisfy an affection, and directed afterwards by a thought. His affection is either to provide for his natural wants, or to acquire fame. This first moving principle of the sculptor is the *end* or aim. Afterwards he has recourse to his intellectual faculties to create a form; the thought which conceives the form to give to the marble is the *cause,* for it is this thought which will direct the hand of the sculptor in the execution of his work. Finally, the manifestation of this form by the chisel, that is to say, the statue itself, is the *effect.*

It thence results that the end, the cause, and effect, are not in relations which precede by continuity, whether from the simple to the compound, or from the compound to the simple, as are for the most part those which exist between things of the same nature. Their relations do not consist in fact either in increase or decrease of the same thing, as the relation of light to heavy, which is only an increment of density, nor as that of heat to cold which is but a decrement of caloric. But if we examine attentively the nature of the end, of the cause, and of the effect, we see that these three things are placed one above the other, in degrees entirely distinct or separate from one another, so that the relations which exist between them are like those of the *anterior* to the *posterior*, or like those of the *superior* to the *inferior*.

It is, indeed, evident that the end or design is *anterior* and *superior* to the cause; the end is *anterior* to the cause; for the sculptor has been moved by the love of riches or of glory, beside having had recourse to his intellectual faculties to create the form of the statue: the end is *superior* to the cause; for the love or affection of the sculptor is above his thought, since it is this love or this affection which has determined his thought, and which does not cease to sustain it. Suppose this love in the sculptor should cease, would not his thought be immediately directed to some other object?

It is in like manner evident, that the cause is *anterior* and *superior* to the effect; for the thought of the sculptor had conceived the form of the statue, or of every part of the statue, *before* his hand applied the chisel to it; the cause is *superior* to the *effect;* for the thought of the sculptor is *above* the statue, since it is this thought which determines the form of the statue. If, before having finished his work, the sculptor rejected his thought, would not the form of the statue have remained unfinished?

Not to confound these relations between things which are of an absolutely different nature with the relations which result from increments or decrements of the same thing, we give to the first the name of *discrete degrees*, and to the others the name of *continuous degrees*. So there are three *discrete degrees* —the end forms the first degree, the cause is the second, and the effect is the third or last. Continuous degrees are in number indefinite. The theory of continuous degrees is not difficult to comprehend, because these degrees, presenting only differences in more or less, can be easily studied. But it is not so with the *discrete degrees:* the theory of these, also, which constitutes a real science, is, at this day, entirely obliterated, and it is the loss of this knowledge which produces all the vague lucubrations of philosophy, when it is engaged in the considerations of ends, causes and effects. As the nature of the questions we treat of will compel me often to have recourse to this theory, I propose to develope to you successively its principles.

The end, the cause, and the effect being three things of a nature absolutely different, but united by relations of anteriority and superiority, it concerns us now to see what results from these relations.

Be it observed, in the first place, that ends and causes can only be comprehended so far as they are manifested in effects. Without the acts which they produce, they would be as if they had no existence; but, by means of their manifestation, they are fixed in effects, repose in them as upon their basis, and remain there so long as the effects subsist. Thus, so long as the statue subsists, the thought of the sculptor will remain in this statue, the form of which is nothing else than this thought definitely arrested and fixed; but, though it may be thus arrested and fixed in such a manner as to strike the eyes and minds of those who contemplate the statue, it is nevertheless certain that this thought does not cease to be in the sculptor; it is then also out of the statue. This is a fact so evident that it cannot be disputed; but how is this fact to be explained if not by the relations of anteriority and posteriority, which exist between the thought of the sculptor and the statue? Really, if the thought of the sculptor presents itself in the statue—which cannot be denied—it is nevertheless not there, but as all that which is *anterior* and *superior* presents itself in the things *posterior* and *inferior* which correspond to it, that is to say, that it does not the less subsist out of the statue, by reason that that which is anterior and superior cannot be absorbed by that which is posterior and inferior. It is thus that the cause subsists out of the effect, though being in the effect.

What I have just said concerning the cause and the effect is applicable to the end and the cause, between which exist the same relations of superiority and anteriority. The end subsists, then, out of the cause, though being in the cause. Farther, as the cause itself is in the effect, it results that the end and the cause both subsist out of the effect, though being both in the effect.

I will resume what precedes in the two following propositions:

1st. The end is simultaneonsly in the cause and out of the cause.

2nd. The end and the cause are simultaneously in the effect and out of the effect.

This granted: all that which exists in the universe having been created with a view to man, to the end that by man the whole creation might return to the Creator, God is evidently the First End of all things.

All that which is of a spiritual nature, consisting in affections and thoughts, that is to say, in living forces always in activity to manifest themselves in acts which are proper to the cause, the spiritual world includes the causes of all things. All that which is of a material nature, consisting in bodies more or less gross, manifested by causes which themselves proceed from the first end, the natural world is the theatre of *effects*.

Lastly, the relations between God, the spiritual world, and the natural world, being thus absolutely the same as those which exist between the end, the cause, and the effect, the two preceding propositions reveal to us these two important truths.

1st. God is simultaneously in the spiritual world and out of the spiritual world.

2nd. God and the spiritual world are simultaneously in the natural world and out of the natural world.

Thus, in the creation, everything is bound together and connected with God, without the possibility of God being confounded with his work. God is the statuary, and the universe is the statue which his divine Thought or his Wisdom has formed and vivified, with a view to satisfy his divine Affection or his Love.

Thus the universe proceeds from God, not by continuity, which would be to deify creation, but by contiguity.

Thus, in that which concerns man, God and the spiritual world are within him, and are also out of him. God is within man, for man finds God in the recesses of his heart, when, by renunciation of his selfish interests, he devotes himself to the general good, or sacrifices himself for one of his brethren. The spiritual world is within man, for man finds in himself his affections and all his thoughts, which evidently belong to the spiritual world, since their nature is wholly immaterial. But when man is disengaged from matter, or when his material body is for him as if it did not exist, then, though God and the spiritual world are in him, he sees them also out of him. He sees God as a spiritual sun, and also as man, when it pleases the Divinity to manifest himself under the human form; and he sees the spiritual world as a real world, containing all that which is necessary to the existence of the man-spirit; for all the affections being spiritual substances, and all the thoughts spiritual forms, there are found there, by means of these substances and these forms, objects corresponding to the objects of our world, which are of themselves correspondences of affections and thoughts.

Thus, the spiritual world which philosophy had made to vanish by subtilizing it, you can now represent to yourself by means of the conception of spiritual substances and forms, as having all the consistence of the material world, without supposing a single particle of matter. But, though the preceding truths are drawn from logical deductions, nevertheless you will be able to comprehend them clearly only so far as you can abstract your thought from space. Indeed, God and the spiritual world being out of the natural world, as the sculptor is out of the statue, they are also out of space; for space is proper to the natural world, and consequently exists only for this world where all is fixed, regulated, and constant, because ends and causes subsist there in their repose.

Here then is the place to examine the two propositions previously announced on the subject of space and time, to wit:

1st. *That space and time are accidents inherent in matter.*
2nd. *That space and time cannot exist but in the natural world.* Let us consider separately these two propositions, and first, as to what concerns space:

1st. *Space is inherent in matter:* This is evident, for it is impossible, by reason of the force of inertia in matter, to conceive this matter without the idea of space.

2d. *Space can only exist in the natural world:* It is easy to convince yourself that everything spiritual, that is to say, all that which is affection and thought, is independent of space. Truly, if man cannot free himself from space when he pleases, it is because he is, as to all the parts which constitute him, enveloped in a material body, and because he thus finds himself subject to the laws of matter in that which concerns his body. Thence it is that, in order to convey himself to any place, he is obliged to pass through places which separate him from it; but if he abstracts himself from this body, by concentrating himself in his affection and thought, the case with him is different, and the trammels of space disappear for an instant. I say for an instant, because it is hardly possible that a man should make this abstraction long, inasmuch as, living in this world in the midst of material objects, his ideas are incessantly carried back upon these objects. When, by your will and your understanding you transport yourself in affection and thought to an absent friend, or to places which awaken agreeable recollections, do you not really abstract space? This space, which so often opposes your desires, only exists, then, for you because the material body with which you are clothed in this world subjects you to the laws of matter. Thus there is, in reality, no space for affection nor for thought; nor, consequently for all that which is spiritual, since the spiritual is composed of nothing else but affections and thoughts.

In that which concerns time:

1st. *Time is inherent in matter.* This results also from the inertia of matter—inertia from which this matter can be subjected to regular movements. The measure of time is owing, in fact, to the two-fold motion of the earth upon itself, and around the sun, or what is the same thing, to the appearance of the double motion of the sun around and in the ecliptic; for you know that it is this double motion which gives us the alternate return of day and night, and the succession of years. Suppose our planet should no longer be subjected to this two-fold motion, and should remain immovable—what would happen? The sun would no longer have his two apparent motions, and would remain for us invariably fixed to one of the points of the azure vault; then there would be no more night for the hemisphere, which would be enlightened, and which alone would be inhabited; no more return of seasons; but one perpetual day, one temperature, whose changes for every locality would depend upon the irregular variations of the atmosphere. How, in such a case, could we measure time? What end would be served by the instruments now in use? Every one, certainly, would be obliged to refer to his own sensations. In such a state of things, it is evident that we should not measure time, for you know that pain and ennui make it appear long, while pleasure and absence of mind shorten it; this would be then rather the *state* of the soul, and the different modifications of that state which we should determine. It thence evidently results that time is owing to the force of inertia of matter, and thus it is inherent in matter.

2d. *Time can only exist in the natural world.* Since time is owing to the force of the inertia of matter, and since it would be impossible to measure it, if material nature were not subjected to regular motions, it results that time cannot exist where the law of inertia does not exist; now this law can only exist for matter. In fact, the spiritual, having been endowed with the liberty or the faculty of moving itself freely, cannot be subject to the law of inertia, for this law and the law of liberty are by no means compatible. Besides, it is easy to see of yourself that time does not exist either for affections or for thoughts; you can free yourself from it, whether by your will and your understanding you carry yourself into the past, even the most remote, which then appears to you present; or whether by these same faculties you represent to yourself the time which is to come.

I will here add, as an observation, that there is in man an innate desire to free himself from the shackles of space and time, and this desire, which is ever appearing, is itself, if not a proof, at least a strong presumption, that the spiritual world, for which man is born, is independent of space and time.

It is also the consequence which flows from my second proposition. In fact, if space and time cannot exist but in the natural world, there is in the spiritual world neither space nor time. Then how can we form an idea of that world? How form a conception of earths, mountains, valleys, meadows, gardens, houses, inhabitants there, if there is not space? How admit there that succession of events which, properly speaking, constitutes existence, if there is not time there?

Although the objection seems strong, a few reflections will suffice to remove it. Habituated as we are to live in a world where we cannot act without being continually subjected to the trammels of space and time, we can hardly conceive of an existence freed from these fetters. Our ignorance of the true nature of spiritual substances and forms, which are nothing else but affections and thoughts, induces us to believe that without space and time there would be nothing there ; no individual thing; that all would be confounded, or rather that all would be annihilated. It is true, it would be thus with our world, since space and time are inherent in matter; but it is quite different in the immaterial world. There substances and forms preserve their individual state, without having need, for this purpose, of space and time. If these substances and forms, which are types of the substances and forms which we see in our world, were not of themselves in the individual state, our world would not exist, since material substances and forms exist from spiritual substances and forms. The material and spiritual worlds are then both composed of individual things, but with this difference, that individual things in the former are subjected to the laws of inertia, whilst in the latter they are governed by the law of liberty.

It thence becomes evident, that there is in the spiritual world the *equivalent* of our space and time, considered only in this, that they cause substances and forms to be in the individual state, and not in this, that they place fetters upon their action; for this last property of space and time proceeds from their inherence in matter, while they owe their first property to the mode itself of the existence of spiritual substances and forms. Yet being obliged, in order to be better understood, to compare spiritual things with natural things, we give to this *equivalent* of space and time the name of *appearance*, and we say that in the spiritual world there is the *appearance* of space and time, though to speak more correctly, we should say that the mode of existence of substances and forms, in our space and our time, is itself a *gross appearance* of their real mode of existence, since instead of acting freely according to their nature, they are confined by space and time in a material prison. Besides, how many appearances are taken for realities, and how many realities for appearances! If man would only reflect a little upon the subject, he would see that in our world everything is filled with appearances which are taken for realities; and, to cite only one example, how many various appearances proceed from the apparent immobility of the earth!

In conclusion, it remains for us to enquire what it is which constitutes for spirits the appearance of space and time. This question being connected with other theories which we will soon examine, I will satisfy myself for the present with giving you a summary solution of it. This appearance of space and time's being the real mode of the existence of spirits, must necessarily result from the life of each one of them. Consequently, the different states of the affections of a spirit constitute for him the appearance of our space, and the different states of his thoughts, the appearance of our time.

I have entered into all these considerations relative to space and time, because it is impossible to comprehend clearly spiritual things if we do not abstract our minds from these two accidents adherent to matter.

To think of God from space, is to think of the extent of nature and to fall into materialism; but when we think of God as *out of* space and time, though *in* space and time, we can conceive Him to be everywhere present, and in all his entireness in the greatest as well as the least things. In his quality of Infinite, he fills all spaces without being himself, like material things, in space; and in his quality of Eternal, he is in all the parts of time, without the divisions of time being applicable to him. Mathematics prove in fact that the infinite is applicable to the greatest as well as to the least thing: and philosophy acknowledges that the eternity of God, being anterior and posterior, there is to God himself neither past nor future.

To think of the spiritual world from space, would be to materialize that which from its nature is immaterial; but when we acknowledge that the spiritual world is out of space and time, though it be in space and time in this sense that it transmits to the material world the life which it receives from God, we can conceive of this spiritual world as really existing, without, on that account, assigning to it a fixed and determinate position; we can conceive that it is in the natural world and out of the natural world; in man and out of man.

I propose soon to show you what is the mode of existence of the man-spirit. It will then be very easy, by the details into which I shall enter, to represent to yourself this immaterial world, of which you cannot as yet have a very clear idea.

Accept, &c.

LETTER VII.

To trace in my exposition the great features of the spiritual world, without stopping to reply to the objections which might arise in your mind was, as you know, my first design. I saw in this the double advantage of enabling you to embrace an idea of the whole at once, and a saving of time in the examination of questions, some of which must necessarily find a place in the course of the discussion; others have been introduced only because you had not this general idea; but your last letter contains so serious an objection, that I find it necessary to examine it immediately. Besides, the desire you manifest, to be enlightened as soon as possible on this subject, is a sufficient reason for me to return to my preceding determination.

Not to diminish in the least the force of your objection, I extract from your letter the whole paragraph which contains it.

"While reading, in your fifth letter, your views concerning the human soul, there arose one objection. I willingly admit that it is the human soul alone that suffers when the body is injured: I admit also that it is this which suffers in the amputated body; but the argument you use would apply as well to animals as to man, for animals experience the same sufferings that we do, and an animal having a limb amputated would in like manner suffer from a member which it would no longer possess. It would seem to result, then, that animals also have a spiritual body. I did not first present this objection, because I expected to see it removed in the course of your exposition, as it has happened with many others which I had previously submitted.

"Nevertheless, far from removing this difficulty, your sixth letter, on the contrary, has rendered it still more serious, since you place in the spiritual world all the objects of the animal kingdom. You say, in fact, that there is not a single object in our world which is not the correspondent of an object existing in reality, that is to say, in substance and form, in the spiritual world; and in the enumeration which you make of these objects you cite the three kingdoms with all that constitues them. Now, to give a spiritual body to animals, and to say, besides, that there are animals in the spiritual world, is evidently assimilating animals to man, for this is not only giving them a soul, but it is making this soul enjoy immortality. Relieve me at once, I pray you, from the disorder of ideas in which these reflections involve me. Your system pleased me; I was rejoiced to see that every one of your letters removed difficulties which I believed to be inextricable. I was not yet, it is true, very familiar with your spiritual substances and forms; but there were so many pleasing ideas in representing man spiritually organised, and thus surviving a complete man, after the dissolution of his mortal body, that you led me eagerly to desire that so beautiful a conception might be a reality. I would, I confess, experience regret in abandoning ideas which were to me a consoling balm; but I should be compelled to reject them if you give a soul to beasts; for my reason would decide for the complete annihilation of man and animals, rather than admit to the privilege of immortality beings deprived of reason."

I cannot reproach you, my dear sir, for having supposed that we attribute to animals an immortal soul, for I expected such an objection. When we are heard to say that there are animals in the spiritual world, there are few persons who would not exclaim: Have beasts also a soul? This exclamation appears to us so natural, that it by no means surprises us. Men's ideas at this day are so vague upon all that concerns man; the discussions of philosophy concerning the soul of beasts, far from throwing light on this subject, have thrown so much obscurity upon it; there are so many of the learned who by their writings have given rise to the belief, when yet they have not postively said so, that between man and beast there is only the difference of more or less—it cannot be surprising that they at first should persuade themselves that we also assimilate beasts to men. We are, however, far from admitting such an opinion, which would be in complete opposition to all our principles. We, on the contrary, use all our efforts to destroy so fatal an error, which introduces materialism into all classes of society; for so soon as there is admitted, between man and beast, only the difference of more or less, men are logically led to believe that man, like a beast, is annihilated by natural death. But to combat this error, instead of having recourse, like the old philosophy, to common-place ideas, the impotency of which is acknowledged, we will demonstrate that the difference between man and beast is so distinct, that it is impossible, when we have once recognised it, ever to assimilate the one to the other.

Now that I have relieved you by making known to you our principles upon this important point, I come to your objection, which may be thus stated :

"If you give a spiritual body to animals, and if, besides, there are animals in the spiritual world, you evidently attribute an immortal soul to the animal."

To this I reply:

Yes, we give a spiritual body to animals: also, there are animals in the spiritual world; and yet an animal has not an immortal soul.

Thus, though I admit with you the two propositions which lead you to conclude that animals have an immortal soul, I maintain the contrary; but yet I am not at all surprised at the conclusion you have drawn, for all other persons would have concluded the same, because they are generally ignorant of what the nature of man is, what that of beasts, and what are the conditions requisite for a being to enjoy immortality.

As you have hesitated in believing that we attributed a spiritual body to animals, it is my duty to insist at first upon this truth which I have just affirmed. You acknowledge, besides, that it is a consequence of the principles which I have explained to you on the subject of man. Logic says, in fact, that if matter in man is insensible, it must be the same in animals; that if there is in man a spiritual organized being, which suffers when the material body receives a wound, it must be the same in like cases with animals; for it cannot be denied that there is suffering with both. Besides, when the insensibility of matter and its inaptitude to take any form of itself is recognised, we are forced to admit the principle of spiritual bodies. It results again from our principles that nature is of itself dead; now it is a fact that life is diffused in different degrees into all natural bodies. How could each one of them take the life which is proper to it if there was not in it a corresponding spiritual body adapted to receive this life from the common source? Thus we declare boldly, because it is a truth which cannot be combatted but by frivolous objections, that vegetables and animals subsist by influx from the spiritual world into the natural, and proceed from spiritual germs included in natural germs, and nature serves only to fix the spiritual which continuously flows into it, in consequence of the tendency of everything spiritual to clothe itself with a body. The animal exists then only because it is the correspondence of certain spiritual substances and forms, of which the whole together has constituted the spiritual body upon which corresponding material particles are moulded.

And here is explained the mystery of the life and generation of all that is born, grows up, and and dies. The seed always produces the same plant. Why does the acorn always produce an oak? It is because in the acorn the spiritual body of the oak already exists. Why have a great many animals and principally the *saurians*, the faculty of reproducing amputated members? How is it that the foot of a lizard, when torn off, grows out again? One of two things—either nature performs a miracle, or else material substances mould themselves upon the spiritual body, as upon a model. This last solution can alone explain why hybrids, mules, &c. cannot reproduce themselves; why the graft can only be performed upon trees of the same class, for though material forms may be coupled, it is impossible in the same manner to establish spiritual forms.

From all that precedes then, it results evidently that animals have spiritual bodies. I proceed now to my second affirmation.

There are animals in the spiritual world. This truth, which has excited your astonishment, is also a consequence of principles previously announced. If you do not admit animals in the spiritual world, you are obliged to exclude from it vegetables, minerals, atmospheres, and, in a word, all that corresponds to the different objects of which nature is composed.

What becomes then of the spiritual world? It vanishes completely; it is no longer a world, for this world carries with it the idea of a thing analogous to the world which we inhabit: you can thence form no idea of it: you fall into the abstractions of philosophy, and consequently into all your doubts concerning the immortality of the soul.

I readily conceive, however, your repugnance to admit that there are animals in the spiritual world. An interior sentiment tells you that you have an immortal soul; but taking a view of all that surrounds you, you see on all sides beings destitute of reason: you know that they live, feel, suffer and have passions like men; you are struck with all the other analogies which we observe between the most intelligent of these beings and him who is called the lord of creation. Then you hesitate to trace the line of demarcation between the reasonable being and the instinctive being, particularly when you reflect that many animals are often more affectionate or ingenious than so many depraved men: and yet, if you grant a soul to the being the nearest to man, you are directly forced to give it to the one which immediately succeeds, and so descend, step by step, to animals which are found in the lowest degree of the scale. At this thought your dignity of man revolts and, in your perplexity you are more inclined to believe in the complete annihilation of man, than in the immortality of all these beings deprived of reason.

All these thoughts, which are those of the greater number of men of this age, were awakened in you so soon as you saw us place animals in the spiritual world. You immediately called to mind that, from their analogy with man, animals must have a spiritual body, and you concluded from this that we give an immortal soul to beast. You know now that we reject your conclusion with all our might; but seeing me nevertheless persist in maintaining as true the two propositions which have led you to this conclusion, you must be anxious to know why I reject it. I proceed to satisfy you.

I admit, it is true, that animals have a spiritual body, but the conclusion that this body is immortal by no means results from the existence of a spiritual body : indeed, if from this alone that the spiritual body exists, we are to conclude that it is immortal, we should be under the necessity of concluding that it possesses existence in itself, and thence it would not only be immortal but eternal; now we know that God alone is eternal. We shall soon see that the spiritual body of man is only immortal because it is the receptacle of the eternal life which reposes in the bosom of the Divinity.

I admit further, that there are animals in the spiritual world; but from this proposition it no longer results that these animal forms, perceived in the world of spirits, are the souls of animals dead or to be born upon the earth, and that these appearances of animals are immortal individualities receptive of the Divine life.

Here is my reply : not to keep you in suspense I give it to you in a few words. As to the proofs of the assertions which it embraces, I do not present them here, because they will result from the examination of the important question which is now about to occupy our attention.

This grave question known generally under the name of the *Problem of the Soul of Beasts* has excited long discussion among philosophers, and has never yet been completly resolved by them. Give me then, I pray you, the whole of your attention.

To ascertain correctly what constitutes immortality, it is necessary to have clear ideas concerning *esse* and *existere* (to *be* or *being*, and to *exist* or *existence.*) These are generally confounded, because the *esse* and the *existere* always present themselves to our view as a one, and thus we cannot see the *esse* but by the *existere.* We see in fact only that which *exists*, and nothing can *exist* without having an *esse*. Nevertheless, we can by abstraction consider the *esse* independently, or separated from, the *existere*, and then the *esse* is to us the thing itself, and the *existere* is the manifestation of the thing. In like manner, we see substances only by their forms, and yet by abstraction we can consider the substance independently or separated from its form; and then the substance is to us the thing itself, and the form is the manifestation of that thing. You may readily see, by means of this distinction, that a thing cannot enjoy immortality, but so far as its *esse* shall be always manifested by an *existere*; for, as results from the very expressions used in common language, "to cease to exist" is not to enjoy immortality.

As it is the *existere* which manifests the thing, and which constitutes its individuality, or its personality, all the objects of nature have their *existere* while they subsist in this world, since each of them is distinct and individual. But is this *existere* so united to their *esse* that it cannot be separated from it, or, in other words, must they always preserve their individuality? And to speak here only of the animal kingdom, as we affirm that animals have a spiritual body, and that this body *exists*, since it is it which acts in their natural body, is it united to its *esse* in such a manner as never to be separated from it? As we affirm besides that there are animals in the spiritual world, are these animals individualities which have previously existed in our world? Such, in fact, is the principal point of the question which we are discussing; for it is very evident from what precedes, that immortality cannot belong to any individualities except to those whose *existere* is united to the *esse* in such a manner as to be incapable of ever being separated from it.

It suffices, then, to enquire which are the bodies that fulfil this indispensable condition, and which are those that do not fulfil it; for the spiritual body even in its essence is not immortal, as I have already told you; it has this prerogative only when it is adapted to receive life in its complete state, or, in other terms, when it is the receptacle of the Love and Wisdom of God. It is, in fact, in this case alone, as you will see presently, that the *esse* and *existere* are inseparably united.

God, we have already said, is Love and Wisdom. Divine Love is the *Esse Itself;* it is this alone which fills and animates everything with its life. The divine Wisdom is *Existere Itself;* it is this which manifests the divine Love, which has created and disposed all things.

All the objects of creation derive their substance from the *Esse Itself*, which is the first Substance, and their form from the *Existere Itself*, which is the first Form (*Forme-Type;*) but they are receptacles of the *Existere* in different degrees. Consequently they all tend more or less to the Form of the Creator, or, in other words, to the human form, since God is Very-Man. Hence the origin of the great chain of beings, every link of which is a lowering from the link which precedes it.

At the head of this chain is man. If we consider man only in his quality of a natural being, he necessarily constitutes a part of the chain; he is the first link of it. But if we consider man in his quality of man, he no longer constitutes the first link, in this sense, that there is not between him and the following link the only difference which we observe between any two other animals taken consecutively; it is no longer possible even to establish a comparison: for the difference which distinguishes him from the other beings is of an order indefinitely more elevated. Man is found, then, above the chain—he rules it as the spiritual rules the natural. Thus, on the one hand, man connected with all nature belongs to this world, and, on the other, he is separated by the spiritual principle with which he alone is endowed; his feet are upon the earth, but his countenance looks towards the heavens.

This truth, which I but announce here, will soon become evident to you. God continually diffuses life into the whole universe; but this life, penetrating into bodies, is modified according to the constitution of each of them.

It is, in fact, evident that man owes the faculty of ascending from the effect to the cause, and from the cause to the end, to his particular organization. If man had not that elevated forehead which distinguishes him from other animals, he would be deprived of this faculty; for experience proves, that the more the forehead is depressed, the less there is of intelligence; and that he is no more than a kind of idiot when the depression is very great. Experience proves, besides, that among animals, the smaller the anterior part of the brain is, relatively to the whole, the more inferior is the degree which the species occupies in the chain of animated beings.

Man being able to ascend from effects to causes, and from causes to ends, the result is that there are in him the three separate or discrete degrees, of which I have spoken in my last letter. The first of these degrees with man, is *love*, because what man loves he proposes for an *end;* the second degree is *wisdom*, because it is by this that the end seeks causes; the third degree is the *operation of the body*, because by it the end and the cause are manifested in *effects*. You know, also, that these three degrees are of an absolutely different nature, and the connection between them is only by relations of *anteriority* and *superiority*. The order in which the *discrete* degrees act is called *successive order*, while that of the *continuous* degrees is called *simultaneous order*.

By means of the three discrete degrees, man can receive the love and the wisdom of God, or life in the complete state; his will is the receptacle of that love, and his understanding the receptacle of that wisdom—the first being warmed by the heat of the spiritual sun, and the second enlightened by its light. It is thus that man is an image of God; and as life descends into him in its fullness, the *esse* and the *existere* are with him inseparably united, so that he enjoys immortality, even when, by his life in this world, instead of having appropriated the love and wisdom of God, he has rejected them far from his heart and his thought; for in this last case the divine influx does not cease to act upon the man, even when he has become a spirit; but man, in consequence of his liberty and rationality which he has depraved, changes love into hatred and wisdom into folly.

Man having been created in the image of God, and the organization of the beast differing from that of man, it results that beasts are not images of God; thus the chain of animals presents to us only successive degradations of the human form. Thence it results, at the same time, that animals do not receive life in the complete state. This last consequence is besides fully confirmed by comparative anatomy. Examine the brain of the animal whose form approaches the nearest that of man, and you will find that his *sinciput* presents no kind of comparison with that of man. Now, it is principally in the anterior part of the human brain where the understanding resides; and you know that the understanding is the receptacle of spiritual light or of wisdom from God. Then, since all beasts without any exception, are deprived of this anterior part of the brain, it is impossible for them to receive spiritual light in the two first degrees which concern *ends* and *causes;* but as they have need of being directed in their actions, they receive this light in its last degree, which concerns only *effects*.

I might here conclude this discussion upon the *soul* of *beasts*, for it results very evidently from what precedes, that beasts do not receive life in the complete state, and thus that the *esse* and *existere* not being in them inseparably united, they could not enjoy immortality. But though solved in principle, this question of the *soul* of *beasts* is so important, I will seek to corroborate its solution by examining with you the principal differences which exist between man and beast: you will see by this examination, that these differences, which have so much occupied the attention of philosophers, are all explained by means of the principles that I have now explained to you.

Man being a receptacle of the wisdom and love of God, has been endowed with *rationality*, or the faculty of comprehending, and with *liberty*, or the faculty of willing freely; consequently he can reason upon ends, causes, and effects.

Beasts not receiving the wisdom of God in the first degrees, there is not in them either *rationality* or *liberty;* they can neither comprehend nor will freely; thus there is in them neither understanding nor will; but instead of understanding they have their science (commonly called instinct), and instead of will they have natural affection. The natural affections, which supply in them the place of the will, are the affection of nourishment, that of shelter, re-production, shunning danger, and avoiding what is hurtful to them. Every natural affection is accompanied with the science which is proper to it, and it is this science which supplies the place of the understanding. They have no thought, for they are only in the last degree; and this degree, without the superior degrees, gives no faculty of thinking of anything whatever of moral or of spiritual life; but, instead of thought, they have an internal sight which makes one by correspondence with their external sight. The differences which we observe between animals proceed from this, that every discrete degree decreases from its most perfect state even to its most imperfect state, as light decreases to shade. Thus, also, animals decrease; and it is this which constitutes the chain of beings in the three kingdoms, without any of these beings having the power to ascend out of the last degree; man alone is in the three degrees.

Man receives the divine influence and appropriates it, because he is endowed with rationality and liberty.

The beast receives also this influence, but does not appropriate it, because it is deprived of rationality and liberty.

Man being endowed with rationality and liberty, is not born into any science, because he is capable of learning them all.

The beast, on the contrary, being deprived of rationality and liberty, is born with all its science, because it is not able to learn any.

In man, the will depends upon the understanding, because he can by his understanding elevate himself above the desires of his will, and because he can thus, from this elevated point, know them, see them, and correct them. In the beast, the understanding is in subjection to the will; or rather its science, which is analogous to the understanding, is in subjection to its affection, which is analogous to the will. Beasts always act according to the laws of order impressed upon their nature; if some appear to act morally and rationally, it is because, being deprived of rationality and liberty, they have not been able like men to pervert their science and affection by depraved reasonings. This is the reason why this science, or this wonderful instinct, with which they are endowed, never deceives them; this is the reason why it is always the same. What seems to be civil and moral in them belongs to their science, and is not above their science, since they are not in the spiritual degree, which gives the power of perceiving what is moral, and afterwards of thinking analytically respecting it. They can also be instructed to do some things, but this proceeds only from the natural which is conjoined to their science, and at the same time to their affection, and is reproduced either by the sight or hearing: but this never proceeds from thought, still less from reason.

Man, being in the three discrete degrees, can think that he wills such a thing, or that he does not will it; that he knows such a thing or that he does not know it; that he comprehends such a thing, that he loves such a thing; and he can express his thoughts by words.

It is not the same with the beast; as it is only in the last separate degree, and cannot elevate itself into the superior degrees, it can only think in a *simultaneous order*, and not in a *successive order*, which is to act from a science corresponding to its affection, and not to think; for it cannot ascend from the effect to the cause, nor from the cause to the end. Now, as it is impossible for it to think analytically, and see the inferior thought by any superior thought, consequently it cannot abstract, nor thence speak; it can only produce sounds which relate to the science of its affection. Thus in all their actions, beasts are led by their affection, by means of their science, without rationality or liberty; they are thus led by influx from the spiritual world; for at the same time that the heat and the light of the natural world act upon their material bodies, they receive heat and light from the spiritual world, and it is this heat and light which constitute their affection and science.

I will conclude this parallel of man with the beast, by this last remark: The man altogether sensual differs from the beast only in this, that he can fill his memory with things which he has learned, and can think and speak from these things; and this, by virtue of the faculty every man possesses of being able to comprehend truth if he is willing. It is this faculty which distinguishes him from the brute; but there are many men who degrade themselves below the beasts, by the abuse of this faculty.

To reply to all the points which your objection has raised, I would have to explain to you the origin of the animals which are in the spiritual world; but this origin cannot be rationally understood without knowing the mode of existence of men-spirits. As we have not time now to enter upon the investigation of this subject, it will suffice for the present to say, that in the spiritual world the representative forms of the affections and thoughts of spirits appear as it were living, hence the appearance of animals which spirits see there.

If your objection has compelled me to interrupt the course of the exposition of the spiritual world, it has at least had the double advantage in leading us to the examination of one of the most important questions of philosophy, and to the proof, by new arguments, not only that man is immortal, but that he alone is endowed with immortality.

Accept, &c.

LETTER VIII.

I had designed, my dear sir, to resume to-day the exposition respecting the spiritual world; but since you have long manifested a desire to have an idea of the creation of the universe, and since this desire is repeated in your last letter, I must hasten to satisfy it. I see besides so much the less inconvenience in treating this subject, as it will furnish you with new means to form more easily a comprehensive idea of the spiritual world. Do not expect, however, a complete treatise—the subject would require a volume. You wish only to have an idea of the creation; it is then simply a sketch which I am about to give you.

But there is a question, in advance, which I must anticipate; it is true you have not yet asked it; but you certainly would ask it, for it always presents itself to the insatiable curiosity of man, when he meditates upon the creation of the universe.

This question is:

Can man know what God was before the universe was created?

You will agree at once that it matters little to man, so far as his happiness is concerned, to know what God was before the creation. What advantage could he draw from this knowledge, if it were even possible for him to acquire it? None whatever. Far from being satisfied, his curiosity would only be increased; and, pursuing his investigations in this unfruitful field, he would wish to go so far as to understand God in his infinity, that is to say, so far as to wish to be God; for to comprehend God in his infinity, it would be necessary to be God. The infinite only can comprehend the infinite.

There are, nevertheless, some spiritualist who imagine that after they have left this world, there will be no secret for them; that they will know the how and the wherefore of all things. This again is one of the thousand errors of philosophy.

Yet with little reflection upon the nature of man, it is easy to discover, that if an intelligent creature, whether man, spirit, or angel, could attain to such a state as to know everything, and consequently to have nothing to learn, it would be to him the greatest of misfortunes. This is not a paradox; it is a truth which it will be easy for me to prove when we come to treat of the existence of man in the other world.

What I have just said on the subject of the *infinite* is applicable also to the *eternal*, for the eternal is that which is infinite as to *existere;* it is then as impossible for any creature to comprehend the *eternity* of God, as it would be impossible to comprehend the *infinity* of God.

Besides, with man living in this world, in the midst of space and time, there is always something of time in the idea which he forms to himself of the *eternal*, just as there is always something of space, in the idea which he forms of the *infinite*. Now as time only exists by the creation of the universe, it is then absolutely impossible for him to comprehend *what God was before time*, that is to say, *before the universe was created*. It is not, however, the same with an angel; though an angel cannot, being a creature, comprehend God in his infinity or in his eternity; he can nevertheless form to himself, in some sort, an idea of *eternity*, because the idea of *time* no longer exists with him, and has been succeeded by the idea of *state;* for with spirits and angels eternity is not an eternity of *time*, but it is an eternity of *states*, without the idea of *time*.

This question concerning eternity having led me to speak to you of the infinite, it will not be out of place to remind you here of certain results to which we arrive, when, upon this point, we consult mathematics. If it is impossible for us, who are continually in space, to place ourselves in a complete state of abstraction; if philosophical meditations offer us only a feeble aid, seeing this aid is very often but instantaneous, and disappears as soon as our ideas fall back upon the things of the world, it is not the same with the exact sciences, the essence of which consists in abstracting all that can oppose the development of thought: the answers which they give us, when we interrogate them, are always clear, precise, and so exactly formed, that they are established with facility in our understandings. Let us see then what they tell us.

It is, in the first place, recognised as a principle that the series of numbers is illimitable, since to the greatest number imaginable, the addition of a unit is sufficient to increase the result. There are then no efforts of the imagination which can fix the limits of the finite, or those of space; should we add to the unit line as many ciphers as there as grains of sand in the sea, what we would thus obtain would not be the infinite; it would always be a number of which an idea could be formed, notwithstanding the impossibility of being able to determine or fix it. Thence it evidently results, that to *pass from the finite to the infinite by way of continuity is absolutely impossible.*

Other incontestable proofs of this impossibility, are found in the surprising results to which we arrive when the *sign of the infinite* (*signe de l'infini*) is introduced into the calculation. Two examples will suffice to convince you of this.

Let us suppose that two parallel lines should have between them the distance which separates the earth from the sun, or any other distance which you may imagine. Let them be prolonged in thought as far as you wish, they would constantly keep this enormous distance without approaching a single hair's breadth during their whole course; this then is the result of the very nature of these lines. But if you introduce into the calculation the sign of the infinite, which is nothing else than to abstract space, you discover that, in spite of the immense distance which separates them in space, they meet however at the infinite, without having previously passed through any intermediate approach.

Let us take, for example, a branch of the hyperbola and its asymptote which would not have between them, at a given point, more than the distance of a millimetre (*un millimetre*). Let us suppose these two lines prolonged as far as the imagination could permit; calculation tells us that they will never meet, though at every step, notwithstanding the slight distance which separated them at the commencement of their course, the right line has always approached the curve. If we wish them to unite, we are obliged to introduce into the formula the sign of the infinite (*le signe de l'infini*); whence it clearly results, that in nature there is no longer any infinitely small, nor infinitely large, and that the word *infinite*, taken in its true acceptation, cannot be applied to anything created.

And it is said that the study of mathematics leads men to materialism! It leads *him* only whose heart, already corrupted, is deaf to the warnings which it gives and whose understanding, already perverted, rejects the living light which it presents. Is it possible, in truth, to prove more evidently that we must not confound the infinite with the finite, nor consequently God with nature?

The science of mathematics is (as you see) far from deserving to incur the reproaches which have been cast upon it. If philosophy and theology had each in its sphere developed this high question, instead of obscuring it by a crowd of sophistries, there would not have been so many materialists. It is then to philosophy and to theology that the fault is to be ascribed, and not to the sciences, which are so exact, that when we wish them to say that which is not true, they immediately give the lie to it.

But should it be replied, the very examples which you have just given prove that nature is without bounds, since it is impossible to determine them. Ah! what matters it if she be without bounds, if these examples prove, even by the clearest evidence, that which has no bounds preserves its quality of *finite* and differs absolutely from the *infinite*? What more could be said of mathematics? Nothing. But religious philosophy should have posessed herself of these first data, and developed instead of obscuring them.

If religious philosophy, setting out on true principles, viz: God is *Being itself* (*Esse*,) from whom and by whom everything exists; he is the first substance and first form (*Forme-Type*,) the only *infinite;* the universe has been created by him to be his image and the representative theatre of his glory, and it is for this reason that the universe, as an image of the *infinite*, is without bounds or *indefinite;* if, I say religious philosophy had held this language, and taught that there is between the *infinite* and the *indefinite*, the same difference as between the first cause and the effect, materialism or naturalism would not have made such ravages in society.

If the universe, as well the spiritual as the natural, had not been separate and distinct from the *infinite*, it could have had no existence; and it is precisely that it may have existence that there is, in its natural part, space and time, and in its spiritual part, the *appearance* of space and time. Without this, the objects of the natural world and those of the spiritual world would not have been either distinct or varied, or to speak with more exactness, there would not have been any objects nor consequently creation; all would have been confounded in the infinite.

I recollect very well, my dear sir, that you have no sympathy for naturalism; but the occasion having presented itself, I thought it would not be inappropriate before passing to the creation, to show you that mathematics themselves establish a distinction between God and the universe. Besides, these general considerations upon the infinite are not foreign to the subject which we are discussing, and cannot but dispose you the better to comprehend the whole.

I come now to the creation; and since you desire to have only a general sketch, I will confine myself to the examination of the three following questions:—

1st. Whence proceeds the universe?

2d. Could the universe have been created, if God were not Very Man? (*l'Homme Meme.*)

3d. How has God-Man created the universe?

I. *Whence proceeds the Universe?*

I have already told you that God has not created the universe out of nothing; this is one of those truths which every man endowed with sound reason may at once acknowledge, because he sees, without being able to doubt, that it is impossible to make something from nothing; for nothing is absolute negation; and from this negation an affirmation cannot proceed; between these two ideas there exists then a manifest contradiction. To pretend that God has taken the universe from chaos, would not resolve the difficulty, but render it more complicated; for it would be necessary to tell what this chaos is, and whence this chaos itself could have been taken. In fine, the universe has not created itself, since it has just been proved, that God and the universe are absolutely distinct; and that the one is the first cause, and the other the effect produced by this cause.

The universe must then necessarily have been created from

a substance, which is itself substance, or substance in itself, for this is Being Itself, from which proceed all things which are; now, as God is substance itself, or substance in itself, and consequently Being Itself, or *Esse*, it evidently results from this, that all that which exists has been created from God and by God. *Thus it is from God that the universe proceeds.*

Remember, always, that created objects are only the manifestation of Being, or *Esse*, without for that reason having Being, or *Esse*, in themselves; since if they had Being, or *Esse*, in themselves, they would be a portion of the Divinity, which cannot be admitted. The cause is in the effect, but the effect is not a portion of the cause: this we have already acknowledged. The being or *esse* or man is nothing else than a recipient of what proceeds from God; for life, as we have seen is one, and God alone is this one only life. Men, spirits, and angels are but recipients or forms which receive life proceeding from God; and the reception of life is what is called *existere.* Man believes that he *is;* he believes even that he *is* of himself, and yet he *is* not of himself, but he *exists.* To be, Being or *Esse*, is only in God. Thus creation was the operation by which the *Esse*, to be, or Being, clothed himself with the *Existere.*

It is so conformable to reason to think that the existence of all things comes from God and from his *Esse*, or Being, that we have met with many religious men who have had this thought; but they have rejected it in the fear of being led to believe that the universe is God, or that the inmost principle of nature is that which should be called God. This fear came from this, that they thought from time and space, which are proper to nature; and from this, that it is impossible to comprehend creation, without abstracting from the thought these two accidents inherent in matter.

Since the universe was created from God and by God, and yet is not God, it must necessarily be an emanation from God.

The truth has also been partly seen by many philosophers; but for want of the knowledge of the existence of *discrete degrees*, these philosophers have fallen into the most serious errors. If this theory had been at their disposal, they would have known that these three degrees exist in all created things, and are with them as the end, the cause, and the effect. Then they would have understood that material nature in the work of creation was only the last degree of the divine ray (rayon,) and that this degree served to envelope, and to clothe the substances and spiritual forms which are in the two superior degrees. Of this I hope soon to convince you.

From all that precedes we must conclude that the universe is from God, aud that he has been manifested by an emanation from his Being or *Esse*.

II. *Could the Universe have been created, if God was not Very Man?*

I have proposed this question in order to meet an objection which you without doubt would have made. You have not forgotten,—for it is a point upon which I have much insisted by reason of its importance—you have not, I say, forgotten that I have established as a principle, in my fourth letter, that God is VERY MAN, and that if we have the human form, it is because we were created in his image. But, now that we have to treat concerning the creation of the universe by God, you will not fail to say to me: Is it possible that God, being Man, could have drawn the universe from Himself, and given it the form which it has? As this apparent impossibility is of a nature to raise doubts in your mind which could not be removed but in another letter, I have preferred showing you at once, here, not only that God was able as Man, to create the universe, but more, that he could not have been able to create this universe, if he were not Man.

The universe very evidently attests the Love and the Wisdom of him who created it; it is only Love divine which has been able to furnish for it all its substance ; it is only the divine Wisdom which has been able, in impressing upon it its form, to order so harmoniously all its parts. Now it is impossible that love and wisdom should exist without a subject ; and this subject is man ; to separate these two attributes from their subjects, is to say that they do not exist. Can you conceive of wisdom out of man ? Would it not be necessary for you to place it somewhere to give it a form ? and what form could you give it superior to that of man ? And what I have just said of wisdom is applicable also to love, for the form of wisdom is that of love, since love and wisdom are inseparable and make one as substance and form.

You can see by this how vain are the ideas of those who represent to themselves God, who is Love itself and Wisdom itself, otherwise than as *Man*, and who place the divine attributes elsewhere than in God-Man. If the divine love and the divine wisdom were not in God-Man, and if one did not constitute the substance, and the other the form of God-Man, these two principal attributes of the Divinity, being nothing more than imaginary entities, the universe could not have been created ; for it is evident that the universe must have been produced by love and formed by wisdom.

If, however, you should represent to yourself God-Man as a man of this world, and if you should think of him by the simple natural idea, it would be impossible for you to comprehend how he was able, as man, to create the universe and all which it contains ; but if you think of him by the spiritual idea, abstracting space and time, you will then be able to perceive that God-man could be present in all his work, and create it instantaneously ; for the universe was *not* created from space to space, nor from one time to another ; it was from a single cast. This besides is what physical laws sufficiently demonstrate ; the motions of the heavenly bodies are so connected with one another, that the whole must necessarily have been arranged at the same instant.*

Is it not true that man, though his thought be in him, and though he remain in one place, may nevertheless by *this thought* be present elsewhere, in any place whatever, and even in a place the most remote from him? Such also is the state of spirits and of angels, even as to their bodies; for you know that they are men, and that their bodies are spiritual. If their thought is fixed upon a place, they are actually there and in body, because in the world which they inhabit spaces and distances are appearances, and only make one with the thought which proceeds from affection. Now, if in the natural world man can already in thought transport himself instantaneously whither he pleases; if in the spiritual world, the man-spirit is always where his thought is, why should we refuse to admit that God who is VERY MAN (l'Homme-Type), should have been able, as man, to be present in all the work of creation; He who in this quality of infinite, is the same in the first as in the last, in the greatest as in the least objects; He who

* We are not entirely sure of apprehending the author in the sense in which he would here be understood, in saying that the creation of the universe was necessarily instantaneous. It is very certain, we think, that our solar system, for instance, was not created at once *in its present state*, for the evidence is overwhelming of progressive formations, from simpler elements, and going on through immeasurable tracts of time; and this would seem to be a fair deduction from Swedenborg's theory of Atmospheric Creations, so strikingly unfolded by the author in what follows. If, however, he means that the original *projection* of the universe as the act of the Divine Mind, was instantaneous, we can better grasp the idea, although we are still doubtful whether even this be not assuming a more distinct conception on the subject than the human faculties are at present capable of attaining. But the reader is referred to Swedenborg's "Divine Love and Wisdom," No. 156, where he treats of this point, and expresses himself in language that seems, at first blush, to convey the same idea with that of the passage before us, but which is, if we mistake not, designedly more abstract and transcendental, and that, too, from the very nature of the theme; for there is nothing that so baffles our feeble powers as the *origin in time* of the material universe.—ED.

fills all spaces without being in space, and all times without being in time; He who consequently could not be continuous as is the inmost principle of nature, since he is not in space?

It would be to have a false idea of the infinite, and to misconceive the true nature of God-Man, if in thinking of his Human Body, any invariable stature whatever, whether great or small, should be given to him; for this would be to think from space. But we can and ought to represent to ourselves God-Man from the appearance of space, for it is thus, when he judges it to be useful, that he presents himself to spirits and angels, who then see his Human Body under a form in relation to the state in which they are as to the reception of love and wisdom; and this visible presence of God agrees perfectly with his continual omnipresence in the universe which he governs.

Thus creation may be understood, if space and time are removed from the thought. Divest yourself of them therefore as much as possible, and then you will perceive that there is no difference between what is the greatest and least of space. Then you will not be able to have any other idea of the creation of the universe than that of the creation of every part of this universe: you will understand that the diversity in created things is from this, that infinites are in God-man and indefinites in the first proceeding from God, that is to say, in the spiritual sun; and that these indefinites exist in the created universe as in an image.

Hence the impossibility of finding in any place whatever, one thing like another; thence the indefinite variety of all the objects which we behold.

III. *How has God-Man created the universe?*

We have already seen that God created the universe, not from space to space, nor from one time to another, but by a single cast; and that the universe is an emanation from the Divinity.

But that you may the better understand the important subject which engages our attention, I will have recourse to analogy, and proceed from the known, for experience proves sufficiently that human reason does not acquiesce in a thing which we ask it to admit, but so far as she can perceive how this was done.

Man having been created in the image and according to the likeness of God, who is VERY MAN, it is in directing our examination to man that we shall be enabled to discover by analogy how God created the universe.

It is now generally admitted by science that a sphere of natural emanations continually proceeds from the body of a man, as well as from the bodies of animals, trees, fruits, flowers, and even from metals. This sphere, composed of fluids for the most part aeriform, and consequently invisible, is more intense than would at first be believed, and extends itself to great distance. The insensible transpiration, whose emission is so voluminous and so surprising may give us an idea of the intensity of this sphere, and the emanations which affect the smell may show us how much it is susceptible of development. Man may then be represented as plunged in an ocean of aeriform fluids which emanate from his own body. All these emanations though not visible, are evidently material; but man in this world being both spiritual and material, that is to say, having a natural body, and a spiritual body, and these two bodies being connected together by laws of analogy, there must also from the spiritual body of man constantly emanate a spiritual sphere analogous to the material sphere which envelops his natural body; a simple examination will at once make this evident.

When it is known that the affections and thoughts are actually spiritual substances and forms, it is directly seen that if a spiritual sphere emanates from man, it cannot consist but in affections and the thoughts which are derived from these affections and which constitute their forms. Thence it is easy to be convinced that such a sphere exists around every man;

it is sufficient for this to direct our reflections to the astonishing phenomena which sympathies and antipathies present. If two persons who have never seen each other, who do not even know each other by name, experience at the first meeting sympathy for one another, it is because their spiritual spheres are homogeneous and directly harmonize; if on the contrary they experience suddenly an antipathy which they cannot account for, it is because their spiritual spheres are heterogeneous and repel each other. How many other phenomena, still more extraordinary, would find their explanation by means of these spheres, and would go consequently to confirm their existence! But this is not the place to occupy ourselves in discussing them; we will examine these phenomena when we shall have acquired a more complete knowledge of the spiritual world. It is sufficient for the present to have verified the existence of spiritual spheres.

I will add that the natural sphere and the spiritual sphere which envelope and surround men, correspond to each other, as all natural objects correspond to spiritual objects; that they are not the man, as it is very easy to persuade himself, is that they derive their existence from man, and do not make one with him but in this sense, that being extracted from his two bodies there is agreement between them and man; that the one drawing its existence from all parts of the natural body, and the other from all parts of the spiritual, they are constantly supported by the natural and spiritual substances which emanate from them; that the substances which are contiguous to these bodies are continually put into activity by the two sources of the motion of life, the heart and the lungs; that these contiguous substances communicate of their activity to those which surround them, these to others, and thus from one to another, so that the more the emanations are removed from the substances contiguous to the two bodies of man, the less activity do they receive.

Now if we ascend from the creature to the Creator, we shall experience no further difficulty in comprehending that God-Man could extract the universe from himself without, for that reason, its being confounded with him. It is very evident that if man, created in the image of God, is surrounded with a sphere of emanations, it is because God, who is VERY MAN, is himself surrounded with a sphere of emanations. It is these emanations from God-Man which have constituted and which vivify continually the whole universe, as well its spiritual as its natural part.

The first sphere which proceeded from God in the work of creation, is the spiritual sun, in the centre of which he resides as a Being infinite, eternal, invisible, unapproachable. Considered thus in his very essence, it is said of him that no one can see God and live; but I have already told you, and soon you will be joyfully convinced, that God, having created man to love him, and to be beloved by him, to satisfy his divine love, has actually rendered himself visible and accessible.

The spiritual sun, being the sphere contiguous to God, is no more God, than the emanations which from the spiritual sphere contiguous to man, are man. This again is a new proof of this important truth that the universe proceeds from God by contiguity and not by continuity, and consequently that it is impossible when the true principles are known, to confound nature with God.

It is by the intermediation of the spiritual sun that the universe was created, and it is also by its means that it subsists. The substances which compose this sun are continually put into activity by the two sources of the motion of the only life, the heart and lungs of God-Man, inexhaustible sources of the divine Love and the divine Wisdom. It is thus that the first proceeding of God is a centre of Life; its heat is love, the principle of all affections, and its light is wisdom, source of all thought.

At the same instant when the spiritual sun was created, the

sun of our world received existence: it was *by contiguity*, and not *by continuity*, the last term of the Divine sphere, whose spiritual sun was the first term; so that, in the work of creation, God was the first end, the spiritual sun the second end or the cause, and the natural sun the last end or the effect. It is by these two suns, the one purely spiritual, diffusing love by its heat and wisdom by its light; and the other, elementary fire, distributing a heat and light purely material—it is, I say, by these two suns that were produced all things which exist in the spiritual uuiverse, and in the part of the material universe which comprehends our solar system; the first of these suns, the centre of life, acting with all the activity of love and wisdom, and the second, deprived of life, receiving and communicating passively the impulsion which is given to it. Thus God is in ends, the spiritual world in causes, and the natural world in effects.

I said before, on the subject of the emanations which proceed from man, that the more remote these emanations are from the sphere contiguous to man, the less activity they receive. This fact is so evident that I rest content with merely announcing it. However, as I am going to rely upon it in presenting to you the principal details of creation, I will here confirm it by this simple observation upon odoriferous spheres, that the farther we remove from the object, whence they emanate, the less the odor is perceived.

Thus the more remote the emanations from the spiritual sun, the less activity have they received. This principle granted, it remains to establish what must have been the first nature of the emanations which proceeded from that sun. The most simple ideas of natural things prove that the individual existence of things depends not solely upon this that they are substances and forms, but that from the nature of things and all necessity, they must be surrounded with atmospheres which retain, by their force of compression every substance in its form. Besides, it is known that the heat and light of the natural sun must necessarily, in order to act with efficacy, be tempered by the atmospheres which they pass through.

Now the spiritual world including objects corresponding to those our world contains, analogy demonstrates that every spiritual substance can only be retained in its form by means of spiritual atmospheres, and that love and wisdom which are the heat and light of the spiritual sun, must from necessity, in order to act with efficacy, be tempered by these atmospheres. Thence it evidently results that the first nature of the emanations which proceeded from the spiritual sun and the sun of our world, was gaseous or atmospheric.

I speak here of many atmospheres, because there are actually several in each world. You know that certain learned men have already admitted, under the name of ether, a substance more subtle and pure than the atmospheric air; it would not then be extraordinary when we say that there exists another still more subtle and pure than ether. It is this indeed which the science of degrees proves: this science which gives a key to unlock the causes of things, teaches us that in every thing there are the three separate degrees, which bear relation to each other as the *end*, the *cause*, and the *effect*, or as *prior*, *posterior*, and *last*; that each degree is distinguished from the other by its proper envelopes; that all the degrees are at the same time distinguished by a common envelope covering, and that the common envelope communicates with the interiors and with the inmosts, which communication by degrees produces the conjunction and unanimous action of all the parts of which the thing is composed. Thus, in animals, the muscle is a compound of moving fibres, which are themselves composed of smaller fibres; the nerve is a compound of fibres themselves formed of fibrils (very small fibres); in vegetables there are assemblages of filaments in a triple order; in metals and stones there are also accumulations of parts in a triple order.

Since all the visible bodies of nature are in this triple order, it must be the same with the natural atmosphere; whence from analogy we conclude that it is also the same with the spiritual atmosphere. Thus there are in each world three atmospheres, which are distinguished from each other according to the three separate degrees, or, to use other terms, which exist in relation to each other as the end, the cause, and the effect or as the inmost of a thing, its interior or middle, and its ultimate or totality.

The distinction of these three atmospheres, according to the three *separate* degrees, causes each of them to have its own *continuous* degrees. Thus each of them, according to the continuous degrees, becomes so much the more inert, and so much the more dense, the more it approaches its ultimate term or inferior places as experience proves in respect to the last natural atmosphere, which is our atmospheric air.

By means of these plain truths concerning the atmospheres, it will be easy now to conceive of the creation at once, and in one connected idea. The emanations from the spiritual sun were three spiritual atmospheres, all three distinct, though the second was composed of the first, and the third was composed of the first and second.

Each of these atmospheres, in its progression away from the spiritual sun, losing continually some of its activity and expansion, became more and more inert and dense; and at last the parts the most remote from it, attained tc such a degree of inertness and density, that they ceased to be atmospheric fluids and became snbstances at rest. They are substances at rest which constitute the earths of the spiritual world: and these earths, like the atmospheres whence they draw their origin, are distinguished from one another according to the three separate degrees. In the sequel I will enter more at large into the details concerning these earths of the spiritual world.

The natural sun acting conjointly with the spiritual sun, and receiving impulsion from it, the emanations which proceeded from it were three natural atmospheres corresponding to the three spiritual atmospheres. So, though all three distinct, the second was composed of the first, and the third was composed of the first and second. In like manner, each of these atmospheres, in its progression away from the natural sun, losing continually some of its activity and expansion, became more and more inert, and more and more dense; and at last, the parts the most remote attained to such a degree of inertness and density, that they ceased to be atmospheric fluids, and became those fixed substances which we call matters. Nevertheless, as these fixed substances owe their origin to the atmospheres, they retained in them an effort and a tendency to produce uses, that is to say, to produce that which is conformable to the order established by the Creator. Each of these substances included in it the three separate degrees, being composed of fixed parts which had their derivation from the three natural atmospheres; the parts derived from the first atmosphere constituted its inmost, and the parts derived from the second constituted its interior. Thence is the origin of the planets and their satellites, and of the indefinitely varied matters which constitute them. Thus nothing exists but from a something prior to itself, and so on from a First. This First is the sun of the spiritual world; and the First of this sun is God-Man. The prior (or things next to the first) are the atmospheres by which this sun penetrates into the last boundaries of creation. Those who do not establish the creation of the universe by continual intermediations proceeding from the first, do but imagine incoherent hypotheses, altogether disconnected from their causes.

This general view of the creation is found confirmed as to what relates to our world, by the recent discoveries of science.

Chemistry has proved the possibility of reducing the most

solid bodies to the gaseous state, whence it reciprocally results that gases could pass to the solid state.

Newton placed in etherial matter the origin of all things which exist; and according to La Place, the greatest geometrician of our age, "it could only be a fluid of an immense extent which has given birth to our planets, and that fluid has at first surrounded the sun as an atmosphere; it was upon the successive limits of this atmosphere, and by the condensation of the zones which it was obliged to separate from in receding, that were formed all the planets of our system, as well as their satellites." (*Exposition of the System of the World, Book V. Ch* 9). P. Cuvier expresses himself thus on the assertion of La Place: "The conjecture of M. de la Place, that the materials of which the globe is composed must have been at first elastic, and have successively in cooling taken the liquid consistency, and afterwards the solid, is much strengthened by the recent experience of Mr. Mittcherlich, who has compounded from parts, and caused to chrystalize, by the fire of high furnaces, many kinds of minerals which enter into the composition of primitive mountains." (*Discourse upon the Revolutions of the Earth, p.* 11).

The more progress the natural sciences make, the more this theory of Swedenborg, on the material creation, will be found to be scientifically confirmed.

I will here close this sketch of the creation. If, however, you desire more light on this subject, I will refer you to the treatise of Swedenborg, where you will be able to find it, viz. "Angelic Wisdom concerning the Divine Love and Wisdom," As to the creation such as it is reported in Genesis, it will suffice to read the record of Moses to be convinced that this in no wise relates to the material creation. I have already told you that I am a Christian in all the extension of this word taken in its true acceptation; thus I have for the Bible the greatest veneration; and my reason agreeing with my heart, tells me that this Book is the Word of God. I hope some day to cause you to partake with me in my convictions on this important point: for I will demonstrate to you that the numerous apparent contradictions which we meet with in the Bible are all consistently explained, when we are in possession of the key which unlocks the inexhaustible treasures that it contains. But, for the present, I will content myself in telling you that, while apparently treating of things of this world, the Bible in reality only treats of spiritual things, and that the first chapter of Genesis speaks solely of the spiritual creation of man, that is to say, of his regeneration. Accept, &c.

LETTER IX.

I have experienced much pleasure, my dear sir, in learning that my last letter has made you familiar with the idea of God-Man, and that you have not the least repugnance to considering the Creator under the human form. In this you have made an immense advance. The difficulties which spiritual theories ordinarily present will henceforth disappear from before you; for everything depends upon the idea which is formed of God: if this idea is just we can easily conceive of the bonds which unite God, the universe, and man; we can comprehend the system of the world; but if this is false, our efforts, however great, will be vain. This explains to you why philosophers rest in the impossibility of conceiving an idea of the creation, and why this impossibility no longer exists with the disciples of the New Church.

To philosophical spiritualists God is a pure spirit, or rather an imaginary Entity, since according to their idea a spirit has neither substance nor form. With so vague an idea of the

Divinity, how could they rationally conceive of the creation of the universe? Is it possible to construct any thing without a basis? and where would they place theirs? The bond which unites the first cause to second causes and to effects, is wanting; and the hypotheses which are heaped one above another, go to prove only the weakness of their efforts.

But with God-Man the impossibility of conceiving an idea of the creation no longer exists. God is Himself the basis, since he is the centre of the universe, and this centre is a focus of love and wisdom; it is the infinite, the eternal Being, in a Human Form; it is VERY MAN, the Archetype whence has emanated all that constitutes the two worlds. Then the human mind seizes upon this central support; it represents to itself the Divinity surrounded by a radiant sun, which diffuses all around spiritual heat and light, or love and wisdom; it sees formed around this sun those spiritual atmospheres which proceed from one another, and which convey even to the ultimate limits this heat and this light with which they are filled; it sees the limits of these atmospheres cease to be fluids, become substances at rest, and thus form spiritual earths; it sees the same things operating conjointly in the material order around our sun by the force of expansion which it receives from the spiritual sun. It can account for all these facts as soon as it knows that the heat and light of our sun extend, by means of the natural atmospheres, even to the last limits of our planetary system; and that according to recent discoveries of science, the formation of the planets is owing to a fluid of an immense extent; it acquires thus the conviction that the universe is a work which is continued from the Creator even to the last objects of the creation; and that consequently God-Man, who is the common centre, holds it suspended, puts it in motion, and governs it as a single coherent whole. Then the human mind incurs no danger of confounding God with the universe, nor the spiritual with the natural; for it can know, by the science of degrees, that the first proceeding and those which are posterior co-exist according to their order, in the more remote or the last, in the same manner as ends and causes co-exist in effects: then it can have the idea concerning God, that he is all in all, that he is omnipotent, omnipresent, omniscient, infinite and eternal; then, also, it can have an idea of the order according to which God-Man by his love and wisdom disposes all things, provides for all, and governs all.

And observe, that when an idea is thus formed of God it cannot be said of him that he is here or that he is there since he is in the inmost of everything. It is then in the inmost of our hearts that he truly is; it is there that we should seek him and it is there that we shall find him.

Do not forget, however, that God, his first proceeding and the posterior proceedings, are not only *in* the last but are also *around* these last, the same as the end and the causes are not only *in* the effects which they produce, but *around* those effects; it is this truth which I have before demonstrated to you by the example of the sculptor and the statue. Thus, though the spiritual world is, like God, in the interior of ourselves, it nevertheless presents itself to our eyes around us, when our soul is freed from the shackles which bind it to this world. If this were not so, the soul remaining absorbed in God would have no enjoyment but for itself, which would be only a selfish pleasure, and for that reason alone opposed to the essence itself of love or of God; whilst by means of this exterior manifestation it can love out of itself in returning upon its likenesses the love which it receives from the Divinity: thus it is in a reciprocal communication of love in which the happiness of eternal life consists. To love his images is to love God.

Let us examine now what the universe at first was in its general constitution.

You have seen that the sun of our world was created at the

same time as the spiritual sun; that it was by contiguity, and not by continuity, the last term of a divine ray whose spiritual sun was the first term, aud that our planetary system was created by the intermediation of the natural sun. Now you know that astronomy assigns to our planetary system but a very small place in the material universe. You should therefore from this conclude that at the instant when the extremity of a divine ray created the sun of our world, thousands of other divine rays from the spiritual sun, created in all directions thousands of natural suns: and that when the three natural atmospheres, corresponding to the three spiritual atmospheres, issued from our sun and constituted its planets, similar atmospheres diffused themselves around each of these thousand suns, and that this natural universe was strewed with millions of terrestrial globes.

Every natural object, corresponding to a spiritual object of which it is the effect, and by which it exists, as every effect exists from a cause, it becomes evident that the immaterial universe includes millions of spiritual earths by means of which the earths of our world exist and subsist. There is, however, an important remark to be made; it is that the three spiritual atmospheres formed immaterial earths distinct according to their degree, whilst the natural atmospheres contributed all three to form, the one the inmost, the other the interior,and the last the ultimate, of the material earths. This difference, of which I have before spoken, results from this, that the spiritual earths not being subjected to the laws of space and of time, those of the second and of the third degree, though contained within those of the first degree, can appear out of these, whilst the natural objects being governed by the laws of space and time, their interior and their inmost cannot be disengaged from their envelope. It thence results that every natural earth corresponds to three spiritual earths, distinct from each other, according to the three degrees.

Thus the spiritual atmosphere of the third degree, or that which, being the purest, remained nearest the source of life, formed as many spiritual earths of the third degree as there are terrestrial globes in the material universe. It was the same with the spiritual atmosphere of the second degree; and the same also with the spiritual atmosphere of the first and least pure degree, in a word, that which was the most remote from the spiritual sun. Remark besides, that according to the principles of the science of the three separate degrees, principles which I have explained in a preceding letter, every earth of the third degree constitutes the inmost of the corresponding spiritual earth of the second degree; that these two earths constitute afterwards the inmost and the interior of the spiritual earth of the first degree which corresponds to them, and that these three spiritual earths are at the same time contained in the natural earth, which is in correspondence with them, but only in the same manner as the first cause and second causes are contained in the effect.

All that I have already said to you concerning the end and the causes which are contained in the effect, though from their nature they are immaterial, would be quite sufficient to convince you that God and the spiritual world are in the natural world, without for that reason occupying there a single point of space. But when the abstraction of space is in question, this cannot be too thoroughly insisted upon; let us not then neglect any means of conviction.

Instead of directing our examination to the whole of the universe, let us consider at first only one of its parts, our earth for example. That which we will say of our planet in particular will apply afterwards to all other parts of the universe, and consequently to the universe in general.

The earth, being an effect which has for causes the spiritual earths to which it corresponds, these spiritual earths are within it, but they are in it as the soul or spirit of man is in his material body. Now, no anatomist has ever discovered the spirit or soul in the human body; if then it were possible to penetrate iuto the interior of the earth, neither would spiritual earths be discovered there, though they are really there, the same as the spirit or soul of man is really in his material body. And why would they not be discovered? It is because every part of a spiritual object, however small it may be, is also in the corresponding part of the natural object as the cause is in the effect. Thus concerning our earth, and the three spiritual corresponding earths, there is not an atom of the spiritual earth of the third degree but what is in the corresponding atom of the spiritual earth of the second degree, not an atom of this which is not in the corresponding atom of the spiritual earth of the first degree, and not an atom of this last which is not in the corresponding atom of our earth; for the spiritual earth of the second degree is an effect in relation to that of the third degree; the spiritual earth of the first degree, an effect in relation to the two preceding; and our earth an effect in relation to these three spiritual earths. Thence it evidently results that our earth can contain the three spiritual earths to which it corresponds, without these earths occupying the least space in its interior. If it is thus with our earth, it is the same with all the planets of our system, and each of these planets contains in like manner the three spiritual earths to which it corresponds; it is also the same with the millions of globes which gravitate in space, and consequently the whole spiritual world is contained in the natural world without occupying there the least space.

I will make at this time on this subject but a single remark: the spiritual exercising thus *within* the natural an action, and this action being necessarily so much the more active as the spiritual is more internal, it results thence that the nearer the bodies which constitute the whole of the globe are to its centre, the more should they be penetrated with heat. Now the experience of modern science, goes to confirm this consequence of our principles, by proving that the more the thermometer is sunk into the interior of the earth, the more the mercury rises. The learned inquire into the cause of this fact, and have written long dissertations to discover it; but alas! it is to them with this cause as with almost all other causes; it is in vain for them to inquire, because they persist in remaining in their false course. How many fruitless labors would they avoid, and what progress would they make in the sciences which they cultivate, if they knew, or were willing to take cognizance of, the true spiritual principles.

As to the exterior manifestation of the spiritual world, as it constitutes the new theatre upon which we must eternally live, it is this which it concerns us above all to examine.

The spiritual universe being divided into three parts wholly distinct, and connected only between them by relations which exist between the end, the cause, and the effect, we denominate the spiritual earths of the third degree with their atmospheres, the inmost or third heaven; those of the second degree, the second heaven; and those of the last degree, the first heaven; this last is called the first heaven, because according to the appearance it is nearer the natural world. You see also, from what precedes, that each of these heavens includes as many spiritual earths as the natural universe includes terrestrial globes.

This division into three heavens consists in this, that the second heaven is to the inhabitants of the first heaven as invisible as this first heaven is invisible to the inhabitants of the natural world; and in this, that it is the same with the third heaven in respect to the inhabitants of the second; but as the inhabitants of the heavens are freed from the shackles of space and time, they can visit the different earths of their heaven, if they desire it, whilst we men who are yet subject to the laws of space and time cannot leave the planet on which we now live.

As to the nature of the spiritual earths, you have seen in the general view given of the creation, that all the bodies of a material nature are in a three-fold order, and that their inmost corresponds to the third degree or to ends, their interior to the second degree or to causes, and their ultimate or first degree to effects. Now the two worlds, by virtue of their creation, corresponding the one to the other, not only in the whole, but also in each of their parts, however small it may be, it results thence that the earths of the natural world can by analogy give us a knowledge of the nature of the earths of the spiritual world. However, to have a just idea of the earths of these three heavens, it is neccessary to form an idea as to what must have been the nature of the natural earths at the epoch of which we are treating. All the objects which then composed the universe were at the same time good and beautiful, since they all emanated from God, and had not yet undergone any alteration. Thus the inmost of objects of which material nature was then composed corresponded to the things which constituted the earths of the inmost heaven; the interior of these same objects to the things which constitutes the earths of the second heaven; and the objects themselves to the things of the earths of the first heaven. The difference which exists between the inmost of a thing, its interior, and its ultimate, should easily enable you to comprehend that which exists between the earths of the three heavens.

Such, in the beginning, was the general constitution of the immaterial universe: but there were afterwards produced changes in the spiritual organism, of which I am now about to speak.

I have shown you, in my second letter, what was the end which God had in creating the universe, and you have acknowledged that this end would have failed if man had not been free to love God or not to love him, that is to say, if he had not been free to conform to the laws of the divine order or to infringe them. It thence results that the free will of man is itself one of the principal laws of this order: so that God who never contravenes the laws which his wisdom has established, is careful not to destroy this liberty of man, and has recourse to other means to preserve the order of the universe, which man, from his present nature, is always disposed to destroy.

Man being in the likeness and image of God, or, in other words, man having been created the receptacle of the love and wisdom of God, received, by this very organization, a power of changing, which was perverted by the abuse which he made of his free will. We have seen in fact that man receives and appropriates the divine influence because he is endowed with liberty and rationality, whilst other beings, having neither free will nor the faculty of reasoning, receive this influence but do not appropriate it. Give me for a moment all your attention. The divine influence is none other than the life which emanates from God, and life is composed of affections and thoughts, which are themselves spiritual substances and forms; this we have already acknowledged. This granted, man continually receiving life appropriates to himself thus at every instant spiritual substances and forms which emanate from God, and these substances and these forms are real objects of spiritual organism. But the affections and the thoughts which man receives from God, being appropriated by him become, by that very reception, affections and thoughts of man; now man being thus himself a centre of continual emanations, they enter, in emanating from him, into the spiritual organism, but changed from their primitive substance and form, if this appropriation is not made conformably to the laws of order, that is to say, if man has separated himself from the divine laws.

You may jndge now of the modification which the spiritual organism must necessarily have undergone when man appeared in the universe; I say when *man appeared* in the universe, for reason teaches and the new sciences prove that the universe must have existed long before it was inhabited by man.

Thus, so long as man returned to his Creator the love and the wisdom which he received from him, that is to say, so long as he lived comformably to the laws of divine order, the affections and the thoughts which he appropriated to himself preserved their primitive purity; and his emanations being for that reason in homogeneity with the emanations which proceed from God by the spiritual sun, the universal organism received from it no alteration. But when afterwards men began to transgress the divine laws, the affections and thoughts which they appropriated to themselves, lost their primitive purity, and were so much the more estranged as the infractions became greater. Man's infractions of the divine laws were at first trivial; for every thing in the universe, as well in its spiritual as in its natural part, proceeds by gradations: and besides, it is even now acknowledged that man does not suddenly pass from an extreme good to an extreme evil. The first transgression that men committed was only a desire—the desire of being led of themselves, instead of suffering themselves to be freely directed by God as at first; but though this desire did not at once precipitate them into evil, it is most true that those who conceived it lost some of the purity of their fathers.

This was the commencement of the perversion of the divine order by man, or in other words, the beginning of man's fall. I can readily conceive the repugnance of men of the world, when the fall is mentioned; it is not that they generally deny the primeval existence of a paradisiacal age; they are ready to admit that the human race is degraded; but when they recollect what, in their childhood, has been taught them concerning the fall, their reason revolts. And could it be otherwise, when they know that the old theology still persists, even in this age, in teaching that the fault of a single man was the cause of the condemnation of the human race? Is not this to attribute injustice to God and is it to be wondered at that the reason of man should refuse to receive such instruction any longer?

This allusion to the fall is but incidental: it is my intention to show you only, in a few words, that it was progressive, and not instantaneous, and that it was the declension of man in the aggregate, and not in the single individual. We will examine this dogma at another time.

There is one law of the divine order whose existence you will readily acknowledge: this is the law of transmission by germs. If the agriculturists make choice of the best grain for seed; if breeders of cattle choose the healthiest and best formed for the propagation of the species; it is because the experience of all time has proved that bodily defects are transmitted in increasing progression from germ to germ. This law exists for the moral and spiritual as well as for the corporeal part of man; it has been recognised by all good observers, but what prevents it from being evident in that which concerns the moral and spiritual part is, because man, by the education which he receives, can conceal his desires and his thoughts; it is, besides, because being endowed with free will and rationality, he can be reformed; but it is always a truth that he is born with a propensity to apparent and hidden defects derived from his parents. I will dwell more on this subject when we come to treat on original evil; for this evil consists in the transmission of evils and falses which accumulate from generation to generation, and not in the simple transmission of the crime of one man.

The men who had not originally the desire for self-guidance, but who had only conceived this desire during their life in the natural world, transmitted it to their offspring according to this general law of order; it was weak with the first, and became stronger with the next generation. Yet these were still good, though their goodness had more degenerated than that of their fathers; but the propensity to depart from the laws of order increasing from generation to generation, men at length fell into evil. There has been, since then, between the divine emanations which constituted the primitive spiritual organism, and the emanations of men fallen into evil, a real antagonism; and as spiritual objects are not subjected to the laws of gravity, but observe those of spiritual attraction, that is to say, of sympathy, all those spiritual objects which resulted from the vitiated emanations of these men, reuniting according to the laws of spiritual attraction, constituted an organism distinct from the first and altogether inverted. We have called the first, heaven, we will call the last, hell. This word, without doubt, sounds harsh in your ears: so many absurdities have been spread concerning hell, that a man of the world now-a-days cannot even hear the name pronounced without smiling; but be good enough to wait a little, and you will soon acknowledge that we can speak of hell, and believe that there is a hell, such as it actually *is*, and *not* such as it has hitherto been described, without for that reason being obliged to make the least renunciation of the use of the intellectual faculty.

Hell, like heaven, has its atmospheres, and its earths arranged according to separate or diserete degrees. In fact, by appropriating to themselves, and by perverting the divine emanations, these men and those who from generation to generation followed their example, did not, on that account, invert the order of their degrees. The exterior good, or the good of the first degree, became evil, but this evil was exterior, or the evil of the first degree; interior good became interior evil, and inmost good, inmost evil; it was the same with truth, which, according to its degree, was changed into the false of the same degree. If you wish to form to yourself an idea of the infernal earths, represent them to yourself as composed of all that is bad and deformed in that which constitutes our earth. The inmost of bad and deformed objects corresponds to the things which constitute the earths of the third or deepest hell; the interior of these objects, to the things which constitute the earths of the second hell, and these objects themselves, to the things which constitute the earths of the first hell. You will also judge of the difference between the infernal earths, by the difference which there is between the inmost of a bad and deformed thing, its interior, and its exterior or aggregate form.

Thus hell is subsequent to heaven; it was not created by God, since God was love itself, and wisdom itself: love could not beget hatred, nor wisdom folly; but hell is from man; man alone created it, and he created it by means of that power to modify which he had received, and which in his hands has become altogether destructive of the works of God, by the abuse which he has made of his free will. If any difficulty is experienced in comprehending that man has such a power, it arises entirely from the erroneous ideas which the false philosophy and theology have incessantly spread about God and creation. Why does the belief that there is no hell so extensively prevail? Because it is repugnant to reason, not only to require faith in the descriptions generally given of it, but also to believe that God created a place of torment. But if God has not created hell, by whom was it created? At this question, moralists are silent; some theologians believe they have overcome the difficulty, by saying that rebellious angels have been cast down into the abyss. But was not this abyss the eternal prison in which they were to be confined? Who then created it? And yet theologians and moralists admit the infinite goodness of God, and recognize the necessity and reality of hell. Why do they find it impossible for them to reconcile the infinite love of the one with the existence of the other? Why! because they have only vague notions concerning God and the world of spirits; because, consequently they have been unable to form a just idea of the creation.

The idea generally prevailing upon this important subject, is, that the universe being once formed, creation ceased. Some philosophers, seeing that every thing is renewed by means of germs, believe that nature perpetuates herself. On the other hand, theologians, relying upon the letter of the scriptures, without seeking to penetrate into their spirit, say that all things were made by the *Word;* and upon this first point they are perfectly correct, as you will afterwards acknowledge, when we come to discuss the dogmatic questions together; but they fall into a gross error in adding that every thing was created by this alone, that God spake a word, or gave an order, as an absolute sovereign would do in a kingdom.

When it is believed that the Creator is a Being without substance and form, and that the universe was created out of nothing, how can errors be avoided? But if is admitted that God is substance itself and form itself (*Form-type*), and that the universe emanated from him, then difficulties disappear; for then it is easy to admit as a principle that all production is a continued creation.

It is true that the universe is from a single outbirth, for it was not created as I have before told you, either from space to space, or from one time to another; but it by no means thence results, that creation was terminated by its formation. The universe being an emanation from God, cannot but subsist by a continual emanation from the Divinity. If it were possible that this emanation could be suspended one instant, the two worlds, the natural and the spiritual, would be instantly deprived of life, and the universe, both material and immaterial, would subsist no longer. Creation then continues every instant, without the least interruption. If it appears stable to us, it is because God is not inconstant as man is, and does not overturn to day what he did yesterday. In God's incessant creation he always conforms to the laws of his own divine order.

If to the considerations which I have previously presented to you, you now add the principle that all production is a continued creation, you will experience no further difficulty in comprehending that man had the power to create hell. Take notice, however, that I do not take the word "create" in the acceptation of producing out of nothing; but in saying that man had power to create hell, I mean that he had power to render bad and deformed the good spiritual substances and the beautiful spiritual forms which emanated from God, and which he appropriated to himself; I will even add that in introducing thus the evil and deformed into the spiritual organism, he introduced them also into the natural organism, according to the laws of correspondence between the two worlds.

The creation of hell was not the only change which man introduced into the spiritual organism; there is still another which I must also make you acquainted with.

When hell was constituted by man's perversity, or in other words, when men after having progressively separated themselves from the supreme good, fell at length into evil, they did not all become perverted to such a degree as no longer to have in them either good or evil. There were even many who still fluctuated between the good and evil, between the true and the false. The emanations of these being a mixture of good and bad substances, and beautiful and perverted forms, could neither enter into the celestial organism, where all is good and beautiful, nor into the infernal organism, where all is evil and deformed; they composed consequently a spiritual mixed organism. In its external manifestation, the earth of this new organism holds the middle between the earth of the first heaven and that of the first hell; it is composed of objects like those of our earth, except the difference between what is spiritual and what is natural; and presents thus a mixture of the good and the bad, of the beautiful and deformed. We give to this part of the spiritual world the name of World of Spirits.

Such are the changes which the fall of man has introduced into the spiritual organism of the globe which we inhabit. I have presented them to you briefly, that you may know what is now the general division of this spiritual world, whose exploration we have undertaken to make together.

I will conclude this letter by impressing upon you this remark, that notwithstanding these changes in the spiritual organism, all its parts are at the same time contained in the natural organism; they are there as good and evil, the true and the false, are in man, for man, we shall see in the course of our discussion, is himself a microcosm, or little world. In fine, if our natural organism remained entire whilst the spiritual organism has been divided, the reason of this is easily to be perceived. The objects which compose the latter have, as I have already shown you, been capable of being separated from each other, and this separation was effected at the instant that there was antagonism between them; but it could not be the same with corresponding bodies of the natural organism, because the laws of space and time opposed, in an absolute manner, their separation.

LETTER X.

I have, in my last letter, made you acquainted with the principal divisions of the spiritual world; I shall speak in this respecting the beings who inhabit them; but permit me first to revert to a question which has already been incidentally treated upon.

I have shown, in my fifth letter, that all the intelligent beings who exist in the immaterial world, it matters not what name has been given to them besides, are men, and have all first lived upon natural earths before inhabiting the other world. This proposition being the fundamental basis of the subject which is about to engage our attention, I must have recourse to all the means which can confirm it, and add to proofs already given those which the present state of our discussion permits me to employ.

As hell is posterior to the primitive creation, I will here treat concerning those spiritual beings only to whom the name of Angels has been given; besides, what I am about to say of angels will equally apply to all other intelligent beings.

If angels had not originally lived upon natural earths, that is to say, if they had not been clothed, as we are, with a material body which they restored to the earth from which it was taken, they must necessarily have been angels immediately created such. It would then be necessary to suppose that God would have been able to create the spiritual without adjoining to it a natural suitable to contain it, and serve it for a basis and support. Now such a supposition cannot be admitted by those who are acquainted with the order which has presided at the creation. You have seen, truly, that the universe is a coherent whole, in the centre of which is the spiritual sun, and that from this sun even to the most compact objects of nature, everything must be connected by contiguity, according to the order of separate or discrete degrees, so that the last degree should be the continent, the basis, and the support of the two prior degrees.

If to this you add that the emanation which has created the universe, being in potency a compound of substances and forms of the three degrees, it was impossible that these substances and forms, as they develope themselves in acts, should not be connected according to the order of these degrees; you will then easily understand that God could not create any spiritual being without there being a natural, which might contain the spiritual, and that consequently to have angels, it was absolutely necessary that he should create intelligent beings clothed with a material body, that is to say, men.

It is true that our modern psychologists do not conceive of the spiritual in this manner; but to what results have they thus come with their vapory ideas? They have so refined away the spiritual, that it has become for them as if it did not exist. But you, who now know that there is nothing spiritual without substance and form, because that which has neither substance nor form cannot either exist or consequently subsist, and is absolutely nothing but a creation of the imagination, or a being altogether chimerical—you will understand without difficulty that spiritual substances and forms, could not have any consistence if they had not for their continent, basis, and support, natural substances and forms, which are their last degree or their effect.

Remark, besides, that if God had been able to create in his likeness and image beings capable of loving him freely, without these beings having been obliged to live first in the last degree of creation, that is to say, in the natural world, it would have been, for this end, useless to create this natural world. What was, in fact, the end which God had in the creation of the universe? We have already seen it, and it is impossible to discover any other,—it was to create beings who could receive his love and freely return it to him. Now, if it were possible to attain this end by an immediate creation of angels, was it not useless to create man and the natural world?

One of the consequences of the principles which we are discussing is, that the spiritual world must have remained a long time without being inhabited. This might, at the first thought, excite surprise; but if our earth, which no one at this day will deny has revolved for ages around the sun, without having had upon its surface any of the beings for which alone it was nevertheless created, why should we be astonished that the earths of the spiritual world, to which it corresponds, should have been for a little longer time without receiving those who were to inhabit them? We who live in the midst of time may think it extraordinary that worlds should have remained uninhabited for ages; but should not our surprise cease as soon as we reflect that ages are but an instant to Him who is eternal? We should not be any more astonished at this, that all the earths of the spiritual world have been inhabited posteriorly to the natural earths which correspond to them. But are we to conclude from this that there were not angels in the spiritual world before man appeared upon our earth? Certainly not. The natural universe, as you know, contains myriads of terrestrial globes, all of which, created to receive men, were certainly not all inhabited at the same moment; some have perhaps been inhabited for millions of years, and it may be possible that others are not inhabited yet. Nothing then can lead us to believe that our globe was inhabited before there were angels in the spiritual world. What we have a right to affirm on the subject of our planet only is, that it had inhabitants before the part of the spiritual world to which it corresponds had any; but it must always have been necessary that one of the earths of the natural world should have been first inhabited, in order that there might be angels in the heavens.

These new considerations, added to those which I have presented to you in my fifth letter, prove very evidently, that the angels at first lived as men in the natural world.

Nevertheless, as what I have said in discussing this subject, has been based upon the principle that the spiritual can have existence only so far as it is contained in a natural, which serves it for a basis and support, it remains for me yet to solve a question which you would doubtless soon address to me if I did not suggest it at this time; the angels having restored to the earth the material body, which in our world, served them for a continent, basis, and support, what is the natural which serves for a basis now?

This question, my dear sir, from its nature enters into the general discussion , and you will there find it explained; however not to detain you longer for an answer, I will say at once, that it is the human race itself which supplies this function. This need not be a matter of astonishment to you, as there can be nothing in the natural world more suitable than man to serve for a continent, basis, and support to beings who have lived men, and who still live in a human form. As to the manner in which angels and spirits are contained in man, it is only in the course of the general discussion that we shall be able to make this clear; to this discussion then I now come.

Since spirits and angels have all once lived as men on the natural earths before inhabiting the other world, the most certain means of forming an idea of spiritual beings is first to acquire a knowledge of man. Being in the likeness and image of God, man must have been, and was really, the summary of the universal creation; and it was for this very reason that the ancients used to call him a *microcosm*, that is to say, a little universe. Thus the enigma of man, the enigma which for so many ages philosophy has sought in vain to discover, this cannot be explained but by meditating upon the creation of the universe. God being VERY MAN, all the emanations which proceeded from him must have been a continual effort to impress upon creation his image or the human form. Do you desire a proof of this? Survey the scale of beings: those which first appeared, presented, it is true, but a rough sketch: but the more creation developed itself, the more you see the newly created beings approach this form; at length when everything was progressively arranged, so that it might attain to its perfection, you see man appear upon the theatre which God had embellished for him.

Observe, on the subject of these successive creations, that the spiritual sun and natural sun, being always in activity, the first by the presence of God who is in the midst of it, and the second by the force of expansion which the first communicates to it, the spiritual and natural atmospheres are continually in effort to preserve and to produce; for it is by them that the substances at rest of the spiritual world, and the fixed substances or matter of our world, subsist and are modified. Now, follow in all its details the formation of the universe, and you will be able to have an idea of the formation of man.

The creation of the three kinds of spiritual earths which are between themselves separate and distinct, according to the three degrees, sufficiently indicate to us, that there must be in the man-spirit three receptacles in the same manner separate and distinct, that the love and wisdom of God may reach him in the three degrees, namely, in the degree of ends, in the degree of causes, and in that of spiritual effects, and that man may thus be able to dwell upon those earths when he departs from our world.

The receptacle of the love and wisdom of God in the degree of ends, is that which constitutes the inmost of the man-spirit. It is in this inmost that God resides surrounded with his spiritual sun; *there* is his sanctuary with man. This inmost, formed of the purest substances at rest, derived from the spiritual atmosphere of the third degree, and disposed in the most harmonious order, is in reality the third heaven for man; for it is by means of this inmost receptacle that he is adapted, as you will see presently, to become an inhabitant of the third heaven, or an angel of the inmost heaven.

The receptacle of the love and wisdom of God in the degree of causes, is that which constitutes the internal in the man-spirit, every part of which envelopes the corresponding part of the inmost. This internal, formed from the purest substances at rest, drawn from the spiritual atmosphere of the second degree, and disposed also in a harmonious order, is the *second* heaven for man; for it is by means of this internal receptacle that he can become an angel of the second heaven if by his life in the world he has not rendered himself fit to be elevated to the inmost heaven.

Lastly, the receptacle of the love and wisdom of God in the degree of spiritual effects, is that which constitutes the interior in the man-spirit, all of whose parts also envelope every corresponding part of the internal and of the inmost. This interior, formed from the purest substances at rest derived from the spiritual atmosphere of the last degree, and disposed likewise in a harmonious order, is the first heaven for man; for it is by means of this receptacle that he may become an angel of the first heaven, if by his life in the world, he has not rendered himself fit to be elevated to the superior heavens.

As to the state of these three receptacles in the material body of man, the formation of the material earths demonstrates to us that all the parts of each of them are enveloped with fixed substances, which are derived from the three natural atmospheres, and which correspond to the substances at rest of which these parts are themselves composed. Such is, in man, the Divine order; but the present state of the spiritual world, such as I have presented to you in my last letter, demonstrates to us again that by his fall man has inverted this order.

You remember that the fall was progressive and not instantaneous. In the degree that man abandoned goodness and truth for the evil and the false, he removed himself from God to turn himself more and more towards himself; the love and the wisdom of God then experienced an increasing difficulty in penetrating into their receptacles, and by degrees there was formed in man an inverse order, having its proper receptacle for the love of self and self-derived intelligence, or in other words for hatred and folly; and when man had entirely fallen into the evil and false, the receptacles of the love and wisdom of God were completely closed, and those of hatred and folly completely open. It is thus that man himself introduced disorder into his primitive organization. Subjected like all other beings to the law of transmission by germs, so long as he lived according to order, his children were born into the order of creation that is to say, good: but as soon as by his life in hatred and folly, he had inverted the order to which he had been created, his children were born into inverted order, that is to say, into evil or into the love of self.

Nevertheless, although the receptacles of the love and wisdom of God were closed by the fall, God did not the less reside in the inmost of man, for God is in the inmost of everything; if it were not thus, man after the fall could not have lived either in this or in the spiritual world. But the love and wisdom of God not being able to manifest themselves in the man-spirit any farther than their receptacles are opened, man would have been forever deprived of that love and wisdom, if God, who had foreseen the fall, had not at the same time in his mercy provided means for reinstating him. This is not the place to examine the means which God employed to restore man to himself; we will speak of this when we come to treat concerning points of doctrine. I will only say that by these means the receptacles of the love and wisdom of God may successively be opened, and thus man can again become an inhabitant of the heavens.

These primary ideas concerning man, being sufficient to enable you to form an idea of spiritual beings, we proceed now to extend our investigations to them.

According to the explications given you in my last letter, the spiritual world is composed of two organisms absolutely opposite, called heaven and hell, and of a mixed organism denominated the world of spirits; then heaven and hell are subdivided each into three great parts distinct in themselves, according to the order of degrees, so that there are three heavens and three hells. Such are the principal divisions which now exist in the spiritual world.

The angels of the inmost or supreme heaven are men who, by their life in the world, rendered themselves fit to receive the love and wisdom of God in the supreme degree, or degree of ends. As the inmost of man is formed of the purest substances at rest, derived from the spiritual atmosphere of the third degree, these angels, living then by this inmost alone, are in the purest state; surrounded with an atmosphere which proceeds immediately from the spiritual sun, they receive without any other medium, the influence of this sun, or rather influx from God; and consequently spiritual heat, or the divine love, and the spiritual light or the divine wisdom, are not tempered in their manifestations to them except by this atmosphere alone.

Here I will make one observation. You know that God, by his spiritual sun, is in every created being, and that it is by the heat and light of this sun, that he vivifies all creation: but the divine love is so ardent and the divine wisdom so transcendantly bright, that all spiritual beings would be consumed in an instant, if God did not temper this ardor and this brilliancy, by veiling himself more or less by spiritual atmospheres, in order to proportion his love and wisdom to the state of every being. Thus God being always present in the inmost of spiritual beings, is never nearer to or more distant from one than another; but he is more or less veiled, so that the intensity of spiritual heat and light depends upon the *media* which they traverse before they affect us. The same thing is produced in the material world, and the analogy is striking: indeed science proves that no being of our globe could support either the heat or the light of our sun, even if that luminary were a thousand times more remote from us than it really is, if there did not exist atmospheric *media* to temper its heat and light; that without these *media* all the globes which gravitate around it, would be set on fire and reduced to liquefaction ; and that consequently the intensity of natural heat and light depends upon the media which they traverse before arriving at objects, and by no means upon the distance of the sun from those objects.

On the other hand, if among beings of our globe some live in the air, others upon the surface of the globe, others in waters, and others in the interior of the earth, it is evidently because they are not all susceptible of receiving the same intensity of natural heat and light; but, besides this, those which fly in the air pass through regions more or less elevated; those which are upon the earth, live in climates more or less tempered; those which swim in the seas keep in greater or less depths; and those which conceal themselves in the earth are more or less remote from the surface: analogy again shows us then, that in the same heaven, angels have mansions which differ from each other, as they are adapted to receive, according to continuous degrees, more or less love and wisdom.

The inhabitants of the deepest hell opposite to the highest heaven, are, on the contrary, men who in the world have lived in the evils and the falses of the third degree or the degree of ends; the purer the angels of the highest heaven, the more impure are those infernal spirits. The inmost inverted form, in which they live, is as hideous as that of the third heaven is beautiful; in a word, everything in this hell is the opposite of the highest heaven.

As to the two other heavens and the two other hells which are opposite to them, it will be seen also, from the preceding, what is the nature of their inhabitants.

The angels of the second heaven are men who, by their life in the world, have only rendered themselves fit to receive the love and wisdom of God in the degree of causes; and the inhabitants of the second hell opposite to that of heaven, are those who in the world have lived in the evils and falses of this same degree. With the first the internal has been restored to order; with the others it has been inverted.

Lastly, the angels of the first heaven are men who, by their life in the world, have only rendered themselves fit to receive the love and the wisdom of God in the degree of spiritual effects; and the inhabitants of the first hell opposite to this heaven, are those who, in the world, have lived in the evils and the falses of this same degree. The interior has been restored to order with the first, and it has remained inverted with the others.

The world of spirits is between the first heaven and the first hell. It is composed of all those who, on leaving the natural world, are not yet good enough to enter into one of the heavens, or not yet wicked enough to plunge themselves into one of the hells. The first remain there until they are divested of the evils and falsities attached to them, and the second until they have rejected the little goodness and truth remaining with them.

It was indispensable to enter upon these preliminary details before we could understand the nature of influx, or the manner in which life penetrates to the inhabitants of the spiritual world, and consequently to men.

God governs the whole universe by influx. We call that *common influx* which concerns the universe in general, and *particular influx* that which specially concerns the inhabitants of the spiritual world and men. There are other kinds of influx, of which I will speak to you at another time, but for the present we will confine ourselves to the nature of *particular influx.*

It is evident that the angel of the supreme heaven receives immediately from the spiritual sun the love and wisdom of God; for this angel lives in his inmost principle, and it is in this principle that God resides surrounded with his spiritual sun.

But the angels of the second heaven cannot receive immediately, from the spiritual sun, the love and wisdom of God; for they live in their internal and not in their inmost, or what is the same thing, they are in causes and not in ends; and as there is only contiguity between ends and causes, and not continuity, the love and the wisdom of God cannot descend from ends into causes, but by an influx of angels who are in ends, upon those who are in causes. By means of this influx, the angels of the third heaven communicate to the angels of the second their affections which proceed from the love of God, and their thoughts which proceed from his wisdom; but these affections and thoughts which with the first are relative to ends, become only relative to causes when the second receive them. This results evidently from the degree of life, or of love and wisdom in which these last are.

You have seen that with the angels of the second heaven the inmost is closed; but as every inmost receptacle is from its very nature a supreme heaven, since it is formed of the purest substances from the spiritual atmosphere of the third degree, and since, moreover, heaven is in the angel and in man, though it manifests itself out of the angel and man, it results thence that the inmost of the angels of the second heaven, closed for them, is open for the angels of the highest heaven; this, then is the receptacle which serves them for a continent, basis, and support, and it is from this that they flow into the internal of the angels of the second heaven.

You will doubtless be much astonished to learn that angels having substance and form, are in other angels; but reflect a moment, I pray you, upon the nature of spiritual substances and forms; remove from your thought the idea of space and time, and your astonishment will cease. In saying to you repeatedly that God is in man, I made use of no metaphor. God is really in the inmost of man, but he is there veiled in his spiritual sun. So the highest heaven is altogether in the inmost of man, but it is not veiled there; yet this inmost being closed with men during their life in the world, and with angels and spirits who have not rendered themselves fit to receive the love and wisdom of God in the degree of ends, is the reason why this supreme heaven is not manifested to their eyes; but if their inmost were opened they would be instantly in this heaven, because this heaven is for them included in their inmost. So of the rest, of which you will be fully convinced when we enter into the details upon the objects of the spiritual world. Now if all the supreme heaven be in general in the inmost of the angel of the second heaven, why be astonished that angels of this supreme heaven should make in this inmost their habitual residence? Yes, my dear sir, you and I have not only God and the supreme heaven in us, but we have in us the whole spiritual world; we have God and the supreme heaven in our inmost, and the lowest hell in our inverted inmost, the second heaven in our internal, and the second hell in our inverted internal, first heaven in our interior, and the first hell in our inverted interior; and lastly, the whole intermediate world in our man-spirit, such as it is now, that is to say, impregnated with terrestrial affections and thoughts; and it is because this is the case that it would happen, if to morrow we should quit this world, we would be there immediately, and without, for that reason, being obliged to make any progression of distance or change of place; we should be, I say in the midst of the world of spirits, with the same affection and thoughts that we now have, and afterwards we should go either into one of the heavens or one of the hells, according as by our life here below we should have rendered ourselves fit to receive in a degree more or less elevated, either the love and wisdom of God, or the hatred and folly which proceed from the love of self and self-derived intelligence. But let us return to our discussion.

If an angel of the highest heaven were not in the inmost of an angel of the second heaven, he could not subsist, and the parts of his body would be dissipated like gases which are not compressed. Indeed, the angel of the supreme heaven, living in his inmost receptacle, has successively divested himself of the other receptacles which invested his inmost, and consequently of the internal receptacle which was its immediate envelope; he would not have then any more envelopes to maintain the parts of his body in permanent cohesion, if these receptacles were not replaced; now it is this which happens to the internal receptacle, that this angel, as soon as he is divested of his internal, resides in the inmost of an angel of the second heaven, and as this last angel lives in his internal, this internal serves the angel of the supreme heaven for a continent, basis, and support.

It is true that the internal of the angel of the second heaven has but little more consistence than the inmost of the angel of the supreme heaven, for the only difference which exists between these two receptacles is that one is formed from substances at rest from the atmosphere of the second degree, and the other from substances at rest from the atmosphere of the third degree. But observe, that as a consequence of the same law the angel of the second heaven has for a residence the interior of an angel of the first heaven, which serves him for a continent, basis, and support; and that the angel of the first heaven in like manner resides in a spirit of the intermediate world. Yet, although these different receptacles are less and less attached as to the substances which compose them, they would nevertheless, have no consistence and would all be dissipated, if they did not repose at last upon a stable basis; and this solid basis is the man whom the spirit of the intermediate world himself has for a continent, basis and support. Thus, according to this law of order, it can be explained how spiritual beings in certain circumstances, may descend from the superior regions of the spiritual world into inferior regions, and appear even be fore men whose spiritual eyes are opened; we can also understand why our soul or man-spirit, in quitting its terrestrial envelope, is not dissipated like a vapor since it finds in the inhabitants of our world a receptacle which serves for a continent, basis and support.

If an angel of the supreme heaven cannot subsist without being in the inmost of an angel of the second heaven, an angel of the second heaven, on the other hand, could not live if he had not in his inmost one or more angels of the third heaven ; for life is composed of affections and thoughts ; and according to what precedes, affections and thoughts cannot flow into this angel, but by the medium of the angels of the supreme heaven.

I have said that there is in the inmost of this angel, one or more angels of the third heaven; this requires some explanation.

The angel of the second heaven, receiving his affections and thoughts from the supreme heaven, if his inmost were always occupied by a single angel or by the same angels, he himself would be an automaton obliged to follow all the impulses which are given to him. But each angel, enjoying liberty and rationality, which are faculties proper to him, is able to appropriate to himself or reject the affections and thoughts which he receives from the angels who are in his inmost. Those then from whom proceed the affections and thoughts which he rejects, finding themselves no longer in correspondence with him, are induced for that very reason to quit him, and others succeed who are more in harmony with him. It is thus that the angel of the second heaven has really a life proper to himself.

You see from what precedes, that the angels of the third heaven are in those of the second, as ends are in causes, or rather as causes are in the effects ; for in considering the second heaven as the effect, the supreme heaven is the cause and the spiritual sun is the end, so in considering the supreme heaven as effect, the spiritual sun is the cause and God is the end. Now, in like manner, as the cause is out of the effect, though being in the effect, so also, the inhabitants of the third heaven are out of the inhabitants of the second heaven, though in their inmost.

The inmost of the angels of the second heaven being closed, it thence results that in their normal state these angels neither see those of the supreme heaven, nor this heaven itself. I say in their normal state, for there exist laws of permission, provided from all eternity, and appertaining also to order, and according to those laws there can be, in certain cases, a communication opened not only between these heavens, but also between all parts of the spiritual world, and even between that world and ours. It is thus that man in his normal state cannot see the spiritual world, and yet that in certain cases his spiritual sight can be opened, and then he sees objects and inhabitants of this spiritual world. When, then, God permits the inmost of the angels of the second heaven to be opened, they are actually in communication with the angels of the supreme heaven; but without this permission, no other communication exists between them than by particular influx, and according to correspondences.

What I have just said concerning the second heaven in relation to the third, is applicable to the first in relation to the second. I will only add that the affections and thoughts which the angels of the superior heavens transmit, although they are inmost and internal, or relate to ends and causes, are transformed into affections and thoughts of the first degree, or having relation to spiritual effects, when they are received by the angels of the first heaven.

Particular influx is transmitted afterwards according to the same laws to the world of spirits. Those who sojourn in this world are destined to inhabit either one of the heavens or one of the hells, according as they have rendered themselves fit during their life upon earth to receive or reject the love and wisdom of God in their different degrees. But as they are still full of terrestrial affections and thoughts—though they are disengaged from their material body—their inmost, their internal and their interior cannot be completely opened, whether for the life of heaven, or the life of hell, until after they have rejected these affections and thoughts. They live in this intermediate world, both by the influx which they receive from the heavens, and by the contrary influx, which comes to them from the hells, influx of which I am now about to speak.

You have already seen that man, by his fall, had destroyed in himself the order of creation, and that by the change of the love of God into self-love, or into hatred against others, and by that of the wisdom of God into self-derived intelligence or folly, he had formed in himself an inverted order, which had its receptacles for the three degrees of hatred and folly, or evil and the false. You have also seen that thence had resulted three hells opposite to the three heavens, the deepest hell consisting in inmost hatreds and follies, or what relates to ends, the second hell in internal hatreds and follies, or what relates to causes, and the first hell in interior hatreds and follies, or what relates to spiritual effects. From the deepest hell then there proceeds also by reaction an influx; but this influx operating upon the two other hells and upon the world of spirits, in a sense inverse of the influx of the supreme heaven upon the two other heavens, and upon this world of spirits, I believe it to be useless to enter again into all the details which I have given you. You will, besides, readily acknowledge that with the spirits of the intermediate world, their inmost inverted includes demons of the deepest hell, their inverted internal demons of the second hell, and their inverted interior demons of the first hell. You will acknowledge also with the same facility that the inhabitant of the deepest hell has for continent, basis, and support the inverted inmost of the inhabitant of the second hell; that of the second hell the inverted internal of the inhabitant of the first hell; and that of the first hell the inverted interior of the inhabitant of the world of spirits; if, however, this presents some difficulty to you by reason of the inverted position which the hells present, it will suffice for you to compare this position to that of the antipodes, and analogy will at once remove the difficulty.

By the effect of these two kinds of opposite influx, the inhabitants of the heavens and those of the hells have for continent, basis, and support those of the intermediate world; but this basis being, like the preceding, of a spiritual nature, would still present no consistence, and all would be dissipated and vanish away, angels, devils, and spirits, if it did not rest upon a solid basis. This last basis which completes the edifice is man by means of his material body. In man are good and bad spirits who transmit to him good and bad affections, pure and impure thoughts; and as spirits include in themselves angels and devils, these angels and these devils are also with man in the different receptacles which his man-spirit contains. Without the affections and thoughts which are transmitted to him from the spiritual world, and which are changed when he receives them into natural affections and thoughts, man could not live, for the life of man consists in affections and thoughts; but in order that man may be man, and not an automaton, he has received free will and rationality as his own, and it is by these two faculties that he appropriates or rejects the affections and thoughts which come to him from the spiritual world by the two influxes. On the other hand, without man spiritual beings could not subsist, since it is necessary that they should have for a support a solid and stable basis to contain them.

These general considerations concerning particular influx will raise numerous questions which I will treat of successively in other letters; however, I will not conclude this, though it is already too long, without drawing from this discussion a consequence which may not have escaped you, but which nevertheless demands from its importance some explication.

Since the spiritual world would not exist nor subsist without the natural world, it results thence that if this were destroyed, its destruction would necessarily draw with it that of the other, so that of all that has been created there would remain absolutely nothing.

Those who have hitherto admitted and preached the erroneous doctrine of the end of the world, have been believed, even by persons who made use of their understandings, because they were in complete ignorance of this strict connection which exists between the two worlds, by which the one cannot subsist without the other. The end of the world in their idea presented only the destruction of the material part of the universe, the spiritual part, by that catastrophe, not ceasing to subsist. But when the inmost connection, which makes the two worlds one coherent whole, is known, it is impossible to admit the complete destruction of the material universe, since God could not destroy it without at the same time destroying the spiritual universe. That God should destroy one part of that which he has made for the preservation and amelioration of the other part, this, I repeat it, may be conceived; but that he should destroy all that he has made, without any vestige remaining, this cannot be admitted, without charging God with improvidence and folly.

Besides, in order to destroy the material universe, would it not be necessary that God should employ means the reverse of those he has made use of in creating it? How, in fact, would these masses which gravitate in space be made to disappear? Would he launch them into chaos? But we have seen that chaos, such at least as it is commonly conceived, is but a word without meaning, and never could have existed. It would be necesary then that the material universe should disappear, or in other words, it would be necessary that it should be, after its dissolution, what it was before its construction; if not, matter would always exist, though under another form. Then this would not be what is commonly understood by the end of the world; it would be a change of form, a general ruin in which the human race would disappear, but it would not be the annihilation of matter. Now where was the universe before its creation? As we have seen by our preceding remarks, it was in the bosom of God. And what was matter before it possessed the forms it now presents? We have also acknowledged, and modern science proves it, that it was composed only of æriform fluids. It would be necessary then that the emanation which, in proceeding from God, has taken forms so varied, in order to constitute by a succession of long periods this vast and beautiful universe, it would be necessary, I say, that this emanation should return to its first state, by following an inverse course, and thus return into the bosom of God without external manifestation. Then God would have labored in vain, and all his work would be to do over again. Can such a supposition for a moment be admitted?

There remains one objection; many persons will no doubt say: How can the spiritual world contain the millions of souls which each of the millions of terrestrial globes transmits to it every day, if this daily transmission is to continue eternally, especially when it is admitted that souls are spiritual substances and forms? How provide for so many spiritual bodies? This objection, it is true, has nothing serious in it, and *you* doubtless would not make it; but I have referred to it because it has often been presented to me by men who have given proofs of intelligence, and were endowed with good judgment.

If we would reflect a moment upon the nature of what is spiritual, which cannot in any manner be subject to the laws of space, we would be very far from making snch an objection; but accustomed as we are to live in space and time, and to refer everything to space and time, our first ideas always will partake of the impressions which we receive from them ; it is not astonishing that a similar objection should present itself to our minds as soon as we speak of such an immensity of spiritual beings. But when we abstract from our minds the idea of space and time, it is easy to understand that the spiritual world, though contained in the natural world, could contain not only all the souls which the terrestrial globes will send to it to eternity, but a much greater number, if it were possible, without its inhabitants being crowded. To see that, it is sufficient to recollect that the spiritual world is contained in the natural world,as the cause is contained in the effect, and that the spiritual not being subjected to the trammels of space, each one of the parts of the other world is always susceptible of taking all the development which is necessary to it, without this development being for that reason prejudicial to the other parts, under the relation of the appearances of space which is enjoyed in the spiritual world. To the considerations which I have just presented to you in favor of the indestructibility of the material universe, I could add many others; but this, I believe, would be useless; for the more we advance in the examinations of spiritual things, the more you will acknowledge the intimate connection which renders the two worlds indispensable to each other. Besides, how much sweet consolation does the thought, that the material universe will subsist forever, present! What a beneficent impulse would it not produce if it were generally admitted! And yet it is engraved upon the heart of man. Consult it, and an interior voice will respond that God has not created this universe to destroy it. What' could God be amused in creating a world to destroy it as a child does with a house of cards! No, God is not reckless— he is not capricious. He is love itself, and wisdom itself. The universe was derived from his love, and it was by his wisdom that he created it in accordance with the laws of that wisdom, that is to say, the laws of divine order. But according to these laws, man, for whom it was created, was endowed with free will, without which he would have been nothing more than an automaton; he has made a bad use of this precious faculty, and has become altogether degenerate. The degradation of humanity has produced disorder in the spiritual world, as we have seen; and the natural world, which is subject to the spiritual world, according to the laws of correspondence, has undergone an analogous alteration. This is the real cause of the state which the world we inhabit now presents. But God, in his infinite wisdom, had foreseen this fall of man, and had, in his boundless love, provided means to save by reinstating him. It is by this renovation of man in particular, that the renovation of men in general will take place, and that our world will gradually arrive at the state of splendor to which it was destined. It is now arising from a long and sad descending series of ages, to enter upon a beautiful and glorious period which shall never end!

Accept, &c.

LETTER XI.

You are anxious, my dear sir, to know in its details, this spiritual world, the generalities of which we have just been investigating. This anxiety gives me pleasure, and I would wish to satisfy it at once, for I am desirous to explain what is the existence of man, when, on leaving this earth, he enters the world of spirits; but the very nature of our discussion requires us to proceed by degrees. Truths can only be well comprehended so far as those upon which they are supported have been at first developed and then admitted. There remain, it is true, but very few truths to present to you that you may be placed in a state to comprehend the existence of man after death; but still it is indispensable that you should know them and admit them.

That which I am now going to establish may at first excite your astonishment, but the least reflection will induce you soon to acknowledge, that it is the consequence of those which you have already adopted. It is this:

Every general division of the spiritual world has the human form, and the spiritual world in the whole presents also this form.

You have acknowledged that God is *Very Man* (or *l'Homme-Type*). and you have seen by our preceding remarks that all that which exists here below tends to reproduce, by insensible shadowings, the forms of the primitive type. If it is thus in our world, with much stronger reason should it be the same in the spiritual world, where life resides free from the obstructions of matter. Besides, since the spiritual world is the emanation of God, and as no object can really exist without having a form, what other form could this world have but the form of the principle from which it proceeds.

Let us at first examine it in its general divisions.

When I explained the creation, in a preceding letter, I made use of the word "sphere," because it is that which is usually employed in treating of emanations; but I did not intend to be understood by this that the emanations proceeding from God-Man formed spheres according to the strict construction of the word, such as those which would result from a body composed of homogeneous parts, and having itself a form perfectly spherical. The form which emanations must take, when no foreign cause opposes, is evidently that of the principle itself. The three spiritual atmospheres that have constituted the three heavens, being emanations from God-Man, have been developed then according to the form of their principle. Thus the supreme heaven, constituted of the spiritual atmosphere of the third degree, has the form of a man; and it is under this form that it is presented in the complex to the eyes of the divinity. The second heaven, constituted of the spiritual atmosphere of the second degree, has also the human form; and as it envelopes, in every sense, the supreme heaven, it is under this form that it is presented in the whole, to the eyes of God and to the angels of the supreme heaven. It is the same with the first heaven, constituted of the spiritual atmosphere of the first degree—it having the form of man; and as it envelopes, in every sense, the second heaven, it is under this form that it presents itself, in the whole, to the eyes of God and angels of the superior heavens. The three heavens, having thus the human form; being from their very nature one within another; and having God for the common centre, the whole of them together present, in the sight of God, the form of one single man. The first heaven is the exterior of this spiritual organism, the second heaven is its internal, and the supreme heaven is its inmost.

But you have seen that through the work of man, there was formed, in opposition to the spiritual organism, an inverted organism, which is called hell. Seen in the whole together, each one of the three hells presents also the form of man; but this form, instead of being that of man created in the image and likeness of God, is that of a man-monster. These three hells, united in like manner, present themselves under the form of one single human monster: the first hell is the exterior of this organism, the second hell is its internal, and the deepest hell is its inmost.

The world of spirits being a mixed spiritual organism presents, in the whole of it together, a form which is intermediate betweeen the true human form and the form of a human monster.

I will not insist further upon these truths; it will be very easy for you to perceive the strict results of the principles which I have previously unfolded. Still I ought, before we proceed further, to anticipate an objection which presents itself, and which would not escape your notice.

"The spiritual world," you might say, "being in the natural world, as the cause is in the effect, and having given to this world the form which it presents to us, since matter has not of itself any form, it results from this that if the spiritual universe has the human form, the material universe also should have this form. Now I do not think that such a position can be sustained. Do we not know that the earth which we inhabit is a spheroid? The principal laws which govern our planetary system are now known. We know that the planets gravitate around the sun, travelling in orbits whose tracts are determined; that every satellite gravitates around its planet; and analogy is there which indicates that it must be the same in the other solar systems. How, in the presence of these acquired knowledges, can it be demonstrated that the material universe has the human form? It seems to me that there is here an absolute impossibility. It is in vain for me to seek this form in the whole of our universe; I should see nothing which could make an approach to it." This I believe is the objection in all its force.

Swedenborg, whose sublime theories I am simply developing in my letters, does not, it is true explain himself upon the form of the material universe; yet his theories, conducting us to the consequence which forms the subject of the objection, I proceed to examine if it is really impossible, since it seems at the first approach, that the material universe should have the form and the constitution of the human body.

To any one possessing a knowledge of astronomy it is evident, that notwithstanding its 25,000 miles of circumference, our globe is yet but a single point in space. The orbit even of the earth, which is more than 630 millions of miles, is still but a point relatively to the immensity of the universe; indeed, if the stars seem to us altogether immovable during the course of the year, though they should from the motion of the earth answer to different positions in the vault of heaven, it is evidently because our globe, notwithstanding the 630 millions of miles it passes over in space, is in respect to them as if it had no motion. But further, the whole of our solar system, of which the orbit alone of Uranus has 12.000,000,000 miles, occupies but an almost imperceptible part of the universe, when we compare this universe to the body of man. This is not a paradox; it is a truth which the telescope has so well revealed that no one can doubt it. A simple survey of the universe, such as modern astronomy presents it, goes to convince us of this at once.

Antiquity, that part at least of which there remains any historical monument counted but twenty two thousand fixed stars. But as soon as the telescope was discovered an innumerable multitude of stars, till then invisible, were presented to the astonished view of observers. The Abbé De la Caille, in one third of the arch of heaven, counted ten thousand of which he gave a catalogue, which would be supposing thirty thousand for the entire vault. The theory of nebulæ afterwards came to increase the number considerably; then the telescope being more and more improved, in a single band of the milky way, of an extent of fifteen degrees in length by two in breadth, Herschell counted fifty thousand; finally this celebrated astronomer presumes the number of stars might amount to seventy-five millions.

Behold then already seventy-five millions of solar systems, of which ours is perhaps but one of the least extent; but admitting for it a proportional mean, still it would constitute but the seventy-five millionth part of the universe; now, I ask you if the seventy-five millionth part of the body of man would not be even by this estimate almost imperceptible?

But who would dare to say that there are but seventy-five

millions of suns spread throughout space, when the interval which separates the stars from us is of such immensity that it even frightens the imagination? Huygen found the distance between us and the nearest of the stars was 2,885,045,634,600 of miles. Other astronomers have carried their investigations to particular stars; that which Lalande observed was at 20,315,310,000,000 miles; that of Baily 21,482,718,240,000 that of Euler at near 42,000,000,000 of miles. This learned man, in a letter to a princess of Germany, has calculated that a ray of light from this star would take six years notwithstanding its incredible velocity, to reach our earth. If it were possible that a cannon ball projected from that celestial body could be transmitted to us, five millions four hundred thousand years would elapse before it could reach us. Another star which was observed by Lambert was more than 51,000,000 000,000 of miles; finally Doctor Derham, canon of Windsor, who observed the nebulæ, in 1732, acknowldged that they were as far from the fixed stars as these stars are from our globe.

If from the 30,000 stars of the Abbe de la Caille, we have reached by the improvement of the telescop', to the 75,000,000 of Herschell, at what number does not so immense extent allow us to suppose we may arrive by means of new improvements? And if an instrument should be discovered, which would be to the telescope what the telescope is to the naked eye, instead of millions we would have to count by the thousand of millions, the suns which enlighten the universe. We may then without fearing to be taxed with exaggeration, assert that in comparing the material universe to the body of man, our solar system would form but an almost imperceptible part.

What do we conclude from this? It is that if we continue to compare the universe to the body of man we are forced to acknowledge that all the motions of the globes which gravitate around our sun, motions which appear to us so magnificent, cannot even be discerned any longer. Then all these masses not only must no longer appear to change position, but they must again be confounded with their common centre, and seem to make with it but one body scarcely visible.

In presence of all these facts revealed by the telescope, what becomes of the argument drawn from the gravitation of the planets and their satellites? But is it not astonishing that men should exclaim against the first idea of the universe under a human form: has it not a long time appeared incredible that the earth is round? What would a philosopher of the middle ages have thought, if this truth, which is now incontestable, had been advanced to him? What again would a Swiss cottager think, should any one tell him that the earth is like an orange, and that its surface presents no more inequalities than that fruit, when that peasant would have but to raise his eyes to see himself surrounded by mountains in the form of spires, and contemplate the gigantic Mount Blanc? Let us beware of judging from appearances; the experience of the past is sufficient to prove that they are deceitful; let us, on this point, be more circumspect than our predecessors were.

I have just compared the material universe to the body of man, and I have proved mathematically that in the hypothesis of the universe under a human form, our whole solar system, however vast it may be, and however magnificent the motions of its planets may appear, would nevertheless correspond only to an almost imperceptible part of the body of man.

I now proceed to show that in the almost imperceptible parts of the body of man, there are motions analogous to those, which are performed in the corresponding solar systems. This second proposition appears at least as extraordinary as the first; but from what we have just seen, what learned man would venture to deny it? If the telescope has made such fine discoveries in the fields of space indefinitely great, the microscope yields nothing to it on this point, and every day new wonders are discovered by it in the no less surprising field of space indefinitely small.

It is generally acknowledged that porosity is a quality inherent in matter; thus all bodies without exception are porous. Now, if there are interstices between the different molecules of a body, how many must there not exist before we come to the parts which are invisible with the best microscopes? And when we reflect on the extreme minuteness of these parts, what intervals relatively immense must there not be between them! From this we may conceive that all that which we have said on the subject of the indefinitely great is equally applicable to the indefinitely least of things; for the distances which separate the objects of the one are proportional to the distances which separate the objects of the other.

If you were not already acquainted with the wonderful things which are discovered by the microscope, in the domain of the indefinitely least of things, I would have drawn a sketch of it to support my position: recall, then, to your memory the principal microscopic experiences, and my proposition will cease to appear extraordinary to you.

A physician, who is doubtless far from knowing the writings of Swedenborg, has published, upon the orbitary motion of atoms, a theory which must confirm in some measure that which I present to you. M. Gaudin, in fact, supposes that the atoms of bodies, maintained at distances very great in proportion to their dimensions, perform around one another motions *analogous* to those of a planetary system.

Imperfect as the microscope may yet be, if we should succeed in verifying the theory of M. Gaudin, we should doubtless find analogy between the motions of what he calls the atoms of bodies and those of a planetary system, but if afterwards the investigations were applied to the particles of the human body we should find there something more than *analogy*; we should find that there is *similitude*. I will state upon what ground this conclusion is based: all the objects of nature tend, as I have already said, more or less to re-produce the human form, which is that of the Creator; it would be then conformable to our principles that there should be found some analogy between the motions of the particles of bodies and that of the planetary system; but as it is man alone who has the form of God, if the material universe, as I suppose, has been created according to this form, it is only in particles of the human body that we could recognize a perfect similitude between their arbitrary motions and those of the solar systems.

I have spoken of the theory of M. Gaudin to show that science itself is beginning to enter upon a way which may lead to great discoveries. Science has been for a long time embarrassed with a crowd of systems which clash with and destroy each other; it knows that there can be but one which is true, and that true system will be that which will be distinguished from others by its extreme simplicity, great economy, and its universality. The less wheel-work a machine has the better does it perform its functions.

The objection which I have anticipated has already conducted us very far; but since the question of the material universe under a human form has been raised, we will continue the discussion. As everything must tend to unity, and as every fixed star is a sun around which a system of planets gravitates, certain astronomers have been led to believe that there exists a central sun, round which all the other suns also gravitate. What are we to think of this sun? does it really exist?

On the first view, the existence of such a central sun appears probable enough; it seems even to accord perfectly with the spiritual theory which I have developed to you; indeed, since there is one spiritual sun, the centre of the whole immaterial universe, should there not be also a natural sun for the centre of the whole material universe? However strong these probabilities may be, you will soon acknowledge that they disappear before a profound examination.

The astronomers who are led to believe that there exists a central sun, base their reasoning upon the analogy of the planets to satellites. Since, they say, planets revolve round the sun, drawing with them their satellites, why should not each sun revolve round a central sun drawing with it, in like manner all the globes which constitute its system?

In the first place there is not here complete analogy. In fact, the planets and the satellites are of the same nature, since they are both earths, and they differ from their sun in this, that the sun is a globe of fire; they are then similar bodies which revolve round a dissimilar body, to receive from it heat and light. It is not the same when we suppose solar systems revolving round a central sun; the suns are not of the same nature with the globes which they would draw with them, and besides, they would not differ from the central star around which they would revolve; for we could not conceive of this central star being any thing else than a vast globe of fire to feed the other suns, which also are globes of fire. But if we supposed this sun of a superior nature to that of the other suns, we should run a very great risk of making it the principle of all nature, and of falling into materialism.

Next we see clearly that the sun of every system is indispensable to the globes which revolve around it, since it transmits to them the heat and light which are necessary to them; but we do not see so well of what use it would be to the millions of suns to depend upon a central sun.

The learned, unable to conceive how the universe could be sustained, desire to extricate themselves from their embarrassment, by uniting through the laws of gravitation all these suns to a common centre; but with this additional wheel-work, will they succeed in diminishing the difficulty? Will they conceive any better how this central globe is itself sustained?

Besides, what would become of the material universe on such an hypothesis? Would it not be a whole composed of parts nearly similar? for this universe in the whole would present but the repetition of that which it possesses in its parts; now we know that the perfection of an unity, consists in the diversity, and above all in the beautiful harmony, of all its parts. You will soon acknowledge that this new wheel work would have been more destructive than useful to the harmonic unity of our universe.

As to the probability of the existence of this central sun, by reason of the existence of one only spiritual sun, it will not bear an examination. What is spiritual, not being from its very nature subject to space and time, the spiritual sun is susceptible of being seen by all the inhabitants of the other world. If it is not visible, if it is more or less veiled, or entirely obscured to a great number, this proceeds only from the disposition of their interiors. It would be necessary, then, according to the laws of analogy, that the central material body, if there existed one, should be universally seen, and clearly distinguished among the other suns; and the single fact that we are unable to distinguish such a body throughout the whole vault of heaven, would be at once a strong presumption against its existence. Besides, from the prodigious number of suns interspersed through space, the first notions of astronomy teach us that for a central body to be invisible to all the globes of the universe, and to be clearly distinguished among the other suns, it must necessarily be so large as to have no proportion between its mass and the laws of gravitation. But further, as the probability in question is supported from the analogy which should exist between the two universes, it will necessarily be destroyed if it is found to be in opposition to the strict analogical consequences, which we have already established. Now I have shown in the beginning of this letter, that the spiritual universe had the form of man, whence resulted, according to the relations which exist between the two worlds, that the material universe should also have this form. Nevertheless, this proposition appeared so strange, that I have been compelled to support it by facts; and those which I have drawn from astronomy have shown you that nothing is opposed to the idea that the material universe has the human form. If then our universe has the human form, it is evident that it could not have a central sun, unless there was in the human body a central organ around which all the others should gravitate. Now it is in vain to seek to discover such an organ in the body of man; it is very certain that it has no existence there.

The probabilities in favor of a central sun for the universe being thus destroyed, I must now show you that this great number of natural suns for one only spiritual sun, does not really constitute a defect of analogy between the two universes.

Observe that the spiritual world, having the human form, is composed of regions innumerable, and in themselves distinct, as are all the parts of the human body; that these regions are all inhabited by societies which present among themselves very sensible differences; that those, for example, which occupy some parts of the feet or the hands of the Grand Man, differ much from those which are in the parts of the head, or of one of the viscera of the breast; that these differences result from the disposition of the interiors of those who compose these societies; that the spiritual sun does not shine with the same force to the eyes of all these societies, since the existence of every one of them depends upon a special degree of spiritual heat and light, the same as in our world the existence of the inhabitants of each planet depends upon a special degree of natural heat and light; and that thus the spiritual sun is always more or less veiled, and must appear to one society different from that which it appears to another. Now as every solar system of our universe corresponds to one of the parts of the spiritual universe, every natural sun corresponds to one of these apparent differences of the spiritual sun; there is actually then no defect of analogy. Thus our sun is the correspondent of the sun of life for the very small part of the material universe which gravitates around it. If there existed a central sun, we could uot comprehend how ours could be the immediate correspondent of the spiritual sun.

There is again, under the relation of analogy, an objection which you might make; it is that the human form belongs, as I have established at the beginning of this letter, not only to the whole of the spiritual world, but further, to each one of these general divisions, whilst in the natural world there is seen nothing, in this respect, of analogy. I have but one simple observation to make upon this subject: The general division of the spiritual world is quite peculiar to that world; for ours, in consequence of the properties of matter, cannot present a resemblance. It is sufficient to convince you of this, to remember what has been said, that the two universes, the spiritual and the natural, were constituted by atmospheres, and that the three spiritual atmospheres formed immaterial earths distinct among themselves, according to the three separate degrees, whilst the natural atmospheres contributed all three to form the one the inmost, the other the interior, aud the last the ultimate of the material earths. [Letter 9.]

I would make, besides, one important remark; it is, that between our system and that which admits a central sun and thus gives to the universe a spherical form, there is, under the relation of the harmony of parts, the same difference as between the beautiful structure of the human body, and that of a round body.

I have sought, in the examination of this question, to anticipate the objections which you might make; if others should present themselves to your mind, be pleased to communicate them.

Now, let us take a view of the advantages which the system of the universe under a human form can present to the philosophical Christian.

Since the laws of attraction and gravitation have been known, men have vainly sought to discover the cause of these laws. Deists, upon this point, have not been more happy than materialists, for in considering, with the materialist, the material universe under a spherical form, it became impossible suitably to explain the relations which exist between God, the universe, and man. What exact relations could they find between their God, who has neither substance nor form, their universe under the form of a ball, and man whose structure is so different? But when it is recognized, as it is by us, that God is Man Himself, or VERY MAN, and the universe is admitted to be in the human form, all is united, everything is connected in a manner as simple as it is admirable, and the structure of the material universe, being like that of the body of man, the knowledge of our body may conduct us to that of the universe.

Why indeed does your body, composed of material elements, move, though from its very nature matter is inert? You have already acknowledged, that it is because there is in you a spiritual man which gives it motion. Well, it is the same with the great material man, or the natural universe—it receives its motion from the grand immaterial Man, or the spiritual universe. As to your spiritual man and the grand immaterial Man, though you have concerning them as yet but indistinct ideas, you however know that they derive the form they have from God-man, and from this alone you may see with what harmonious simplicity, and with what admirable economy of means, the Divine Architect has constructed and sustains all that which exists; but farther on, you will find in the explications which I will give you concerning the man-spirit and the spiritual world, new motives of admiration and new means of confirmation. However, I ought even now to observe, that if I call the universe the Grand Man, it is not that it is properly speaking a man, that is to say, a being endowed with will and understanding, it is only an immense organism, all the parts of which, disposed according to the body of man have been destined to be the representative theatres of the glory of God, serving for the habitation of men, who alone are completely created in the image and according to the likeness of the Divinity. I make this observation, because certain philosophers still pretend that the universe is a being endowed with intelligence.

I might here conclude this discussion; however, as I ought to neglect nothing in so grave a subject, I will examine yet one question which may occur to you; but this will only be to prove to you how useless it is for a man to employ his meditations about things, which it will never be given to him to comprehend. This question is: "The universe having the form of man, what existence is there out of that form?" In advance, I must make one remark, viz: that this question does not concern only the universe under a human form; but that it may quite as well be addressed to those who represent it to themselves under a spherical form. But whether the universe has the form of a man or that of a sphere, there will always be the same difficulty in conceiving it in all its extension, and this difficulty arises from the fact, that our thoughts are continually influenced by ideas of space, because living in the material world we are unable to make a complete abstraction from space, which is an accident inherent in matter. Men usually reason concerning the infinite as if they could comprehend it, and yet it is impossible to have the least idea of it; in the spiritual world, where there is only the appearance of space, it is possible to form some idea of it; but to comprehend the infinite, it is necessary to be infinite, that is to say, God. Between the infinite and the finite there cannot be any relations, and the word infinite should never be employed but in speaking of God and his attributes.

It cannot then be pretended that the universe is infinite, for this would be making it God, but we may say that it is indefinite. In fact between the indefinite and the infinite there is this difference, that the indefinite is extended as far as our imagination can go, while the infinite admits neither the idea of the greatest nor of the least; and besides, though the indefinite cannot be expressed by a number, nevertheless, relatively to the infinite, it is itself finite, and so finite that there cannot exist between the two any relation.

Though the material universe has a form, yet as this universe is indefinite, it results thence that space is indefinitely extended; now, to ask, *what exists out of the form of the universe?* is in other words to ask, *what exists out of space?*—an idle question, as the terms which we are obliged to make use of to form it sufficiently indicate. *Out of*, is in fact an expression which belongs in an absolute manner to space, and has no meaning when separate from the idea of space. Reflect a moment on the idea which the expression *out of* excites in you, when you ask yourself: *what exists out of the universe?* and you will admit at once that you are then under the impression of an idea of space. All that you could suppose then to be *out* of the universe would be still in space, and would still be part of the grand material man, or our universe. It is in vain to seek abstraction from space, whether in saying *out of the universe*, or by employing any other words of this kind; we always remain fixed to space not only by the employment of expressions, but by the thought which is itself composed only of ideas of space. Should not this very evident impossibility dissuade men from occupying themselves with questions which are above human intelligence?

These considerations upon space apply also to *time*. When I said to you in my last letter that the material world would subsist *always*, I did not mean that it would be eternal. *Always* is not *eternity*. We cannot here below, enveloped as we are by time, have any idea of eternity; in the spiritual world, where there is but the appearance of space and time, spiritual beings can form some idea of it; but the Eternal Himself can only comprehend eternity. Multiply ages by ages as long as you please, you never will obtain eternity, because you will remain in time without ever going out of it, and you will thus have behind you a past, and before you a future. *Always*, or *the indefinite of time*, differs from eternity in this that *always* extends itself as far as the imagination can carry the succession of time, with the unavoidable idea of the past and the future, whilst eternity admits neither the idea of the past nor the future. Man is destined to live always, because he is immortal; but immortality is not eternity; for if man in the spiritual world is no longer in time, he is in the appearance of time, and consequently in that of the past and future. God alone has the past and future in the present, because he alone is Eternal.

All this is because the indefinite is the image of the infinite, and because the infinite is in God, and indefinites are in the spiritual sun, whence proceed the two universes.

To resume, I see not, my dear sir, any impossibility in the material universe having the human form. The more I reflect upon this question, the more it seems to me that this form is that which accords best with our theories as a whole, and presents at once the greatest simplicity and the most beautiful harmony.

The old theology is affrighted at the discoveries of science; it persecuted Galileo, aad, if it could, would again prevent the soaring of the human mind; but true theology, far from wishing to restrain the intelligence of man, would rather encourage its development. The more the telescope shall multiply worlds to our eyes, the more the microscope shall expose to our wondering gaze the marvellous structure of the human body, the more will men be brought to acknowledge the sublime truths of Christianity.

But why do those who cultivate the sciences make so little progress in them, notwithstanding their ardor in the pursuit? Why are they always groping, and incessantly turning in a circle, instead of advancing in a straight line? It is because they want a fixed basis; it is because they have no *criterium.* The learned may in general be divided into two classes; in the first are those who by means of a system which they have built up themselves, or which they have modified, claim to be leaders of sects; these so identify themselves with their system, that it would be like committing suicide to abandon it. The second class is that of the more modest learned, who seek truth and attach themselves to some system in the hope of finding it; these would become much more useful to the sciences if they studied Swedenborg, and took his revelations as their *criterium;* for whatever branch of human knowledge they might explore, a vast field of discoveries would soon open before them. They would not, it is true, acquire one of these ephemeral reputations which, in our age, we have seen dissipated even during the life time of those who have so laboriously sought after them; but what is of far more value, they would contribute effectually to the true progress of humanity, and instead of attributing the least glory to themselves, they would render it all to Him alone to whom it belongs. Accept, &c.

LETTER XII.

There is, my dear sir, in your last letter, a passage which has so awakened my attention, that I consider it necessary again to suspend the course of our exposition, in order to examine with you the difficulty you speak of.

You are struck, you say, with the sublimity of the new theories drawn from the writings of Swedenborg; the more you meditate upon them, the more you find them conformable to sound reason, and the chain of connection between them tends still more to increase your admiration; but when you reflect that we continue, with such rational theories, to call ourselves Christians, you are arrested by a serious difficulty; it is impossible for you to conceive how the ideas we entertain concerning God can be reconciled with the doctrines of Christianity.

This difficulty arises from several causes, but chiefly from the following:—

The first is, that Christianity having for its foundation the acknowledgment of Jesus Christ as God, it has not yet been possible for you to see how this acknowledgment can agree with the philosophical idea of one only God, such as has hitherto been developed to you.

The second is, that still confounding Christianity with the different Christian sects, which all really admit three Gods, though with the lip they say there is but one, you are therefore compelled to believe, that to be a true Christian it is necessary, when the question is about dogmas, to renounce entirely the use of reason.

Permit me to tell you that if, during the whole of our discussion, I have not yet once spoken to you concerning the Lord Jesus Christ, though I have often repeated to you that I was a Christian, it was not certainly through forgetfulness; but because the state of your mind obliged me for the time to keep silence. I could not speak to you concerning the Lord without entering upon the doctrinal part of the Christian religion, and of what use would it have been for me to have drawn your attention at first to dogmas? you, who are disposed to believe, it is true, but have since rejected all those doctrines which were taught to you in your childhood? Would I for a single instant have been able to gain your attention? It was best then to begin with the philosophical part of Christianity, and this I have done; when you become fully convinced of the important truths which we have already discussed, and those which remain to be explained, then only will you be able to give your attention to the doctrinal part.

Nevertheless, as it is important to show that our ideas concerning the Divinity, are not in the least incompatible with true Christianity, I will speak to you briefly concerning the redemption and the Trinity.

Concerning Redemption. Man, created free and rational, abused his liberty and reason; he fell: but his fall, foreseen by God, was to be succeeded by a restoration; for God, who is love itself, could not leave him in the miserable state into which his fall had plunged him. Now in what manner was this restoration to be effected? To replace man in his primitive state, would not this have been to destroy his free will, and consequently annihilate him? for this misery, as we may be assured of by the state of things at the present day, was pleasing to man, and constituted even all his life. Conforming to the laws of his own eternal order, God preserved the liberty of man, and proceeded to the restoration of the human race.

You have seen, in my ninth letter, how by his fall man had given birth to a spiritual organism altogether opposite to the primitive one, and how this new organism afterwards acted upon our world with a force continually increasing. In the struggle which thence arose between the two spiritual organisms, or between heaven and hell, the Divinity by his influx was always acting, it is true, to diminish the progress of evil and the false, preserving still the liberty of man; but hell at length became so preponderant, that spiritual order was about to be broken, which would have brought with it the subversion of thé universe; for in consequence of this preponderance, the divine influx, transmitted through heaven, was no longer sufficient to maintain order and preserve the creation. It was then that God had recourse to the great act of redemption, which had been foreseen by him, and for which he had provided from the beginning of time.

This act consisted in reaching hell, confining it to its limits, by combatting it, so to speak, hand to hand; for it was necessary that man should be restored to spiritual equilibrium in order that he might be able, by means of his free will and rationality, to re-enter into the way of good and truth then closed to him. But how could the Divinity, being in essences the most pure, reach the enemy of men that is in essences the most corrupt? Indeed, you have seen that God the Creator, or Jehovah, resides in the bosom of the spiritual sun, and that the heat and light of this sun cannot even approach the angels of the highest heaven without being tempered by the spiritual atmospheres. Now Jehovah, not being able in his spiritual sun to approach the supreme heaven without enkindling and consuming this heaven, it is very evident that from the bosom of that sun he could not reach the hells, which are beyond the heavens and world of spirits. But if Jehovah could not employ this means without destroying the laws of his divine order, this order, nevertheless, far from being opposed to the work of redemption, presented all that was necessary to effect it.

You know that God or Jehovah is VERY MAN, and it is owing to this that we his creatures, formed in his likeness and image, are men, that is to say, beings endowed with a will and understanding, susceptible of receiving his love and wisdom, or the good and the true; you know also, that it is by reason of the form of God, that everything in creation presents either the human form, or a tendency more or less evident towards that form. Now, if you recollect the developments contained in my tenth letter, concerning the formation of man, and the two opposite influences which he receives from the spiritual world, it will be easy to acknowledge that in order to approach the hells, combat, conquer, and subdue them, and thus accomplish the great work of redemption, it was altogether conformable to the laws of divine order, for Jehovah to become flesh and dwell among us.

Observe first, that Jehovah, being life itself, resides wholly, in this quality, in all creation, and in each of its parts, for the Divinity is indivisible; thus we say that God is everywhere. So Jehovah, who is in the inmost of every man, without this residence preventing him from presiding over the government of the whole universe, could easily clothe himself with the external of a spiritual body, without abandoning any of the attributes of Divinity. Observe next, that in making himself flesh, and descending thus into the last degrees of the creation, Jehovah, who, in his spiritual sun, could not even approach the heavens without consuming them, was able on the contrary, without producing the least perturbation, to reach the deepest hells; for the struggle of the hells against the heavens renewing itself every day with man, Jehovah, in clothing himself with humanity, placed himself upon the only proper arena for the combat, and where he could, without deranging his work, struggle with, conquer, and subdue the enemy.

As my object here is to give you only a general idea of Redemption, I will not at present treat on the important subject of the Incarnation; besides it would require some preliminary ideas which can only be explained in the doctrinal part. I will merely say that in Jesus Christ the internal man was Jehovah himself, while the external man and the material body which veiled and enveloped Jehovah, was from Mary; that Jesus Christ, whose internal man was Jehovah, not having been, like other men, conceived of a man, had not in him the hereditary evil with which we are all born; but that his external man and material body, having been produced in the womb of a woman, he had from the mother hereditary evil, evil which with him,—by reason of the resistance of the internal man—never became actual evil, as he said in these words. "Which of you convinceth me of sin?" (John viii. 46.). If he had not had external hereditary evil he never could have been tempted, for his internal man being Jehovah, that is to say, Good itself and Truth itself, was not in any manner susceptible of being tempted; thus, without this evil which was in his external man, he would not have been able either to combat with hell, or consequently, to subdue it. By his temptations, his struggles, and his spiritual victories, he successively put off all that he had from Mary, and attained to the complete conjunction of his external man with his internal man which he calls the Father, thus making his humanity divine so that if Jesus Christ was for a time the son of Mary, by reason of his external, he is no longer so, since he rejected all that he had from her, and thus Jesus Christ is no other than Jehovah God, the Creator of all that exists, now become the Redeemer of the human race by his incarnation.

All these truths, and many others which concern the incarnation will be proved hereafter, and I will then enter upon all the details which you may desire. I will here make only one observation; God or Jehovah is in us all, as I have already told you, for if he were not in us, we should not have life; but he is only in the inmost of our being, and he is not in our internal man which we have from our father, as we have our external man from our mother; but the internal of Jesus Christ was Jehovah himself. Thus, though Jesus Christ had his external man and a material body from Mary, he was altogether different from any other man.

Concerning the Trinity. You already see from what precedes, that God the Father or the Creator, and God the Son or the Redeemer, are one only and the same God, one only and the same person and not two distinct persons. But the Creator of men, in becoming their Redeemer, became also their Regenerator and Saviour, for God by redemption did not save a single man; If he had been able to save one, he would have saved all; but he gave to all the possibility of being saved or regenerated—a possibilty which no longer at that time existed, by reason of the superabundance and overflowing profligacy of the most fatal errors and the most depraved passion.

Now, regeneration or salvation was the consequence of redemption; indeed, before redemption, Jehovah, not having yet descended into the last degree of creation, could not act from the bosom of his spiritual sun, but by a mediate influx, that is to say, by the intermediation of angels and good spirits; but as soon as he made divine the assumed Humanity, all power was acquired to this divine or to the divine body of Jesus Christ, whose soul is Jehovah himself, and it is this Divine Humanity, which from this moment, governs the whole universe, as well by the mediate influx of the heavens, as by his immediate influx. From that time men could receive this immediate influx. He is the Sanctifier or Holy Spirit, and it is by him that men can be regenerated or saved, if they consent to follow the impulses which he gives to them.

The Holy Spirit is then no other than Jehovah-Jesus-Christ acting to regenerate men and preserve the universe. Thus God the Father or Creator, God the Son or Redeemer, and God the Holy Spirit or Regenerator, are one and the same God, one and the same person, and not three distinct persons. Thus the divine Trinity exists in the unity of God, and this only God is the Lord Jesus Christ in his glorified humanity; the soul of this humanity is Jehovah or the Father, his body is the Son, and the incessant action which his soul exercises by his body to regenerate men and preserve the universe, is the Holy Spirit. I can here do no more than announce these high truths; they will be developed in the dogmatical part of our discussion, and you will then see that they are in perfect harmony both with the Scriptures and with human reason. I regret to speak thus briefly upon a subject which, from its nature, demands the greater elucidation; but on the other hand, since I shall return again to the subject, I experience a satisfaction in having presented to you these few ideas, for I have been desirous for a long time to speak to you concerning the Lord. Henceforth, instead of using exclusively the expression *God*, I will from preference employ that of Lord, for it is this which we generally make use of. Jehovah excites more particularly the idea of God considered as Creator; Jesus Christ the idea of God as Redeemer, whilst the word Lord presents to us the idea of the one God considered in his three grand manifestations of Creator, Redeemer, and Regenerator.

Thus, my dear sir, by this brief sketch you can see that our ideas respecting the Divinity are perfectly reconcilable with Christianity, and what is more, that we are the true Christians. The word *Christian*, indeed, is derived from *Christ*, and no one can properly be called a Christian who does not acknowledge Jesus Christ to be God. Now, Jesus Christ being for us God himself, and not the second of three divine persons, have we not the right to claim the name of Christians in preference to those who acknowledge him only as the Son of God, and worship him only as a Mediator between God and men, though with the lips they acknowledge him as God?

It is true, however, that Jesus Christ is a Mediator between God and man, but not as a Person distinct from the Father; he is Mediator in this sense, that he is the Divine Body in which resides the Divine Soul or Jehovah. Now, as in addressing a man, we cannot approach his soul, but by the mediation of his body, so we can only approach Jehovah by the mediation of the Divine humanity, or glorified Body of Jesus

Christ. For this reason he himself said, "no man cometh unto the Father but by me," (John xiv. 6,) and for this also he said, "no man hath seen God at any time," (John i. 18.) Indeed, always enveloped with a body, whether natural as in this world, or spiritual as in the other life, the soul of man always remains invisible, and only manifests itself by the action of its body; it is the same with the Divine Soul or Jehovah; enveloped now with the humanity which Jesus Christ assumed in this world and which he glorified or made divine, it is only manifested by the action of this Divine Humanity. Thus no one has ever seen, or ever will see, Jehovah or the Father; but the inhabitants of the heavens see the Divine humanity or Jesus Christ, whose soul is Jehovah himself, whenever it pleases the Lord to manifest himself to them; and further, they continually enjoy the presence of his spiritual sun which vivifies them by its heat and light. But it is not thus that Christians of the old church conceive of the mediation, since they represent to themselves the Mediator as a person distinct from God the Father.

Why do we see at this day so few Christians? for to be really a Christian, it is not sufficient to have received baptism, nor even to follow certain religious practices; it is absolutely necessary, not only to acknowledge from the heart, as I have said, the divinity of Jesus Christ, but to live according to the precepts which he has given us; why, I say, do we see at this day so few Christians? It is because the theologians of the old church persist in maintaining that there are three divine persons, and because it is difficult to persuade men at this day that three Gods make but one. Besides, how could the clergy of the various Christian sects convince their auditors, and convince themselves, that Jesus Christ, risen again, according to the Evangelists, with the body which was laid in the sepulchre, is but one with God the Father, whom they consider as a pure Spirit, that is to say, as a Being without substance and form, though they make of him, nevertheless, a real person distinct from the person of Jesus Christ? And do they know even where to place the body of the Lord Jesus Christ in that world which also, in their idea, being without substance and form, can consist of nothing but a kind of vacuum or emptiness? But these difficulties, which prevent our contemporaries from being Christians, completely disappear when it is known that the Creator of the universe is himself VERY MAN, and that all creation tends to the human form, and above all when the relations as simple as they are admirable are known, which bind the universe to man, and man to his divine original.

This is a long digression, but the subject is so important, that you will excuse me for having interrupted the course of our discussion to answer a simple observation which you had made.

Let us resume our exposition of the spiritual world, and enter upon matters of detail.

If we see so many unbelievers, if even the man who so loudly proclaims the immortality of the soul, feels his faith waver when he seriously fixes his thought upon the passage from this life into the other, is it not because it is impossible for him to form a clear idea of this passage, after all the incoherent vagaries put forth by theologians and philosophers upon the soul and its mode of existence? Not knowing in an exact manner what the soul is, nor in what part of the body it resides, is he not compelled either to consider it as a breath, that disengaged from its prison wanders in a vacuum, which is repugnant to his reason, or to regard it as one of those imponderable fluids which, being set free, unites with its common reservoir, which is repugnant to his conscience? This, however, is the desolating alternative to which a reflecting man is reduced when he has nothing for a guide but the data of the old theology or those of the philosophy of the day. But it is altogether different when he has a precise idea of the soul, and of the world in which it is perpetually to reside; then, to comprehend how his passage from this life to another is effected, it is sufficient to have present in his mind the truths which I have previously set forth, and which it is important here to repeat;

(1.) The soul or spirit of man is a real being, having a spiritual body, endowed with all the organs constituting the material body with which it is clothed.

(2.) The spiritual world is a real organism, having objects analogous to those which we see in ours; it has its earths, seas, atmospheres, a celestial vault, which like ours is a result of the conformation of the eye; it has, in fine, its three kingdoms—animals, vegetables, minerals; but nevertheless, there exists between the two worlds this difference, that in the one, all the objects are of a spiritual nature, while in the other, they are all of a material nature.

(3.) The spiritual world, being independent of space, is not a place; it is a state of the soul or spirit. Thus it cannot be said that it is above or below; above the skies or in the bowels of the earth; here or there; but it is in man himself—every one has actually in himself his heaven or his hell.

(4.) Though independent of space and time, accidents which are inherent in matter alone, the spiritual world presents still appearances of them, appearances which result from interior states in which those who inhabit it are successively placed.

Now, we have seen in the sixth letter, that there are in man as many receptacles having the human form as there exist general divisions of the spiritual world, and that these receptacles are opened or remain closed, according to the manner in which man has lived in the natural world. You have seen also, in the ninth letter, that each general division of the spiritual world, though it be within us, is nevertheless manifested without us, when after our death the receptacle which it has in our soul or spirit is opened.

When therefore man is stripped of his mortal covering, he has no need of being conveyed from one place to another, or of making the least progression; he finds himself, with the same affections and the same thoughts, upon a spiritual earth, and precisely upon that which belongs to the general division whose receptacle is opened in him.

But as the heavenly receptacles are not completely opened in man, unless he has neither bad affections nor false thoughts, and as the infernal receptacles in like manner are not completely opened in him, until he has rejected all good affections and all true thoughts, it results that the greater part of men, in leaving our earth, find themselves *without conveyance or transit*, upon an earth of the world of spirits, or intermediate world, where they remain a longer or shorter time, before they go definitively either into the heavens or the hells.

Thus the passage of man from this world into the other consists simply, *without conveyance or transit*, in the emancipation of the man-spirit by the loosening of the bonds which confined him to our earth, which is effected as soon as the systolic and diastolic motions of the material heart have ceased forever. Then the material part of man is nothing but dead matter, but the man, as to all that constitutes him a man, lives, and his senses no longer imprisoned in matter acquire properties much more exquisite. It is the same with his two constitutive faculties, will and understanding; they then manifest themselves in a higher degree of strength and activity.

The passage from this world into the other is besides so much the easier to conceive of, as man during his life upon our earth is himself, without knowing it, in the spiritual world. He is actually there, since his affections and thoughts which cause him to be man, and which certainly are not matter, belong only to the spiritual world: but he does not see that world, and knows nothing of that which is passing around his man-spirit, because his spiritual eyes, as well as his other spiritual senses, being covered with matter, are then only used for that which concerns his existence upon our earth. But as soon as man is disengaged from his mortal envelope, his senses being no longer confined in an obscure prison, and entering upon their full exercise, it is not then surprising that he now sees the part of the spiritual world in which he had been already, though unknown to him in his natural life, and that he is then conscious of all that passes about him.

Since the greater part of those who go from our globe pass into the world of spirits, we will first turn our attention to the part of that world corresponding to our earth; but before entering into details it is necessary to give you an exact idea of the nature of the objects of which the intermediate world is composed.

The intermediate world, being a mixed spiritual organism, presents a mixture of good and evil, of the beautiful and deformed; and in this respect, as in many others, bears a strong relation to our material world. There exists even between them, at first sight, so great a resemblance that many of those who enter into the world of spirits, believe themselves yet to be in ours, and do not perceive their error until they meet there those who have died before them ; and see none of those whom they left upon our earth. As to the objects of which this intermediate world is composed, they have their origin in two opposite sources. All that is good and beautiful comes from the heavens, and has its origin from the love and wisdom of God; all that is evil and hideous comes from the hells, and has its origin in hatred and folly, or the evil and the false which the fall of man has produced.

You have seen in fact that the divine Love, the source of all good affections, is the first substance whence proceed all substances which are good, and the divine Wisdom the source of all true thoughts, is the first or original form (*Forme-Type*), whence proceed all the beautiful forms in which these substances are clothed. You have seen also, that since the fall of man, all the affections of his selfish will were bad spiritual substances, and all the thoughts of his perverted understanding were unsightly spiritual forms with which the bad substances were clothed.

Thus, every affection being a spiritual substance, and every thought a spiritual form, the mixture of good and bad substances and of beautiful and hideous forms which the objects of the intermediate world in general present, is the effect produced by the state of its inhabitants, whose interiors are a mixture of good and bad affections, of true and false thoughts.

Besides, as the intermediate world, the same as every general division of the spiritual, is an exterior manifestation of that which is included in the man-spirit, it must present, in all its parts, objects whose substances are affections, and whose forms are the thoughts of those who inhabit it. If the objects are presented there in number indefinite, and are indefinitely varied, it is because the affections and thoughts themselves of spirits present varieties whose number is unlimited.

I have already often repeated to you that the spiritual world, such as it is presented to the sight of spirits and angels, is an exterior manifestation of that which is in their interiors. A consequence which, at first sight, would seem to flow from this principle is, that each man-spirit would see only objects which represent his affections and thoughts, and therefore, would live altogether isolated from other men-spirits. Now, if spirits did not live in society like men in our world, if they were prevented from communicating their affections and thoughts to others, however beautiful and delightful might be the theatre upon which they live, their existence would be the most sad that can be imagined, and would soon become insupportable. It is then important to prove that in the intermediate world spirits live in societies like men in our world, and that thus the consequence which seems to result from the principle above stated is but specious; but to arrive at this proof, I shall be obliged to give you some general ideas relative to correspondences. This again is a digression which it is necessary for me to add to many others already made; I hope, however, that you will continue to be as indulgent towards this as towards the preceding. I will first speak of the correspondences which exist between the spiritual world and ours.

The spiritual world and the natural world being related to each other like the interior and exterior, it results from this that spiritual things and natural things make one by *Influx*, and that there is *Correspondence* between them. This is the principle; but what are we to understand by this *Correspondence* and this *Influx*? Some examples to which I am about to have recourse will enable you easily to comprehend it.

It is evident that the variations of man's face, or the different expressions of his countenance, *correspond* to the different states of the affections of his soul, for the expression of the countenance varies according to the state of the affections. These variations, which are natural effects, we call *Correspondences* of the affections which are the spiritual causes of them, and we say that the face itself is the *Correspondence* of the interiors of the soul. But, in order that these correspondences may manifest themselves, it is necessary that the soul should act; this action of the soul is what we call the *influx* of the spiritual principle into the natural. [See *Apocalypse Explained*, number 1080.]

It is in like manner evident that the understanding of man, or the sight of his thought corresponds to the sight of his eyes, for the light and flame which shine in his eyes manifest the thought which his understanding produces; the sight of the eye is the *Correspondence* as well as the eye itself, and the action of the understanding upon the eye is *Influx.*

So also, the active thought which depends on the understanding *corresponds* to the language which depends on the mouth and its accessories; language is the *Correspondence* as well as the mouth and the organs which serve to produce language, and the action of the thought in language and in the organs of language is *Influx.* Lastly, the action of the body *corresponds* to the will; that of the heart to the life of love; that of the lungs, which is called respiration, to the life of faith; and the whole body, as to all its members, viscera and organs, *corresponds* to the soul, as to all its functions and all the forces of its life.

By these few examples you can see that the spiritual and the natural make one by *Correspondences*, as the interior and the posterior, or as the efficient cause and the effect; or again as the cause principal which belongs to the thought and will of man, and the cause instrumental which belongs to his language and action.

I have taken these examples from what passes in man, that you may easily comprehend what we are to understand by *Correspondence*, and the *Influx* which manifests it; but the correspondence of the natural and spiritual is general; it not only has place in all that which constitutes man, but it also exists in all that constitutes the universe, and is a result of the influx of the spiritual univérse into the natural. Moreover, it is a consequence of the principles which I have previously explained, and which you have admitted. Every natural object including in it an analogous spiritual object, the spiritual is always in activity, and its action being the influx of which we are now speaking, it results that all the objects of the natural universe are Correspondences.

The knowledge of these Correspondences constituted in ancient times a science; it was even the science of sciences, for it was the key to all knowledges; but it was gradually corrupted by men, and at last entirely lost. From this corruption arose the symbols of the eastern nations, of the hieroglyphics of the Egyptians, and all the mythologies. This science is at length restored to the world, and may now be studied in the writings of Swedenborg. When hereafter we shall examine the doctrines of Christianity, you will be easily convinced that the sacred Scriptures are filled with correspondences, and that this science of sciences dispels all the apparent contradictions which have led our contemporaries to doubt their holiness, and even to deny it.

As there is correspondence between all things of the natural universe and all those of the spiritual, and the spirit of man being a little spiritual universe, it results that there is also a correspondence between all the objects of the natural world, and all the thoughts and the affections of man, for it is his affections and thoughts which constitute his spirit. I cannot give you now the nomenclature of all these correspondences; this would not be the place; but it is indispensable to the understanding of what follows to present you at first with some of them.

The earth in general corresponds to man; its different productions, which serve for the nourishment of men, correspond to different kinds of goods and truths, the solid aliments to various kinds of goods, and the liquid to various kinds of truths.

A house corresponds to the will and the understanding, which constitute the human mind; by house, we have to understand all that serves for lodging or retreat, the palace as well as the hut.

Garments correspond to truths or falses according to the substance, color, and form which they present.

Animals correspond to the affections; those which are useful and gentle, to good affections; those which are hurtful and bad, to evil affections: gentle and beautiful birds to intellectual truths; those which are ferocious and ugly to falses; fishes to the scientifics which derive their origin from things sensual; reptiles to corporeal and sensual pleasures; and noxious insects to falsities which proceed from the senses.

Trees and shrubs correspond to different kinds of knowledges; and herbs and grass correspond to various kinds of scientific truths.

Gold corresponds to celestial good, silver to spiritual truth, brass to natural good; iron to natural truth, stones to sensual truths, precious stones to spiritual truths. With these few correspondences you will easily be able to follow the discussion.

All that I have just said concerning the correspondences which exist between the spiritual and natural worlds, is applicable in general to the correspondences which the great divisions of the spiritual world have between them; for from the lowest degrees of creation up to the spiritual sun everything lives, everything is conjoined by influx which produces correspondences. Thus, the intermediate world, of which we are now treating, being placed between the first heaven and the first hell, receives an influx from both, and consequently is in correspondence with both. Nevertheless, between this correspondence and that of which I have just spoken to you, there is an important difference to be observed, namely: that here below the objects which surround man being natural, and consequently subject to the laws of space and time, are not dependent upon changes which are effected in his spirit, while in the intermediate world, the objects which surround spirits, being of a spiritual nature, depend upon the states of these spirits, and vary according as these states change. As the objects in the intermediate world are the very *representations* of the affections and thoughts of spirits, correspondences are manifested there clearly to the sight, and then they are called *representatives*.

By means of these ideas concerning correspondences, I am now able to prove to you that in the intermediate world, spirits live in societies as in our world, and thus that the consequence which appeared to result from the principle above advanced is but specious.

Let us first take spirits separately ; each one of them according to this principle, having for the theatre of his existence the exterior manifestation of his affections and thoughts, and no one spirit resembling another, it results, it is true, that there exists as many individual representative theatres, or different little intermediate worlds as there exist spirits; but we shall presently see that all these individual theatres or little worlds make in fact but one.

It is evident that the intermediate world of a Chinese or of a Hottentot must differ much from the intermediate world of an European, since the affections and thoughts of the one have but little affinity with the affections and thoughts of the other; you will also agree that the intermediate worlds of two Chinese, or of two Hottentots, or of two Europeans must differ much less; observe however, that the question here is only concerning external effections and thoughts, such as are those of spirits; for as regards internal affections and thoughts which are manifested later, those of a Chinese and European may even have a closer relation between them than those of two brothers. You will again agree that the intermediate worlds of two Frenchmen must differ less than those of a Frenchman and an Englishman, these of two Parisians less than those of a Parisian and a countryman, and those of two lawyers less than those of a lawyer and a merchant.

But before extending further the inquiry into the resemblances which these little intermediate worlds must present, let us first see what, according to the science of correspondences, is in general the intermediate world of a spirit. As a spirit is really a man, and the earth is the correspondence of man, this spirit finds himself upon an earth; as he has a will and an understanding, he dwells in a house; as he is imbued with truths and falses, he has garments; but the nature of this earth, as to its fertility and aspect, depends upon the general state of this spirit; the grandeur and beauty of the house are in relation to the state of his will and understanding; the substance, the color, and the form of his garments depend upon the mixture of his truths and falses. Lastly, as this spirit possesses affections and thoughts, and a multitude of things which are the consequences of them, he sees in his horizon and around him objects of the three kingdoms, and products of industry; but the nature of these objects and these products depends upon the state of his affections and thoughts.

The representative theatre of the state of this spirit cannot resemble in an absolute manner that of any other spirit, for in the whole universe of beings, there are no two that completely resemble each other; nevertheless, diversity in unity being a general law of creation, everything tends to unity; to attain this, everything is arranged into groups, and it is by means of harmonious relations that the different groups are formed. Now, if there are not two men, nor consequently two spirits, who resemble each other in an absolute manner, at least there exist, in a greater or less number, those whose affections and thoughts present among them many resemblances, and have, so to speak, a kind of neighborhood. The representative theatres of the states of these spirits having consequently analogous relations between them, find themselves, so to speak, neighbors one of another, or to express it more exactly, they constitute one country of the intermediate world, which is common to them, and are only distinguished from one another by slight differences, and by the particular habitation of each spirit: and these habitations exist more or less near to one another, according as the affections and thoughts of spirits have more or less similitude between them. Thence result united masses of which the villages, towns, and cities of greater or less extent are composed, which are spread over the earth of our intermediate world.

You can easily conceive from this, how the millions of representative theatres or little individual worlds concur in forming a whole. There is actually but one only intermediate world for all the spirits who depart from our globe; but there exist millions of different horizons; in the same country the horizon of one is never completely like that of another, and the horizon of each spirit varies even at every instant according to the mobility of the state of his affections and thoughts. Ah! do we not see something analogous in our world, in both a physical and moral respect? In the physical, are not the horizons in number indefinite, and does not a man change his horizon at every change of place? And in the moral, in the domain of affection and thought, is the horizon of one ever like that of another? Does not the horizon of the same man change at every instant?

But there are also spirits whose affections and thoughts present more intimate relations, and have a kind of kindred and family, so that there is with them so to speak, the same will and the same understanding; the representative theatres of the state of these spirits present not only a country which is common to them, but also one and the same edifice for a habitation; and under this relation these theatres are distinguished only by particular parts of the same house; or only by other details of the interior of this house. It is thus that families are formed in the world of spirits; they are the result of a more intimate conformity in affections and thoughts.

If to all that precedes you add, that in the spiritual world there must necessarily be, as in this, and even in a much higher degree, communication of affections and thoughts between those who have some relations between them, it will be easy for you to comprehend that spirits of the same country see one another, and see also the exterior of their neighbor's house, and penetrate even into the interior of those houses, or visit those who inhabit them, when for the time they have with them the same will and the same understanding.

Observe, moreover, that if, in this natural world, our affections and thoughts are not exclusively fixed upon things, but are also determined to persons, it must be the same in the intermediate world. There, when the affections and thoughts are fixed upon religious, moral, political, or civil matters, they are manifested visibly by spiritual objects which are the correspondences of them ; but when they are fixed upon other spirits, they are immediately present, though their proper habitation may be in the most remote part of the intermediate world. And this is easily conceived, since affection and thought know no distance. Have you an intimate friend beyond the seas, at Philadelphia, for example ? If you think of him, you see him, you speak to him ; and if he does not hear you, if he does not answer your questions, it is only because you are both in a material world, and space and time oppose your communication of ideas ; but abstract matter, put away space and time, and you are in the presence of your friend ; he then hears you and you enter into conversation. It is thus that it should be, and really is, in the intermediate world, since space and time are there replaced by states of affection and thought, states which are manifested only in an appearence of space and time.

You see from this, that spirits do not live separately but in society, although the intermediate world is for every spirit the exterior manifestation of what is contained in him. The affections and thoughts are what every spirit has within him, and these are a consequence of those which he had in our world ; the latter are never entirely effaced, but are only removed from his memory, so that occasionally they are reproduced. The life of man is not interrupted by his passage from this world into another; it is continued, and his memory then is in all its vigor; for there is not a single action of his life, nor a single idea, which may not be recalled. If man, after becoming a spirit, had no recollection of his life in the world, he would be deprived of his individuality, and consequently of immortality, because it would not be he who would exist; it would be really *another being* in his place.

The ordinary residence of the man-spirit being the correspondence of the habitual state of his will and understanding, so long as this state is not entirely changed, the man-spirit preserves the same residence, without being forced to remain continually in his house or city; for certain affections and thoughts may lead him to travel over the different countries of our intermediate world, and even to visit the earths of the intermediate world which correspond to the other planets of the natural world, without the habitual state of his will and understanding being remarkably altered; but if this state is entirely changed, he himself changes his abode.

Changes of residence are very frequent in the intermediate world; for man only goes into this world to be prepared there by successive transitions, either for the heavenly or infernal life. He is then obliged to pass through many states, and consequently often changes his abode, before repairing to his place, whether in heaven or hell.

The future life of man depends entirely upon that which he has formed for himself upon our earth; if during this life his will had been bad, it is no longer possible for him to make it good, and his understanding, at the same time enlightened by truth, will lose its light or its truth, in the intermediate world; on the other hand, if his will had been good, it is in no danger of becoming bad, and his understanding will exchange any false opinions it may have for truths. I will return to this subject at another time.

Thus, all depends upon the will which man has made for

himself in the natural world, or, in other words, all depends upon his ruling love. The will or ruling love of man is the man himself; his understanding is but a servant at the disposition of his will. All that appertains to the will is a spiritual substance, and all that belongs to the understanding is a spiritual form; so far then as the substance excels the form, so far the will governs the understanding.

Nevertheless, as the life of man is not interrupted by his passage from this world into another, the situations of those who arrive in the intermediate world is generally, at first, very similar to that which they had upon our earth; but this is not of long duration, for the scene soon changes. Every spirit being directed by his ruling love, if this love is good, since it rules over all the other affections, it successively removes those which are bad, and favors those which are good; then the interior state of the spirits continually improves, and his exterior situation becomes more beautiful, by means of delightful representatives, which are the correspondences of his interior state. But if the ruling love is bad, it successively removes the good affections and favors the bad; then the interior state of the spirit continually becomes worse, and his exterior situation becomes more and more miserable, by means of hideous representatives, which are the correspondences of his interior state.

I will continue the description of the world of spirits in the following letter; but I cannot conclude this without presenting to you some reflections.

The imminent peril which social order is in at this day is at length understood, and great efforts are made to avert it; those who lately smiled with contempt at the bare name of religion, now think it might come to their help, and are the first to invoke its support; but religion will remain impotent in this respect, so long as they persist in relying upon the falsified doctrines of the old Church. If Christianity no longer exists, so to speak, but in name, or if it is no longer effectual to render those moral who call themselves Christians, it is owing to the causes which I have already explained; but it is chiefly because its two principal branches have each adopted a pernicious error, which they persist in spreading among the people; Roman Catholicism, in affirming that the absolution of the priest, or even a single prayer of repentance, at the moment of death, opens heaven; Protestantism, in maintaining that it is sufficient for man to believe that the blood of Christ has saved him. These two doctrines are no doubt consoling; they even present a charm to whoever believes in another life; but they are absolutely false, and so much the more dangerous, as they give to man a kind of security, which prevents him from thinking seriously of reformation.

Man, indeed, is naturally led to procrastinate, when the occupation of his life should be to struggle against his bad passions; now, to tell him that a single prayer of repentance may save him, is not this flattering his natural propensity? It will be in vain to add that he may die without having time to address one single word to the Divinity; it will be in vain to cite to him examples in support of what you say; he will soothe himself with the hope of not dying suddenly, or even if you succeed in making some impression upon him, that impresion will be but momentary.

On the other hand, if it is sufficient for man to believe that the blood of Christ has saved him, why should he struggle against his bad passions, since he has need of nothing but this faith?

In each of these two branches of Christianity reformation of life cannot then be really undertaken except by very few persons; and the generality of Christians will not be in the least interested in changing their course of life, asevery day's experience sufficiently proves.

Suppose men on the contrary, to be inwardly penetrated

with the great truths which the New Church of the Lord proclaims they would certainly manifest the greatest inconsistency if they hesitated a single moment to enter upon the way of reformation and regeneration. Convinced that repentance is nothing, and that faith is nothing, if there is not a change of life—convinced that man carries with him, into the other life, his ruling love—that there this ruling love will strip him successively of all his vices if he is good, and of all his good qualities if he is bad, and will thus render him fit to become either free in heaven or a slave in hell—would he not use all his efforts to make this love good, especially when the rational knowledge which he would have of the spiritual world would no longer permit him to have the least doubt of its existence ?

Hereafter, when you become acquainted with our doctrines, and the admirable morality which they teach, I will return to this subject; and then you will acquire the inward conviction, that it is only the New Church of the Lord, that is to say, the New Jerusalem, that can cause peace and tranquility to reign upon the earth. Accept, &c

LETTER XIII.

In my last letter, my dear sir, I showed you that the world into which man enters immediately after death is altogether like ours, except the difference existing between what is spiritual and what is natural; you have seen besides, that though the world of spirits was for man the exterior manifestation of his affections and thoughts, he could, nevertheless, in that world, have relations not only with those whom he had known during their natural life, but also with spirits who, in our world, had lived in foreign countries, or even upon other earths.

Now, as it is impossible that relations should be established between spirits the same as among men, without the use of some language, the first question which we have now to examine is this: In what language do spirits converse with each other?

This question would no doubt appear absolutely idle to our philosophers and theologians. Why, indeed, should they ask about the language of spirits, since, in their view, a spirit is without organs? since, in their view, the other world, containing neither substances nor forms, is but an immense vacuum, or something which has but an imaginary existence?

It is thus they think when they are shut up in their studies; but let a painful event drive them from their pretended science, and immediately the truth, piercing through the darkness which obscures their understanding, becomes manifest to them.

Behold the philosophical spiritualist who has just lost a beloved child; it is in vain he calls to his aid the arguments of his school concerning the immortality of the soul; they remain altogether impotent to console his grief; with them, there is nothing which can retrace the form of his infant, its smile, its graces, and its infantine language, every word of which came so agreeably to his ear; all this is destroyed, destroyed for ever. This he says, this he repeats in his despair; but suddenly a ray of truth pierces the clouds of his understanding—he raises his eyes to heaven, and represents to himself his child, like one of those angels which painters have in their pictures; immediately he feels his heart dilate, his respiration becomes more free; oh, how precious is this thought to him! how it sooths his grief! he would give everything to retain it; but his reason, which science has perverted, soon deprives him of this only consolation, and he falls again into his mournful despair. Oh, philosophers! you often pay dear for the frivolous pleasures which your science procures for you; unite it then to true theology, and you will render it beneficent both for those whom you wish to instruct, and for yourselves.

When a theologian is with his mother, whom death has just deprived of her husband, what are the arguments which he employs to soothe her affliction? Does he tell her that she will again see, after a lapse of ages, him for whom she weeps? Does he himself believe, in the effusion of his grief, that he will not find again his father, until after the complete destruction of our world? Oh surely, such a thought is far from him. He then believes that the object of their regret yet exists really in a human form. Hear him addressing his mother: You will see him again, says he; moderate your grief; we shall meet him again as soon as it pleases God to call us. Such then is his language; for in the overflowing of his filial grief, his false science is forgotten, and a ray of truth penetrates even to him.

It is thus our philosophers and theologians give the lie to their own science, whenever truth is able to penetrate the clouds of their understandings.

But when they have re-entered their studies, say nothing more to them about the soul or spirit under a human form; present to them no more the other world as a real world containing spiritual substances and forms; tell them not that the inhabitants of that world converse together as we do in ours; they will laugh you in the face, grave as they are; but, my dear friend, let us, far from laughing at their blindness, rather pity them, for the more they think themselves clear-sighted the more are they objects of pity.

The question which is now to engage our attention will not then consist in the enquiry whether spirits speak or not; for the moment that we acknowledge that they have a mouth, a tongue, and ears, and that they live surrounded by a spiritual atmosphere, it at once becomes evident that they can produce sounds and hear those which others produce. So we have only to examine what must be the language which spirits make use of in their intercourse with one another. This examination will again require some digressions; for if in this world the language of man depends upon his memory and his thoughts, it must be the same when he lives in the world of spirits; it is absolutely necessary then that I should give you some explanation, first concerning the memory of man, and afterwards concerning his thought.

Since men have lost true spiritual knowledge, they have in vain endeavored to resolve the problems which most concern the happiness of humanity; so they are as much in the dark when they speak of the memory of man, as when they treat of the immortality of his soul. And how could it be otherwise? Must not all the questions of philosophy be referred to one general principle? Now, this principle they misunderstand; they are not willing to comprehend that every natural thing envelopes an analogous spiritual one, with which it is in correspondence. If they admitted this principle, they would then know that there are in men two memories, the one natural and external, the other spiritual and internal; they would consequently know that these two memories, though they seem to be confounded, must nevertheless be distinct from each other.

If our two memories seem to be confounded and make but one, this should not by any means surprise us; is it not the same with our spiritual man and our natural man? If then man does not perceive that in his natural man there is a spiritual man, no more should he perceive that in his natural memory there is a spiritual memory: besides, he reflects but little upon this subject, because he immerses his life in corporeal things, and can with difficulty withdraw his mind from them.

All that man thinks, wills, says, and does, all that he hears and sees, everything, in a word, is received instantly in his interior memory, and there remains impressed forever: nothing thus received is entirely effaced from this memory; they are not there confounded whatever be their number, which may seem astonishing; but this proceeds from the very constitution of man who was created in the image of God; for if the infinite is in God alone, indefinites are in his spiritual sun, as I have already told you, and exist as in an image in the created universe. It thence results that the interior memory of man can receive things in number indefinite, and preserve all their impressions; it retains even the impressions of things which, having become a habit in the life of man, are entirely effaced from his exterior memory; in a word, it is in reality the book of his life.

When man leaves this world, he comes into the full possession of his interior memory, which is the memory of his spirit, and though he has no longer his natural body, he is not deprived of his exterior memory. In what way he can also enjoy this memory shall now be shown. As the things purely natural which are in it cannot be produced in the other life, the spiritual things which are adjoined to them by correspondences are represented in their place in a form altogether similar, so that the life of man is really continued in the spiritual world, by means of this representation of things purely natural. It is thus that the man-spirit does not cease to be the same man that has lived in the natural world; his identity is perfect, since he can thus remember all that he has done during his life in this world. If it were not so would there not be something wanting to his immortal existence?

I have just said that the happiness of humanity depended also upon the solution of the problem of the memory; as this assertion may have appeared to you rash, it is necessary to corroborate it here by some reflections.

Though you may have given but little attention to the study of man, it is easy to see that he himself is most generally the cause of his own happiness, and that it would again be possible for him to live happy upon this earth, if he knew and would moderate his passions. This truth is proclaimed in all the pulpits; it is written in all treatises on morality; we find it in all books of popular instruction. Why, then, does man remain deaf to the lessons of his instructors, to the advice of moralists, to the threatening exhortations of the priests? Why does he continue to let himself be drawn away by his bad passions? It is because it is not sufficient to tell him that God sees his secret thoughts; it is necessary also to show him that these thoughts will be publicly divulged, and above all, to prove to him how this will be done. Now, so long as God is represented to him as a pure spirit, without substance or form, so long as the soul is in his view but a breath—so long as the spiritual world is looked upon by him as something void, without any objects whatever—the sermons the best prepared to produce effect, will make no impression upon him; if he is affected by them, it is only for the moment, and he will very soon fall again into his former errors. But when he knows that God is VERY MAN—when he is informed that on putting off his natural body, his soul is still invested with a spiritual body, and that he then enjoys all his senses in a degree much more elevated than during his existence upon our earth—when he knows that the world of spirits, into which he will enter after putting off his material body, is like ours, except the difference between what is spiritual and what is natural, and that this world includes innumerable spiritual objects which correspond to natural objects—it will be sufficient then to give him some explanations concerning his interior memory in order to produce the conviction that his most secret thoughts will one day be publicly divulged. Suppose now that he should be penetrated with this truth, would he not strive with all his might to repress within himself every thought which is of a guilty nature? From this there would be but one step to reformation, which would conduct him to happiness so far as it can be hoped for upon earth.

As to the manner in which the secret thoughts and actions of man are divulged, it is easy to conceive. All that man has thought, willed, said, and done in this world, being inscribed in his interior memory, and the intermediate world being for every spirit a representative theatre of his thoughts and affections, it is only necessary that a shorter or longer period of the terrestrial life of a man-spirit should be suddenly recalled to his memory in order that all things which relate to that thought, and even their smallest particulars, may be immediately manifested by representatives to the sight of all the spirits near him.

It is thus that the book of man's life is opened, and it is thus he is judged. Such is the law of the divine order, a law as inflexible as justice, but admirable as all that is divine, since it provides that every one shall be judged according to his works.

Yet this divulging of the thoughts and actions of man is not effected as soon as he enters into the intermediate world, for he is then in the exteriors of his spirit, and he preserves them for a longer or shorter time, according to his greater or less attachment to external things; but it is effected when, being entirely divested of his exteriors, he comes forever into the interiors of his spirit. This is not the place to speak of the different states through which man passes during his sojourn in the world of spirits; we will give some attention to this hereafter. But as the subject is now concerning the manifestation of the thoughts and actions of man by means of his memory, I will present you with an extract from Swedenborg, in which you will find in the first place several explanatory examples, and afterward the principles which govern this subject. In the Treatise concerning Heaven and Hell, Nos. 462, 463, he says:

"But still the difference between the life of man in the spiritual world, and his life in the natural world, is great, as well with respect to the external senses and their affections, as with respect to the internal senses and their affections. Those who are in heaven perceive, that is, they see and hear more exquisitely, and also think more wisely, than when they were in the world; for they see from the light of heaven, which exceeds by many degrees the light of the world; they hear also by a spiritual atmosphere, which likewise exceeds by many degrees that of the earth, the difference of these external senses is as the difference of sun-shine in respect to the obscurity of a mist in the world, and as the difference of light at mid-day in respect to shade in the evening: for the light of heaven, because it is divine truth, gives to the sight of the angels to perceive and distinguish things the most minute. Their external sight also corresponds to their internal sight, or the understanding; for with the angels one sight flows into the other, so that they act as one; hence they have so great acuteness; and in like manner also the hearing corresponds to their perception, which is as well of the understanding as of the will; hence, in the sound and words of one speaking they perceive the most minute things of his affection and thought; in sound the things which are of affection, and in the words the things which are of thought: see above. But the rest of the senses with the angels are not so exquisite as the senses of seeing and hearing, because seeing and hearing are serviceable to their intelligence and wisdom, but not the rest—which, if they were in a like degree exquisite, would take away the light and delight of their wisdom, and would bring in the delight of pleasures, which are ef the various appetites of the body, which obscure and debilitate the understanding in proportion as they prevail; as also in the case with men in the world, who are dull and stupid as to spiritual truths, in proportion as they indulge the taste and tangible blandishments of the body. That the interior senses of the angels of heaven, which are of their thought and affection, are also more exquisite and perfect than what they had in the world, may be manifest from what has been said and shown in the article concerning the wisdom of angels of heaven, (No. 265–275). But as to what concerns the difference of the state of those who are in hell in respect to their state in the world, it also is great; as great as is the perfection and excellence of the external and internal senses of angels who are in heaven, so great is the imperfection of those who are in hell. But the state of these will be treated of in what follows.

"That man, when he passes out of the world, has also with him all his memory, has been shown by many circumstances; concerning which many things worthy to be mentioned have been seen and heard, some of which I will relate in order. There were those who denied the crimes and villanies which they had perpetrated in the world, wherefore lest they should be believed innocent, all were disclosed and were recounted from their memory, in order from their earliest age to the latest; they were principally adulteries and whoredoms. There were some who had deceived others by wicked arts and who had stolen; their deceits and thefts were also enumerated in a series, many of which were known to scarcely any one in the world, except to themselves alone; they also acknowledged them, because they were made manifest as in the light, with every thought, intention, delights and fear, which then together agitated their minds. There were some who had accepted bribes, and had made gain of judgement; they from their memory were in like manner explored, and from it were recounted all things from the first period of their office to the last; every particular, as to quality and quantity, together with the time, the state of their mind, and intention, all which things were at the same time brought to their recollection, and shown to their sight, which were more than several hundreds. This was done in some cases; and what is wonderful, their memorandum books themselves, in which they had written such things, were opened and read before them, from page to page. There were some who had enticed virgins to acts of fornication, and who had violated chastity. and they were called to a similar judgment; and every particular of their crimes was taken and recited from their memory; the very faces of the virgins and women were also produced as present, with places, speeches, and purposes, and this as suddenly as when any thing is presented to view; the manifestations continued sometimes for hours together. There was one who had esteemed backbiting others as nothing, and I heard his backbitings recounted in order, and defamations also with the very words, the persons concerning whom and before whom he had uttered them—all were produced and presented to the life at the same time; and yet every particular was studiously concealed by him when he lived in the world. There was a certain one who had deprived a relation of his inheritance, under a fraudulent pretext: he was, in like manner, convicted and judged, and, what is wonderful, the letters and notes which passed between them were read in my hearing, and it was said that there was not a word wanting. The same person also, shortly before his death, clandestinely destroyed his neighbor by poison, which was disclosed in this manner; he appeared to dig a hole under ground, from which a man came forth as out of a sepulchre, and cried out to him, 'What have you done to me?' then everything was revealed, how the murderer talked with him in a friendly manner, and held out the cup, also what he thought before, and what afterwards came to pass; which things being disclosed, he was sentenced to hell. In a word, all evils, villanies, robberies, artifices, deceits, are manifested to every evil spirit, and brought forth from his very memory, and he is convicted; nor is there any room given for denial because all the circumstances appear together. I have heard also from the memory of a certain one, when it was seen and surveyed by the angels, what his thoughts had been within a month, one day after another, and this without fallacy, which were recalled as he himself was in them on those days. From these examples it may be manifest, that man carries along with him all his memory, and that there is nothing, however concealed in the world, which is not manifested after death; and this in the company of several, according to the Lord's words; "There is nothing hidden which shall not be uncovered and nothing concealed which shall not be known; therefore the things which ye have said in darkness shall be heard in light, and what ye have spoken into the ear shall be preached on the house-tops."—Luke, xii. 2. 3.

"When man's acts are disclosed to him after death, the angels then to whom is given the office of inquisition, look into his face, and the search is extended through the whole body, beginning from the fingers of one hand, and of the other, and thus proceeding through the whole. Because I wondered whence this was, it was disclosed to me, viz., that as all things of the thought and will are inscribed on the brain, for their principles are there, so also they are inscribed on their whole body; since all things of thought and will proceed thither from their principles, and there terminate, as in their ultimates. Hence it is, that the things which are inscribed on the memory, from the will, and thence its thought, are not only inscribed on the brain, but also on the whole man, and there exist in order, according to the order of the parts of the body. Hence it was made evident that man in the whole is such as he is in his will and thought thence, so that an evil man is his own evil, and a good man is his own good. From these things also it may be manifest what is meant by the book of man's life spoken of in the word, that is, that all things, both which have been acted and thought, are inscribed on the whole man, and that they appear as if read in a book when they are called forth from the memory, and as seen in effigy when the spirit is seen in the light of heaven. To these things I will add something memorable concerning the memory of man remaining after death, by which I was confirmed, that not only general things but also the most singular, which have entered the memory, remain, nor are they ever obliterated. There appeared to me books with writtings therein, as in the world, and I was instructed that they were from the memory of those who wrote, and that there was not a single word wanting there, which was in the book written by the same person in the world; and that thus from the memory of another may be taken the most singular things of all, even those which he himself in the world had forgotten. The reason was also disclosed, viz., that man has an external and internal memory, an external which is of his natural man, and an internal which is of his spiritual man; and that everything that man has thought, willed, spoken, done, also that he has heard or seen, is inscribed on his spiritual memory; and that the things which are there are never erased, since they are inscribed at the same time on the spirit itself, and on the members of its body, as was said above; and that thus the spirit is formed according to the thoughts and acts of its will. I know that these things appear as paradoxes, and thence are scarcely believed, but still they are true. Let not man therefore believe that anything which a man has thought in himself, and has done in secret, is concealed after death; but let him believe that each and all things then appear as in clear day."

I have transcribed this passage for two reasons; first, because the details and principles which it contains throw light upon the subject which engages our attention; and next, I was desirous of showing you with what candor Swedenborg relates what he has seen, though he well knew how difficult it would be for men to believe his relations.

Let us now return to the exterior or natural memory. I have already said that all things purely natural, which are in that memory, cannot be reproduced in the other life, but in their place are corresponding spiritual things in a form absolutely similar ; now, things purely natural, being those which are neither intellectual nor rational, we must rank among them all the words of earthly languages, for there is nothing intellectual or rational in these words. It thence results that our natural languages cannot be of any use in the world of spirits; if there exist books there which seem to include, as you have just seen, the same words as our books, they are representative appearances, which have but a simple relation of correspondence with the language of spirits, and you will acknowledge presently that in this language words become absolutely useless. In our world, it is true, men cannot converse with one another without the use of languages divided into articulate sounds, that is, into words, and do not understand each other unless they are acquainted with the same language ; but it is because they are immersed in things purely natural and corporeal, and cannot withdraw their minds from them.

The language of man depending not only upon his memory, but his thought, we have now to carry our investigations to the nature of thought ; will you for a moment lend me all your attention ?

If man would reflect upon what passes within him, he would acknowledge that his language is nothing else than his thought speaking by means of the organs of his body. Indeed the thought of man is active or passive ; it is active when he speaks and passive when he is silent. Now, his active thought, which we may also call his speaking thought, expresses itself according to a mode proper to itself ; and by the activity of its language, it excites the organs of the body which correspond to this language. I confess however, that at the first examination it seems to man, that the words of his language are in his thought ; but should not every reflecting man hesitate before concluding from a first appearence ? Does he not know that he lives in the midst of illusions of every kind ? If the progress of the physical sciences has discovered so many illusions of the senses which had, for thousands of years, been taken for realities should not a progress of theology and philosophy also unveil them ? Well, this appearance that the *words* of the language of man are in his thoughts is pure illusion; it is only the *sense* of a language which is in thought. In a word, when man speaks his thought is the language of his spirit, and if it does not then appear to him to be a language, it is because it conjoins itself to the language of the body, and is in this language. Besides, it is easy to acknowledge that the language of the thought differs much from the language of words; since man can think in one minute what it takes him a long time to speak, it is very evident that he could not speak with so much readiness, if the language of thought was composed of words, like that of the body. (See the *Arcana Celestia*, no. 3679. 4052. 6987.)

But, you will say, In what then does the language of the thought consist ? This I can now explain to you in a few words.

The thought of man is composed of ideas, as a phrase is composed of words; thus in the language of the mind one idea of his thought follows another, as in the language of the body one word follows another word; but the ideas of the thought succeed one another with so much rapidity, that during our life in this world, it seems to us that the thought is continuous and does not present any distinction in it. (See the *Arcana Celestia*, no. 6599.)

The language of the mind of man then is composed of ideas of his thought, and it is by the influx of this language into the correspondent organs of the body that the language of words is produced. Thus when man leaves this world, as he divests himself of all that was of use to the body, he leaves with it all the words of human languages with which he was acquainted and as he carries with him all that belongs to his mind, he finds himself in possession of all his thoughts and memory, as well interior as exterior, excepting, as to the latter, the modifications of which I have spoken to you; and it is by means of his interior memory and of the ideas of his thoughts, that he expresses himself in his new abode. Human thought, says Swedenborg, then becomes more distinct and clear, and the ideas of the thought become discrete, so that they serve for distinct forms of speech. What was obscure is dissipated, and thus the thought, delivered from the fetters, as it were, with which it was bound, consequently from the shadows in which it was involved, becomes more instantly perceived; thence it results that the intuition, perception, and utterance of every particular contained in it are rendered more immediate. (A .C. 1757.)

It is then ideas of the thought which take the place of words; and these ideas, which we cannot distinguish here on earth, being clearly manifested when we are freed from our natural body, become then distinct forms of our language. It must not be supposed, however, that this language is mute; it is manifested exteriorly like that of men, by means of sounds which are produced and are heard like those of our language; for spirits, as you know, having a mouth, tongue, and ears, and being surrounded by a spiritual atmosphere, respire in this atmosphere; and by means of that respiration and of organs of language, they produce words like men in our world. Then the ideas of their thought, and the words of their speech make one, as the efficient cause and the effect; for that which exists as a cause, in the ideas of thought, is manifested as an effect in words.

You may now see what is the principal difference which exists between the language of the ideas of thought and the language of words; the latter is altogether conventional, as its very construction proves; and the former is above all convention, as it flows from the affection itself, and the thought itself of the man-spirit; in this language, sound corresponds to affection, and the articulation of the sound corresponds to the ideas of the thought which proceeds from the affection.

The language of words being with us altogether conventional, it results that the inhabitants of our world cannot, in their present state, understand one another except they are acquainted with the same conventional language. The language of the ideas of thought being, on the contrary, above all convention, it results that it is spoken and understood by all spirits without being obliged to learn it; for one affection always manifests itself by the sound which is proper to it, and one idea of thought by the articulation which alone agrees with it.

From all that precedes we must necessarily conclude, that the language which is spoken in the world of spirits is the real universal language; and that this language can never be understood upon our earth, so long as men are immersed in things purely natural and corporeal, and will not elevate themselves to things really rational and intellectual.

Thus, every man who leaves this earth, is able to speak the universal language as soon as he enters into the intermediate world; and he can by this means converse, not only with the spirits who have inhabited our earth, whatever may have been their language here, but with spirits who may have belonged to one of those innumerable earths which compose the natural universe. The correspondence which exists between the language of thought and the language of words, causes man, in the first moments of his new sojourn, to speak this language without being aware of it, believing that he is expressing himself in the language he made use of in the world.

You have, no doubt, my dear sir, met with, among your acquaintances, some enthusiastic admirer of mucic, an honest man, who believes in the immortality of the soul, after the manner of our psychologists. Speak to him, I pray you, of our ideas concerning spiritual substances and forms; tell him that in the other world we shall live in a spiritual body in the midst of an immaterial atmosphere. He will regard you at first with attention, to assure himself whether you are speaking seriously, and if he does not see you smile, he will think you have lost your senses, though he may not tell you so to your face; that will depend upon the degree of familiarity which exists between you. Let not this contempt for your new faith disconcert you, but ask him if he believes in the immortality of the soul: he will answer you in the affirmative; ask him if he thinks that the soul of the good man will live in a happy state: he will tell you, yes; ask him if he knows in what consists the happiness of that soul; upon this point his answer will be in the negative; ask him next what it is in this world which affords him the most delightful enjoyment; he will answer, "Music; nothing," he will tell you, "electrifies all the faculties of my soul like the melodious accents of the human voice, united with the sound of instruments; it is to me the most lively pleasure; it is then only that I enjoy life in fulness." Interrupt him quickly, (for this subject being inexhaustible, he knows not when to stop,) and say to him, "You love it well, my dear friend, and when you think of the other life, you hope your soul will be happy there. You do not know, it is true, in what its happiness will consist; but I ask you, can it be happy if deprived of a concourse of sweet sounds?" At these words you will see him hang his head and reflect. Continue: "If the good man must live happy in the other life, and you do not doubt that, God is too just to deprive him of what constituted the charm of his life; and as God must have foreseen everything, should there have been upon the earth but one single musician, a good man, the divine justice would have provided for him, in his immortal existence, those innocent pleasures which were here the recreation of his earthly existence." Your friend, whom these words will relieve from the painful reflections into which you had first plunged him, will then raise his head with an air of satisfaction, and say: "You are right; why should there not be music and singing in the other life? The Grecian philosophers thought that music prevailed in heaven, and constituted the principal amusement of the Gods and virtuous souls; and do not our theologians speak of choirs of angels?" "This is true," you will reply, "but I would have you to observe, that without an atmosphere it is impossible there should be sounds. And these accents of the human voice which you prefer to the sounds of all instruments, how could they be produced if souls do not speak, at least, if they do not sing? And how could they sing if they had not a spiritual body, and if they were not surrounded with an immaterial atmosphere? And your own soul, how will it be possible to hear sounds, if it has neither substance nor form, as from your philosophical principles you believe?" Do not press him further; tell him to compare these principles, of which he seems so proud, with those whose simple enunciation has almost made you pass for a fool in his eyes; and, if after having maturely reflected upon spiritual substances and forms, upon the existence of the soul in a human form, and concerning immaterial atmospheres, he still persists in his principles, of which I doubt, he will respect yours, and never permit himself again to laugh at them.

Accept, &c.

LETTER XIV.

Let us continue, my dear sir, our examination of questions of detail.

In the preceding letters, we have taken man at his departure from the world and introduced him into the spiritual world. You have seen him, in the midst of spirits, speaking their language without having learned it, associating with those whose character has some analogy with his own, and preserving, as in our world, his individuality by means of a human form which, being proper to him, thus distinguishes him from all other spirits. Let us now enquire what this form is, and first see if it is the same as that which he had at his departure from our world.

As the other life is a continuation of this, and death is merely a passage from one world into another, the first moments of a new existence must be conformable to the last moments of the preceding. You recollect besides, that there is a gradation in everything which is subject to the Divine Order, as well in the spiritual as in the material universe. Man entering into the other life preserves then the physiognomy by which he was known in the world: the infant enters an infant; the young man with all the freshness of youth; the old man with all his wrinkles and frailty; and this, because man, as a spirit, though divested of his imaterial body, is then in the exteriors of his spiritual body. But he does not always remain in those exteriors: he by degrees puts off this second clothing of his real spiritual body and retains no more traces of it when he leaves the world of spirits, whether to enter into heaven, or to precipitate himself into hell. (See the 10th letter). Thus during this new phasis of his life, man is preparing to manifest the interiors of his spirit, and his countenance becoming by degrees the mirror of his affections, or rather of his ruling love, which always tends to development, his physiognomy must appear more and more beautiful, if his ruling love is good, and more and more deformed if his ruling love is bad. All this evidently results from principles previously established.

But here a question arises which you would certainly present, if I should pass by it in silence, for it is very rare that it is not addressed to us when we are speaking of the mode of existence in the other world. *Do we there become young again?* exclaim almost always with eagerness those who have passed the spring time of life.

This question is not resolved by what precedes; for from the circumstance that the physiognomy of man will become more and more beautiful, it does not follow that he will himself again return to the flower of youth. Thus to speak only of the old man, all that results from what has been said is, that the old man whose ruling love is good, will, in the other life, be a beautiful old man, and possess the tastes and inclinations of a wise old man; but the question is repeated, will he again become young with the tastes and inclinations of youth?

The reply, which we make in the affirmative, generally pleases those who interrogate us, because there are so few who do not regret their youthful age; but the greater part, not contented with this simple answer alone, enquire further, how such a transformation can be effected. As I do not believe that you are a man to be contented with a simple *yes*, I will explain how, in the spiritual world, the old man can become a young man.

But, previously, permit me to make some reflections. They will lead us to establish first, that although, in our world, man grows old, it cannot be the same with him in the spiritual world. Like all the bodies of the animal and vegetable kingdoms, the human body, after having reached its maximum of youth and strength, enters upon a period of decay which terminates in a complete dissolution. Such is the law of natural order. The aged never return to their youth, and the virtue of the fountain of youth exist only in the writings of poets, and the imagination of some superstitious persons.

How many regrets this law of natural order every day excites! how many complaints it continually gives rise to! and yet it is altogether conformable to the love and wisdom of the

Creator. Consider what would have happened, if it had been possible for man to be always young and live eternally upon this earth, and you will readily acknowledge that this law of natural order, which excites so many murmurs, proves also, like all his other laws, the merciful views of God towards the human race.

Our globe renews its inhabitants three or four times in an age, and yet some are apprehensive that it may become too populous! And statistics prove that the earth would be very soon unable to nourish its inhabitants, if the population continued to follow its increasing progression. What then would have happened if man had not been subject to natural death? A consequence of this terrestrial immortality would inevitably have been a limitation as to numbers; and already thousands of years would have passed since the closing of the list. There would have been no more births from that time. Imagine then the earth covered with inhabitants, the youngest of which would be many thousand years old: admit further, according to our supposition, that they all remained in the prime of life, and tell me if, in that case, from the nature of the human heart which under the penalty of satiety demands a continual variety in all things, the terrestrial immortality of these men would not have become a burden to them?

Besides, if it had been thus, the infinity of God would no longer be manifested in his works; for the limitation of the number of men upon the terrestrial globe would have been a proof of the limitation of his power. God being infinite, all things produced must be unlimited, or in other words, the infinity of God must manifest itself in creation by indefinites. Now, in order that indefinites may exist in the natural universe, which is subject to the laws of space and time, it is absolutely necessary that all the bodies of the vegetable and animal kingdoms, to give place to others, should successively pass through periods of growth and decay.

It was then conformable to the love and wisdom of God, that man, for whom the universe was created, should be but a sojourner upon this material earth, whose limits are fixed and invariable, and that he should only enjoy immortality—his incontestable heritage, as a creature in the image and likeness of God—on a spiritual earth, unlimited as all that is independent of time and space, and consequently capable of receiving to all eternity the generations that will successively pass on our globe.

In what blindness then are they, whose greatest desire is to live eternally in our world, and who blaspheme the Divinity, by murmuring against that law which subjects man to natural death? They thus abuse that conservative instinct which God has impressed upon the heart of man, and which makes him dread death. If it is the will of God that man should be, by an irresistible attraction, attached to his existence here below, it is because man has a function to perform upon this earth, as well for his own interest as for the accomplishment of the designs of the Divinity towards the human race in general. In impressing upon man the fear of death, it is the will of God, without however forcing his liberty, to prevent him as far possible from arrogating to himself the right of discontinuing this function, and thus opposing his merciful views. Without this fear of death, would the religious principle, which classes suicide among the most enormous crimes, be strong enough to prevent men from precipitating themselves in crowds into the other life? and what then would become of the plans of the Divine Providence? In fearing death, we do but obey the laws of order, and so long as our fear does not surpass our confidence in the divine mercy, it is moderated, and does not produce any prejudicial effect, because we remain in order; but in the contrary case, it renders us unhappy, because in thus abusing the conservative instinct, we are in order no longer.

Man being merely a passenger upon this earth, it is by natural death that he should leave it; for violent and premature deaths are only exceptional cases; it is necessary then that his material body, after having attained, by an ascending progression its maximum of strength, should retrogade to the last degree of decay, by passing successively through the periods of infancy, youth, manhood, old age and decrepitude. In short, man grows old in our world, because it is necessary that he should leave it.

But should it be the same with him in the spiritual world? Why should he grow old there since he is to remain there eternally? The cause ceasing, the effect must disappear. It is true that the world of spirits is itself but a preparatory state, and man must also leave it to enter into his definitive spiritual state; but this new passage cannot be compared, upon this point, with the first; it is the passage from one spiritual state to another spiritual state, and not from a place to a spiritual state, such as is the passage which it performed by natural death. Besides, you will presently acknowledge, that to effect this new passage, far from being obliged to grow old, the spirit on the contrary must resume all its powers.

I come now to our question: How does man become young again in the spiritual world? To render this discussion more clear, let us have recourse to examples.

Let us take, for the first example, an old man whose ruling love is good. On leaving our earth, this old man enters into the world of spirits with his own physiognomy: his dotage, the tastes and inclinations of old age follow him there, as he is then in all the exteriors of his spirit; in a word, he would believe himself still upon our earth, if where he now lives he were not deprived of the sight of persons whom he has left in our world, and if he did not see some of those who have preceded him into the other life.

In his new dwelling place, what will become of his feeble spiritual body? The analogy which exists between the laws of natural order and those of spiritual order will inform us.

You are not ignorant that, in our world, the material body is at every instant subject to changes; they are insensible, it is true, but they are not the less real; and strictly speaking, it may be said, that our body of to-day is not identically the same which we had yesterday. You know also that these changes are owing to the continual loss which the body sustains in its exercise, and to the reparations which it continually receives from the atmosphere which surrounds it, and the aliments by which it is nourished.

Why should it be otherwise with the spiritual body in the world of spirits? Is not this body organized spiritually, as ours is materially? Does it not live upon an earth like ours, covered also with productions and surrounded with atmospheres? Why should it not exercise the same functions, and be subject to continual changes in consequence also of loss and reparations?

But, you will say, that by these successive changes, in this world, we become old, while in the other, on the contrary, if we enter there old, we shall become young; whence this manifest opposition? It proceeds from the characteristic difference of the two worlds. Here we live in time, we must therefore be subject to the laws of time; thence the successive periods which we call ages of life. In the other world, on the contrary, as we are completely set free from the laws of time, these periods or ages of life disappear and are succeeded by states. Created in the image and likeness of God, who is VERY MAN, our normal state must be that of a man, and not that of an infant with whom the constitutive faculties of man are not yet developed, nor that of an old man with whom these faculties have been blunted. Nevertheless, as all that proceeds from order is effected, as we have seen, without violence, those who enter as infants or old men, into the other life cannot but by degress attain to the state of man, the one by increasing in stature and the other by growing young again. This is the principle. Let us return now to our old man, and to analogy, and we shall be able to discover how such a change is effected. You know that man is continually governed by his ruling love, and that in the other life this love remains eternally, without the possibility of its ever being changed. As the ruling love of our old man is good, this love must remove successively from his heart all the bad affections which still beset it, thus this old man, although still retaining the tastes and inclinations, which he had when leaving our world, begins, from the moment of his entrance into the other life, to profit by the new lights which he has there acquired, to discriminate attentively between the good and evil, and the true and the false: it is thus that he is able to struggle against his bad affections and to root out his errors. He chooses with care his societies, and seeks principally the company of old men, who are in a spiritual state in affinity with his own. Then the air which he breathes becomes more and more pure, the food with which he is nourished becomes more and more healthy.

Here you would no doubt stop me to enquire if I make use of a figure when I speak of food in the spiritual world. No, my dear sir, I am not speaking figuratively, but really of the thing itself. And why should you be astonished that they eat and drink in the spiritual world, since you admit that they breathe there? Why cry out against the word substantial food, since you admit in the other world earths, animals of all kinds, fields with their crops, gardens with their fruit trees, and in a word, all that exists in our world? As the man-spirit has a spiritual body, is it not necessary that it should be nourished? And how could he nourish it if he did not make use of the products of the spiritual earth which he inhabits? But, you will answer, "If I have admitted all these things, it is only, in regard to spirits, as correspondences of their affections and thoughts, and I supposed that the nourishment of the man spirit consisted in good affections and true thoughts, if he was good; in bad affections and false thoughts, if he was wicked." Well, it is just so that I understand it; but observe, I pray you, that it is a principle that every interior act manifests itself by an exterior act which corresponds to it. Without this manifestation, the spiritual world would no longer be a world, and we would then fall into the systems of philosophers and theologians who, by idealizing the other life, have presented to men upon this subject ideas absolutely chimerical, and consequently inadmissible, which is the reason why there are so few persons now who believe in the existence of man after death. You had consequently adopted only the interior part of the fact, and entirely overlooked its exterior part. The man-spirit, it is true, is nourished interiorly with affections and thoughts; but as the affections and thoughts are real things, having substance and form, and not imaginary entities, as philosophy pretends, and besides, as the spiritual world, though within the man-spirit, is nevertheless manifested exteriorly to the eyes of his spiritual body, as I have explained to you in my ninth letter, it is thence altogether evident that the affections and thoughts with which the man-spirit is nourished interiorly, manifest themselves exteriorly in palpable aliment with which he nourishes his spiritual body, absolutely in the same manner as we nourish our material bodies on this earth.

I have said, before this new digression, that by degrees our old man breathes a purer air, nourishes himself with healthier aliments; *he breathes a purer air*, because the spiritual atmosphere which surrounds spirits always corresponds to their present state; it becomes then purer for him in the degree that he lives in society with more upright spirits: *he nourishes himself with healthier aliments*, for the aliments with which spirits nourish their bodies, always correspond to their affections and thoughts at the moment; the solid aliments to their affections, and the liquid aliments to their thoughts; they become then healthier for him in the degree that his ruling love removes the bad affections and false thoughts. Thus his spiritual body, at first frail, will by degrees resume strength and his strength will be always increasing, because his affections will be always better and his thoughts always more beautiful. Add to this, that man takes with him into the other world, all his memory, and that it is only necessary for him to think of any fact whatever of his natural life, to reproduce all the circumstances which accompanied it in their least details, (13th letter,) and you will see that our old man must pass, in the world of spirits, through states analogous to those of his terrestrial life; but as his ruling love is good, he will reject with disgust those which were impregnated with evil and the false, and be delighted with those which included the good and the true.

All that precedes is, besides, conformable to the general principles which we have previously discussed. You know that in the whole spiritual world there exist, properly speaking, only affections and thoughts; that these affections are good or bad, and these thoughts beautiful or deformed; that the good affections and beautiful thoughts proceed from good itself and truth itself; and deformed affections and thoughts proceed from the evil itself and the false itself, which have been introduced by the fall; that all the innumerable objects, which specially constitute the world of spirits, or the intermediate world, are but various combinations of good and bad affections, of true and false thoughts, and that all these objects are themselves modified in their substance and form, by reason of the modifications which the affections and thoughts undergo, of which they are the exterior representations.

Apply these principles to the body of the spirit, and you will see that, simply a receptacle as the spirit itself is, of which it is the exterior manifestation, this body should be modified according as the spirit receives and appropriates good or evil, the true or the false, or in other words, according as the spirit receives and appropriates good or bad affections, true or false thoughts; and then you will be forced to conclude that the spiritual body of the man-spirit whose ruling love is good, must be continually strengthened, will become more and more lovely in the intermediate world, until a degree of perfection is attained which will permit the spirit to enter heaven and become an angel.

Thus, our old man will not only become young again, but he will besides partake of all that constitutes the beauty of a young man, whatever may have been his visage or the conformation of his body when living in our world.

This conclusion might give rise to an objection which it is expedient to meet at once: If man, in the world of spirits, becomes so different from what he was on the earth, how can we, on entering that world, recognize those who have gone there long before us? The answer is easy: Although the face may have undergone many modifications, it ordinarily preserves some characteristic feature; and in most cases, it happens there, what is very often observed on this earth, that they recognize one another after a few seconds examination. If, however the inspection of the face were not enough, as spirits retain all their memory, and recall to their minds all the events of their earthly life, better than on earth, (13th letter,) it becomes easy for them to prove their identity, by citing the most minute details of facts which passed between them in our world.

Let us take for a second example an old man whose ruling love is bad. Entering into the world of spirits, he also retains his physiognomy, his decrepitude, his inclinations and tastes, as he is in the exteriors of his spirit. His ruling love which is bad, must remove successively from his heart all the good affections which yet remain; thus also on his arrival, this old man, far from struggling against his bad passions, and seeking to root out his errors, begins on the contrary, to take a disgust at good affections and to ridicule the truths which he had in his memory; he disdains the society of old men who act and speak with wisdom, and seeks the company of those who are in a spiritual state in affinity with his own.

While this old man lived in our world, his bad passions had been for the most part deadened, so to speak, by the frailty of the material body, whose worn out wheel-work yields with difficulty to the impulse which comes from the interior; but when he is disengaged from this material body, they gradually resume some strength, and afterwards become more and more active, in the degree that his ruling love removes the few good affections which remain with him. Thus the air which he breathes becomes heavier, the aliments with which he is nourished become more and more gross; but nevertheless his spiritual body, at first feeble, continually gains strength, for his affections becoming more and more violent and his thoughts more and more deformed, the spiritual body, which is nothing but their exterior manifestation, becomes for that very reason so much the stronger. This old man then also becomes young again; but far from manifesting the freshness of youth, he becomes more and more hideous, and when at last their no longer remains in him any good affection, nor any true thought, he precipitates himself into hell and becomes a devil.

From all that precedes, you see that we become young again in the other life. I could, it is true, have confined myself in this discussion to presenting to you the principle, that is to say, to supporting myself only upon the characteristic difference of the two worlds; for it is very evident that old age, being an accident inherent in time and matter, must be dissipated when we are disengaged from the laws which govern matter and time. But, as in this letter I have entered into particulars concerning the world of spirits, I have dwelt upon the subject in corroborating the principle by all the considerations which I have just presented to you.

To complete this picture, it is expedient to add a few words on the subject of the child who enters into the other life. You have already seen that it there becomes a man, and this, on the sole consideration that God being VERY MAN, and having created man in his image and likeness, to people the spiritual world, the normal state of the spirit must necessarily be the state of complete man. You have seen also, that the child does not attain to man's estate but by degrees, and in a manner analogous to the growth of the child in our world, and this because in all that depends upon order there is gradation; and no violent interruption. I will only add that all those who die before they have enjoyed liberty and rationality in our world—faculties which alone render man spiritually responsible for his actions—are all without an exception taken to heaven and become angels, when they have by degrees attained to the state of complete manhood. As to the manner in which the infant increases in stature in the spiritual world, to explain this to you, it would be necessary to enter into developments, which you will find in the treatise of Swedenborg concerning Heaven and Hell, and principally in his posthumous treatise concerning the Divine Love and the Divine Wisdom, where he enters into the most profound and most interesting details concerning the formation of man.

My letters having at length induced you to undertake the reading of the works of Swedenborg, which treat particularly of the spiritual world, it is unnecessary now for me to enter into other details which relate to that world; you will find in these works all that you can desire to know, and your conviction, already formed, cannot but be more and more corroborated by the studies in which you are about to engage.

But, my dear sir, I have hitherto only fulfilled for you the least difficult part of my task. I promised to explain to you the doctrines of the True Christian Religion, after you have understood and admitted the principles of true religious philosophy. I am far from retracting my promise; but, though you now acknowledge these principles, and however strong may be your desire to proceed to the investigation of these doctrines without delay, the exposition of them cannot however be presented to you, until after a new preparation, which will oblige me to enter into extensive developments. You are aware that all the doctrines of Christianity repose upon what are commonly called the Sacred Books, or Sacred Scriptures, which we by a single expression call the WORD. Now, on the subject of the Sacred Scriptures or the WORD, you have, like all men of the world, a crowd of prejudices, which it is indispensable to root out. Though you may have preserved for it some of that respect which you were accustomed to pay to it in your childhood, you are far from having the conviction that it is divine in all its parts; and yet this conviction is absolutely necessary; it is consequently necessary to make it penetrate deep into your heart before I attempt to explain to you its doctrines.

This is the task which I am about to undertake in a second series of letters. Accept, &c.

LETTERS

TO A MAN OF THE WORLD.

SECOND SERIES.

LETTER I.

You were conscious, my dear sir, at the commencement of our correspondence, of a deep necessity of believing. Weary of an incessant whirl in the empty void of our philosophers, and scarcely gaining a glimpse of any foundation on which to stand, you at length became convinced of the nothingness of their systems; but though always on your guard against the doctrines of the theologians, who carry written on their banners, "*Shut your eyes and believe*," yet you knew not how to escape from your painful position. You desired to believe, it is true, but you wished your eyes to remain open, and on no account would you consent to their being bandaged; you felt yourself, therefore, but little disposed to return to the religious beliefs inculcated upon your childhood, and which you put away immediately upon your entrance upon the world; thus, despite of your earnest desire, you saw yourself reduced solely to the belief in a God, the Creator of the universe, and still, how vague was this belief, when you found yourself unable to form any idea of this God! It was then that, having heard mention made of the doctrines of the New Jerusalem, you evinced a determination to become acquainted with them, and for that purpose saw fit to address yourself to me. If I have been agreeably surprised at your application, I have, on the other hand, considered it a duty to respond to so laudable a wish, and have therefore been prompt to enter upon the exposition which you desired, endeavoring at all times to adapt myself to the present state of your mind, that is to say, to develope first in order those propositions which it would be most easy for you to admit.

Although I have as yet brought to view but a small part of the sublime truths revealed by Swedenborg, yet your position has already become essentially altered; your belief in God has risen from its former vagueness to the strength of a firm conviction, and, to say nothing of the great number of truths you have admitted, you have heard also that man in dying continues still to be a man, and merely passes from one world into another, altogether as real and even more real than the former. Here, then, are certainly two points of belief, which, of themselves alone, ought to effect a happy revolution in all your ideas, and I am not therefore at all surprised by the intimation, that you have experienced an inward satisfaction and joy of which you had never before been conscious. Still it is not this which has afforded me the most pleasure on your account; to believe in God and in the immortality of the soul is, it is true, something; but this something is reduced to near nothing, provided one goes no farther. The circumstance which affords me most pleasure is, to have become apprised of the fact that you are now conscious of an inward want no less urgent than the former. Your first want was to believe; that which you now feel is, to become really a Christian. You have been struck with certain ideas which I have presented to you on the subject of the Trinity, and of Redemption; and now that you have learned that true Christianity acknowledges but one only God in the single Person of the Lord Jesus Christ, you experience a lively desire to arrive at the knowledge of this One True God. There is here, my dear sir, a very important progress, on which I am impelled to congratulate you.

But to attain to an interior conviction that the Lord is indeed the Creator of the Universe, the Redeemer of men, and their Regenerator—that is to say, the Father, Son, and Holy Spirit—you have still much ground to travel over; for you have still many prejudices to overcome, many philosophical errors to extirpate, and a great number of truths to admit. We cannot advance otherwise than very slowly, for you, doubtless, desire that, in this second series, I should continue to follow the course adopted in the first; that is to say, that I shall all along address myself to your intelligence, as is also my intention. The intelligence, or, rather, the understanding, is in fact, one of the two faculties which constitute man; it is the torch which enlightens his will. Without intelligence man would not be man; and to pretend that he is to forego the use of it, in dealing with religious questions, is to propose that man should renounce one of the most precious gifts of the Creator, that faculty which distinguishes him from the brutes, and by which alone he can know and admire his God. I shall, therefore, be especially on my guard against demanding of you the sacrifice of your intelligence; yet, as the intimate conviction that the Lord Jesus Christ is the only God of the universe springs from genuine faith, this is the moment for recalling to your recollection certain expressions in my First Letter, on the subject of the conviction which one acquires by reasoning: "Be it well remembered that, however strong this conviction may be, nevertheless it will not be faith; but it will conduct you to the faith which God alone gives to man, when man is prepared to receive it."

Thus you have been already instructed that there is a distinction to be made between a conviction acquired by reasoning, and to which the name of faith is often given, and the true faith which the Lord alone bestows upon man. In the position which you now occupy, with the precautions that ought still to abide with you, it is evidently needful that you first acquire, by human means, a strong conviction before you will be able to receive a true faith. This faith is not given arbitrarily, nor in an instant, as many suppose. Those who think to have thus received faith are in the greatest delusion, and have only an enthusiastic faith, which is therefore rather injurious than advantageous to them, because it does not come to them of the Lord. God never departs from the laws of his Divine Order, which are the laws of eternal justice; but the first notions of human justice, which is merely a reflection of the Divine Justice, do they not declare that a father would be unjust who should distribute arbitrarily his goods among his children? How, then, can we suppose that God, who is Justice itself and the common Father of men, should arbitrarily bestow faith? If faith could be given without some kind of co-operation on the part of man, He would certainly give it to all without exception. As to the conditions in which man ought to be, in order to be enabled to receive true faith, you will see very soon, that they lie principally in his interior life, or, what is the same thing, in the love which directs his actions; so far as man remains in the love of self, it is impossible for him to obtain true faith, but the moment that he compels himself to resist this love, and to live devoutly, he becomes capable of receiving it.

Nevertheless, true faith, of which the principal point consists in the recognition of the Lord Jesus Christ as the God who has created the universe,—this faith, I say, cannot be received by man unless he believes sincerely in the Divinity of the Sacred Scripture, or of the Word; and it is on this account that this series of letters will be, as I have already intimated, devoted to proving that the Word is divine in every part.

But since, in the position in which you now stand, it is necessary that you acquire a strong conviction, before hoping to attain a true faith, I am in duty bound to neglect no means which may at present tend to prepare you for this result; I shall, with this view, submit to your notice certain passages of Swedenborg, taken from the *Arcana Cœlestia:* you will then see that, although man is not interdicted the use of his intelligence while dealing with the doctrine of faith, it is at least necessary that he should be interiorly in a suitable state; as otherwise the use that he makes of his intelligence, far from benefitting, will be positively injurious to him. I earnestly solicit your whole attention to these passages; you will meet in them, it is true, certain new terms, or terms taken in a new sense; but in the main they so carry their import with them, that you will have little difficulty in grasping it. Swedenborg as is permitted in every new science, has had recourse to neology, but still without in the least abusing it; and, if you will allow this slight digression, I would add, that it is important to consecrate these new terms in our modern languages, and to endeavor even, at all times, to translate them literally; to allow the least paraphrase in the text would be to incur the risk of misconstruction; there is not, in fact, a single word in the writings of Swedenborg which does not suit its place, and for which another could well be substituted, for he always employs the proper term.

"To respect the doctrine of faith," says Swedenborg, "from rationals, is very different from respecting rationals from the doctrine of faith; to respect the doctrine of faith from rationals, is not to believe the Word, or doctrine thence deduced, before there is a persuasion wrought from rationals that it is true; whereas to respect rationals from the doctrine of faith, is first to believe the Word, or doctrine thence, and afterwards to confirm the same by rationals; the former case is inverted order, and effects that nothing is believed, but the latter case is genuine order, and effects a better belief.

"There are, therefore, two principles, one which leads to all folly and madness, another which leads to all intelligence and wisdom; the former principle is to deny all things, as when a man says in his heart that he cannot believe such things, until he is convinced by what he can comprehend, or be sensible of; this principle is what leads to all folly and madness, and may be called the negative principle; the other principle is to affirm the things which are of doctrine from the Word, as when a man thinks and believes with himself that they are true because the Lord has said so; this principle is what leads to all intelligence and wisdom, and may be called the affirmative principle. They who think from the negative principle, the more they consult things rational, scientific, and philosophical, do but so much the more plunge themselves into darkness, till at length they come to deny all things; the reason is, because no one can from things inferior comprehend things superior, that is, things spiritual and celestial, still less things Divine, inasmuch as they transcend all understanding: and moreover in such case, all things are involved in negatives from the principle: but, on the contrary, they who think from the affirmative principle, may confirm themselves in things spiritual and celestial by whatever rationals, by whatever scientifics, yea, by philosophicals, as far as lies in their power, all such things being given them for confirmation, and affording them fuller ideas. Moreover, there are some persons, who are in doubt before they deny, and there are others, who are in doubt before they affirm; they who are in doubt before they deny, are those who incline to a life of evil, and when this life bears them away, then as much as they think concerning things spiritual and celestial, so much they deny; but they who are in doubt before they affirm, are those who incline to a life of good, to which life when they suffer themselves to be bent by the Lord, then as much as they think concerning those things, so much they affirm them." A. C., n. 2568.

"They who are in the negative principle in regard to the truth of what is in the Word, saying in their hearts, that they will then believe, when they are persuaded by rationals and scientifics, are in such a state, that they never believe, not even when convinced by the sensuals of the body, as by the sight, the hearing, and the touch, for they always frame new reasonings against such convictions, whereby at length they totally extinguish all faith, and at the same time turn the light of the rational into darkness, because into falses. But they who are in the affirmative principle, that is, who believe what is in the Word to be true, because the Lord has declared it, are in such a state that by rationals and scientifics, yea by sensuals, they are continually confirmed and their ideas illustrated and corroborated; this is the case with every one who is in the affirmative principle, for man has light from no other source than by means of rationals and scientifics."—A. C., n. 2588.

Swedenborg gives, in the same article, a number of illustrative examples; I will transcribe only one of them.

According to the doctrine of the "Word, the first and principal thing of doctrine is love to the Lord and charity towards the neighbor; they who are in the affirmative in this, may enter into whatever rationals and scientifics, yea, sensuals, they please, every one according to his gift, his science, and his experience, yea, the more they enter, the more they are confirmed, for universal nature is full of confirmation. But they who deny this first and principal of doctrine, and wish first to be convinced that it is so, by scientifics and rationals, never suffer themselves to be convinced, because they deny in heart, and continually insist on some other principle, which they believe essential: at length by confirmations of their own principle, they so blind themselves, that they cannot even know what love to the Lord is and what love towards the neighbor is; and inasmuch as they confirm themselves in things contrary thereto, they also finally confirm themselves in this, that there cannot be any other love attended with delight, but the love of self and of the world, and their confirmation herein is such, that, if not in doctrine, yet in life, they embrace infernal love, instead of heavenly love. But with those, who are neither in the negative, nor in the affirmative, but in a doubting (principle) before they deny or affirm, the case is as was said above, n. 2568, viz., that they who incline to a life of evil, fall into the negative principle, but they who incline to a life of good, are led into the affirmative."

Your actual position, my dear sir, seems to me to be indicated with sufficient clearness in these passages. It is certain that you are not in the Affirmative on the subject of the Word, since you do not admit that it has been uttered by God himself. It is certain also that you are not in the Negative, since, under the conscious need of becoming really a Christian, you have reached the point of desiring to recognise the Divinity of the Word, which forms the basis of Christianity; it is, therefore, the Dubitative position that you now occupy. If you were *in doubt before denial*, I should anxiously avoid attempting to convince you of the Divinity of the Word, for in that case, I should be really culpable in directing your meditations to a subject like this, without any probability of success; but as everything evinces that you are *in doubt before affirming*, I do not hesitate to present to you the means of emerging from this doubt, and of arriving in the end at a complete conviction of the Divinity of the Word.

I shall follow, then, in this new discussion, the course which I have all along adopted in the former. It is not by employing the common places of the old theology that one can hope to convince on this point a man of the world, as experience has but too well shown their utter impotency for such a purpose; but the end may be gained by a successive development of the sublime truths revealed by Swedenborg. As to yourself, my dear sir, when you have learned these truths, you will believe in the Word, as you have believed in the God-Man; as you have believed in a soul in the human form; in a word, as you have believed in another world, composed of spiritual substances and forms. You will then be fully in the Affirmative principle, and you will be able, without difficulty or danger, to make use of the Rationals, Scientifics, and Philosophics, which will furnish you with new confirmatory proofs; but in the mean time, while this process of conviction is going on, I have one thing to ask of you, and that for your own sake, which is, that you would unceasingly bestow the greatest attention upon the subject matter of the various passages which I shall cite.

Accept, &c

LETTER II.

If I have suffered a long time to elapse between my last letter and this, it is not, my dear sir, without a motive, as you may presume. Before entering upon a subject so important as that which is going to occupy our attention, it was the part of prudence to allow you time for mature reflection upon the passages of Swedenborg which I had cited. Everything proved to me, in truth, that you were rather in *doubt before affirming*, than *in doubt before denying;* but, nevertheless, that the proof might be complete, I desired to receive from you a formal declaration. I have now, since, after sufficient examination, you have acknowledged yourself that you were led to the study of religious matters, not by mere curiosity, but by an urgent necessity of knowing your God, the most perfect conviction that you are in an *affirmative state*, and hence am ready to enter with you upon the examination of the *Bible*, or the Word, in order to dissipate your doubts upon its sanctity, and to convince you that it is really the Word of God, and, consequently, Divine in all its parts.

I will commence this examination by an exposé of the Word, presenting it to you from the origin of all things, and giving you, so to speak, its history down to the present time.

If you will recur to what was said upon the Creation in the preceding letters, you will find that the universe emanated from Divine Love, but that it is by Divine Wisdom that it was formed or created. This is still farther evident from the fact, that without the operation of Divine Wisdom the universe could not possibly have existed; for the emanations of Love could have been neither distinct nor varied: or, in other words, there would have been no objects, and, consequently, no creation, because there would have been no forms; it is Love that furnished the substances, but it is by Wisdom that each substance was clothed with a form which constituted its existence; thus the universe owes its being to Divine Love, and its existence to Divine Wisdom.

Hence, when it is said in John i. 1, 3,—"In the beginning the Word was with God, and all things were made by It," it is very evident that by the Word nothing else is meant than the Divine Wisdom.

The Word [*La Parole*], or Divine Wisdom, by which all things were made, is what the Greeks called *Logos*, the Latins, *Verbum*, and what is generally called, at the present day, the Word [*le Verbe*]. Taken in this sense, you can by no means doubt that the Word is Divine; but when you consider the written Book, to which the name Word is given, you question with yourself its Divinity, because you do not seize upon the identity of this Book with the Word by which all things were created; and yet the identity is perfect, as you may be convinced by the sequel of this exposé.

Since the Word has caused the existence of the universe, or has created it, it is also the Word which causes it to subsist, or preserves it; for preservation is perpetual creation, just as subsistence is perpetual existence. In order to preserve the universe, the Word is everywhere in action, and in all things it acts according to the recipient, that is, according to the conformation of the thing which receives, and according to the use for which it was created; viz.: in every object of the mineral kingdom, according to its form and its use, as also in every vegetable, in every animal, and likewise in man; but with man, whose form is the image of God, and whose use is to become an angel of heaven, it acts with plenitude.

In the earliest times, when everything was still in a state of integrity, the Word found nowhere the least obstacle to its reception, and everything then maintained itself in order; the human receptacles were continually open, and nothing prevented the Divine Wisdom from penetrating them. Men, thus directed by the Word, lived happily upon the earths by conforming themselves to the laws of Divine Order, and when they laid aside their mortal bodies they found themselves immediately in the heavens.

Such were the men upon our earth who constituted the Most Ancient Church, designated in Genesis under the name of Adam or Man. "In the Most Ancient Church," says Swedenborg, "the Word was not written, but was revealed to every one who was of the church, for they were celestial men, thus in the perception of good and truth like the angels, with whom also they had fellowship; thus they had the Word written in their hearts. And inasmuch as they were celestial, and in society with angels, all things which they saw and apprehended by any sense were to them representative and significative of things celestial and spiritual, which are in the Lord's kingdom ; so that they saw indeed worldly and terrestrial things with their eyes, or apprehended them by their other senses, but from them and by them they thought concerning things celestial and spiritual: it was for this cause, and not otherwise, that they were able to speak with angels, for the things which are with the angels are celestial and spiritual, and when they present themselves to man, they fall into such things as are with man in the world."—A. C., n. 2896.

You may readily obtain an account of the state of these men, if you will recur to what was said of the spirit of man, and of the correspondence of the things of the spiritual world with those of the natural world, in the preceding letters. You have seen there that man has in himself the spiritual world, and that this world is manifested exteriorly before him as often as his spiritual man is open. Now, with the men of the Most Ancient Church, the spiritual man was constantly open, and it was for this cause that they were in society with the angels, not with all indiscriminately, but with those who were at the moment in their spiritual man; hence they saw them face to face, as man in the world sees his fellow-man. When they conversed with them, the angels, who were not in the least occupied with worldly and terrestrial things, spake of celestial and spiritual things in angelic language which was entirely unintelligible to man; but, in consequence of the correspondence of the things of heaven with those of the earth, the expressions which they used were changed for man into analogous expressions concerning the world; and as man then understood correspondences perfectly, and consequently had a full understanding of representatives and significatives, he immediately apprehended in these worldly and terrestrial expressions the celestial and spiritual things which they contained.

Thus, with these men of the Most Ancient Church, Divine Wisdom, which is the *ensemble* of all the laws of Divine order, was graven interiorly upon the depth of their heart, and inscribed exteriorly upon natural objects and natural events; entire nature was with them the book of God, or the representative theatre of the Lord's kingdom, and each object, each event, was a leaf of that admirable book in which they read fluently. That book, always displayed before their eyes and engraven upon their heart, was the Word, inasmuch as it contained the Divine Wisdom.

If man had always remained in the state in which he was when the Most Ancient Church flourished, the operation of the Word would always have made itself felt in the same manner; but man having been endowed with free-will, that is to say, with the liberty of following the laws of order or of breaking them, there came a time when the men of the Most Ancient Church began to deviate from the laws of Divine Order; from that moment the perception which they had of good and truth, and which was to them the Word graven upon the heart, became less clear, for by infraction upon the laws of order their spiritual man became closed, and no longer afforded the same access to the Divine Wisdom; and the more their descendants deviated from these laws, the more obscure their perception became; until finally, this infraction having arrived at extremes, their spiritual man was entirely closed, the Divine Wisdom had no longer any way of entrance to them, and this most Ancient Church totally perished, which is represented in Genesis by the Deluge.

The destruction of this church must necessarily have been followed by that of the entire human race, if the Lord had not instituted a new church, designated in Genesis by the name of Noah, which is called the Ancient Church, to distinguish it from the preceding. In fact, if the Word or Divine Wisdom did not penetrate men, or at least some of those constituted into a church, the human race could not possibly subsist; for men would lose all idea of good and truth, of justice and equity, of honesty and decency; they would act contrary to all the laws of Divine Order, and would finally become reduced to utter destruction. But the Lord never leaves men without a church, and when the last which He had instituted is destroyed, he institutes another, as will be shown in the sequel of this exposé; for if the human race should entirely perish, as it is the only seminary of the heavens, it would follow that the heavens,—destined, by reason of the infinity of God, to receive perpetually and indefinitely new inhabitants, without ever being filled,—would receive no more, and would become limited in population; which would be in manifest opposition with the love of God, for whom the natural world is only a means of indefinitely and perpetually creating beings capable of loving their Creator. Moreover, you have seen elsewhere that spiritual beings and men could not subsist without each other.

In order that a new church might be instituted, it was necessary that the Word should be received among some men who were less depraved than the rest; but as the Word could not be engraven upon their heart, inasmuch as,—their spiritual man being closed, and the evil and the false operating against its being opened,—they could have no perception of the good and the true, it manifested itself to them by another kind of dictate, which may be called Conscience. Thus, instead of perception, they had conscience, which is comparatively very obscure, and instead of being celestial, like the men of the Most Ancient Church, they were spiritual: their state was entirely different from that of the most ancient people, for they had with heaven only a communication of which they had no knowledge. The Divine Wisdom, it is true, did not cease to be inscribed upon natural objects, even in the least natural events; for nature, on her part not vitiated by the fall of man, never ceased to be the representative theatre of the Lord's kingdom; but the spiritual man being no longer open, and the Word manifesting itself no longer to the interiors, except by conscience, it was indispensably necessary that this new church, in order to be a guide for conscience, should have exteriorly a fixed rule; then the Word [*Verbe*] became the written Word [*Parole*], without however ceasing to be the same [Word], that is, without ceasing to be the Divine Wisdom, as you will see.

The Lord, in his foreknowledge of the fall of the celestial church, had provided the means of instituting a spiritual church; and as the spiritual man, deprived of perception, could not be enlightened in the same manner as the celestial man, his Divine Providence had caused to be preserved, from the very commencement of the degradation of the Most Ancient Church, some doctrinals of faith and some revelations of that church for the use of the new church. These doctrinals, at first collected by men designated in Genesis under the name of *Cain*, were put in reserve, that they might not be lost: this is what is meant when it is said, "*that a mark was put upon Cain that no one might kill him.*"—iv. 15. At a later period representatives and significatives were collected into a compilation of doctrine by other men designated in Genesis under the name of *Enoch ;* and as this doctrine was to serve for posterity, and not to be used at that time, it is said that " God took Enoch."—v. 24.

The written Word that was given to the Ancient Church was derived from this origin ; it was composed of recitals, all of which, even to the least word, were representative and significative of things celestial and spiritual, and, consequently, contained the laws of Divine Order. Thus the Word, instead of being read fluently [*couramment*], as in the Most Ancient Church, upon the objects of nature and in natural events, was read in a compilation written according to the correspondences of the earth with heaven ; it was therefore always the Divine Wisdom itself; but that Divine Wisdom was found in a natural envelope, or, rather, it was, as an inestimable treasure, inclosed in a casket whose key was then in the hands of men ; the casket was the literal sense of the representatives and significatives, and the key the science of correspondences ; by this science, which was universally disseminated in the Ancient Church, the men of that church knew what the representatives and significatives contained ; but they differed from the men of the Most Ancient Church, inasmuch as they had no perception of them, —they merely derived from them a doctrine for the guidance of their spiritual life.

That you may have a better apprehension of this difference, I will quote the following passage from Swedenborg :—" To know by perception and to apprehend by doctrine are very different things ; they who know by perception have no need of the knowledge acquired by means of systematized doctrines ; let us take an example which will illustrate this point ; he who knows how to think well has no occasion to be taught to think by any rules of art ; for in this way he would lose his faculty of thinking well, as is the case with those who grovel along in scholastic dust. Those who act from perception receive from the Lord the faculty of knowing by an internal way what is good and true, whilst those who act from doctrine derive their knowledge of such things through an external way, or by means of the corporeal senses; the difference between these two ways is like that between light and shade. Moreover, the perceptions of the celestial man are wholly indescribable, for they extend to the most minute and particular things, with the greatest variety, according to states and circumstances."—A. C., n. 521.

As regards this written Word of the Ancient Church, only a few fragments of it, which are found in the books of Moses, are known, for it was lost in the course of time; it consisted, like the Word of the Old and the New Testaments, of both historical and prophetical books; the historical books being called the *Wars of Jehovah*, and the prophetical, the *Enunciations*.—Numb. xxi., 14, 27. Finally, the historical narrations, being written in the prophetical style, were factitious, for the most part, like those in Genesis from the 1st to the 11th chapter.—A. C., n. 2897.

The Ancient Church extended over the greater part of the globe, and flourished principally in Syria, the land of Canaan, Mesopotamia, Arabia, Chaldea, Assyria, Egypt, Nineveh, Tyre and Sidon. Whilst the men of that Church followed the laws of Order, they preserved the key of that Word; that is, they knew by the science of correspondences what the representatives and significatives, of which it was composed, contained; as these representatives and significatives contained Divine things, they were reduced among them into practice, and were applied to their Divine Worship; and this was done that there might be a communication with heaven; since things in the world represent and signify analogous things in heaven. But from the moment the Ancients deviated from the laws of Order, they departed from the true meaning of correspondences; and when they became entirely abandoned to the love of self and the world, the science of correspondences was lost, and their worship became wholly idolatrous.

At the fall of this Ancient Church men had become so external that it would have been impossible to institute a new church; for they would have been incapable of comprehending the internals of worship; and even if they could have comprehended them, they were in such a state of depravity, that they would have profaned them. At that time, that there might always be a communication between heaven and earth, and that by this means the human race might be preserved, the Lord instituted a representative of a church, and not a church, as is generally believed; for that which causes a church to exist with man is the internal of worship, and the worship that was then established was entirely external, for reasons which I have just mentioned. Man could be brought back again into the internal of worship only when the Lord Himself should institute a church by coming into the world; because it was only by making Himself man that He could conquer the power of evil and falsity by subjugating the hells; and the Lord was to come into the world only when man had fallen into the last state of degradation, that is, when from external-sensual, as he then was, he should become corporeal-sensual; it was therefore to preserve the human race during this last period of degradation, that the Lord instituted a representative of a church. For this end He chose the Jewish nation, not because that nation was less corrupt than others, for the history of the Jews proves that they were as barbarous, and often more ferocious, than the neighboring nations; but rather because, by the tenaciousness of their character, and by their national egotism, the Jews were better adapted to preserve untouched the depôt of a new written Word.

You will doubtless ask, Why a new Word,—since the Lord might, before the Ancient Church was entirely destroyed, have secured the Word, and at a later period have deposited it among the Jews, when the representative of a church should be instituted among them. I will reply by enlarging a little upon what I have just said, viz.: that the Lord, who is prescience itself, knew that the representative of the church would have no more efficacy than the preceding churches for reinstating the human race; that He alone could reinstate them by coming himself into the world; that according to the laws of his Divine Order, He must not come till the middle of the times [*le milieu des temps*], that is, till the human race, by successively declining, should become reduced to the last state of degradation; that the middle of the times had not then arrived; that it was indispensably necessary to provide, in the mean time, that the human race should not perish, by giving a Word that might be carefully preserved; that if the Lord had caused the Word of the Ancient Church to be deposited with the Jewish nation, or with any other nation, it could not long have existed, for no nation could have preserved it; because that, no one being capable of understanding the spiritual sense of it, the literal sense would have been without interest to them; that then the loss of this Word would have been followed by that of the human race, since the Divine Wisdom having no further access to men, the communication of heaven with the earth would have been broken; but that, on the contrary, by giving to the children of Jacob a new Word, whose external sense was conformable to their character and to their national egotism, it would be preserved by them with the greatest veneration till the appointed times. This is what took place; in fact, this Word being destined, like the preceding, to be the bond of conjunction between heaven and the human race, was entirely composed of representatives and significatives; it was also, like the preceding, divided into historical and prophetical books; the historical relations anterior to Heber, or the father of the Hebrews, are fictitious, like most of those of the Ancient Word;

but those posterior to Heber are real. Now all these relations refer directly or indirectly to the Jewish nation, and, moreover, all the prophetical books treat, in the literal sense, of future events relative either to the principles of the nation or to the nation itself, and announce to them the most important destinies; in fine, this Word, which, beginning from the creation, comes without interruption down to the time of Abraham, and afterwards traces their religious, political, and civil history, was to them a precious monument, of which they have always showed themselves very proud. All this may satisfy you why the Jews, men so attached by character to terrestrial things, have preserved this Word with so much fidelity and constancy, and, at the same time, why, by reason of the inherent tenacity of their nature, this Word has been intrusted to them in preference to any other nation.

I shall have occasion, further on, to return to this subject, and to remove many objections by presenting to you the Jewish nation and the principal personages of the Bible under their true character; but for the present, to avoid digression, I will pursue my task by explaining to you the manner in which the Word has been transmitted.

The spiritual man having been entirely closed with the people of the Most Ancient Church, there was no longer any open communication with heaven; that is, men no longer conversed with angels, as at the time when that Church was in a flourishing state; there was only a communication by means of the Word, but so obscure with man, that he had no knowledge of it. Such has been, since that epoch, the ordinary state of man upon this earth; this state, which goes back anterior to the period of historical record, seems to be the normal state of the human race; but it is, as you see, only a consequence of the degradation of man. The Lord cannot cause it to cease, although it may be very easy for Him to open the spiritual-man with all men, for the Lord can desire only the good of men, and in the state in which they now are, if He opened their spiritual man, He would precipitate them into evil; in fact, they are more in the love of self than in the love of God, and more in the love of the world than in the love of the neighbor; now, as the love of self is diabolic love, and the love of the world is satanic love, men would enter immediately into communication with diabolic and satanic spirits, and would disdain the society of angelic spirits. Nevertheless, although the spiritual man has been closed with all men, and notwithstanding the dangers of which I have just spoken, it has always been capable of being opened with some few of them, either when the Lord wished to transmit revelations for the church,—and then all dangers were carefully guarded against,—or when men, driven by an evil love, ardently desired to enter into communication with the other world,—and then they suffered the penalty of their audacity. Thus those with whom the spiritual man was open momentarily found themselves in communication with the beings of the spiritual world; namely, either with angels, who most frequently announced themselves as being Jehovah, or with infernal spirits, who ordinarily assumed the appearance of angels of light, and presented themselves under diverse names, as being also gods. Hence the true and the false prophets, hence also Divine miracles and magic miracles.

I have just said that angels announced themselves most frequently as being Jehovah; this requires an explanation: before that Jehovah had made himself flesh, it was impossible for Him to communicate directly with his creatures, and to speak with them face to face; you have seen the reasons for this in my 12th letter, where it is treated concerning redemption: when, therefore, Jehovah wished to make revelations, he filled an angel with His divinity, to the extent that the angel believed himself Jehovah, and remained in that belief until his communication with man or with men had ceased. Thus it was always by the ministry of an angel that Jehovah spake with the prophets and other personages of the Bible; for neither man nor angel has seen or can see Jehovah; but since the Incarnation, they can see the Lord, whose soul is Jehovah.

You may already perceive by these details how the Word of the Old Testament was given: Moses, the Prophets, and in general those whom Jehovah employed to transmit to us the Word, were all, at the time, in communication with the spiritual world; or, in other words, their spiritual man was then open. When they say, "Jehovah hath spoken to me,"—" The Angel of Jehovah hath said to me,"—" I saw, and behold,"—etc.,—such expressions show that they were not in the ordinary state. The beings and objects which they saw were spiritual beings and objects, and they saw them as distinctly as the natural man sees the natural beings and objects that surround him: for their spiritual man being open, they were really in the spiritual world. The words which they heard were spiritual words which had reference only to celestial and spiritual things, and which on arriving within their hearing were changed into analogous expressions concerning the world. But when they wrote the Word, they wrote according to an inspiration coming from their interior; each phrase, each word, even to the least iota, was inspired into them; there was absolutely nothing of man; for what they wrote could be the Word only so far as all the literal or worldly expressions should be, without the least exception, in perfect correspondence with the celestial and spiritual ideas which they were to represent. " This Word," says Swedenborg, " was written in like manner by representatives and significatives, in order that it might contain in itself an internal sense understood in heaven, and that there might thus be a communication by the Word, and that the Lord's kingdom in the heavens might be united to the Lord's kingdom upon the earth. Unless each of the things which are in the Word represents, and each of the expressions by which the things have been traced signifies Divine things belonging to the Lord, consequently celestial and spiritual things belonging to His kingdom, the Word is not Divine; and since the case is so, the Word could have been written in no other style, for it is by this style, and by no other, that human things and expressions correspond, even to the least jot, with celestial things and ideas; hence it is, that if the Word be read only by a child, the Divine things which it contains are perceived by the angels."—A. C., n. 2899.

You may see from this quotation what is the nature of this communication of heaven with the earth by the Word; you know, from my preceding letters, that there are in every man beings of the spiritual world, namely, angels and devils, good spirits and evil spirits; when therefore man reads the Word, the angels that are in him perceive the spiritual sense of it, and the good spirits understand it, and there is thus without his knowledge a communication of those angels and good spirits with him, which is a source of great spiritual advantage to him, if he is disposed to obey the interior impulse that results from it.

This passage and that which precedes show also that the Word of the Old Testament has precisely the same characters as the first written Word; and since the word of the Ancient Church was no other than the Word or the Divine Wisdom in a natural envelope, it follows that the Word [*la Parole*] of the Old Testament is likewise the Word [*le Verbe*], or the Divine Wisdom.

When the middle of the times arrived, or what is the same thing, when the human race, having become entirely corporeal-sensual, had fallen to the last state of spiritual degradation, Jehovah, came Himself into the world. This is not the time to explain the Incarnation; that grave subject will be treated upon when we discuss the question of doctrines; but all that has been said thus far is sufficient to enable you to understand that Jehovah, in consequence of the incarnation, being the soul of Jesus Christ, the Divine Saviour, whilst He lived upon our earth, spake only according to the science of correspondences, for every expression that proceeded out of His mouth was at the same time intended both for the inhabitants of the heavens and the men to whom He addressed Himself; and that thus whatever He pronounced was representative and significative of the celestial and spiritual things of His kingdom.

When the Lord had glorified or rendered Divine the Human, which He had assumed in the world for the purpose of living among men and performing the great work of Redemption, He desired that certain expressions which He had uttered by word of mouth, and certain actions of His life upon our earth, should be collected and transmitted to posterity as a new evidence of His mercy. Hence the Word of the New Testament, which was written in the same manner as that of the Old Testament; that is, each phrase and each word, even to the smallest iota, was inspired, and in the Evangelists and in the Apocalypse there is absolutely nothing that was derived from man. Everything, therefore, is in like manner representative and significative of celestial and spiritual things of the Lord's kingdom, so that the Word [*la Parole*] of the New Testament is also the Word [*le Verbe*], or the Divine Wisdom.

The question may here arise, why did the Lord, since the Word of the Old Testament was then in existence, and has always existed, give that of the New Testament? I will reply, by saying that the Lord having come into the world in the middle of the times, that is, at the epoch when humanity, having arrived at the last limit of the period of degeneration, was going to enter through Him into an ascending period of regeneration, it was indispensably necessary that the external worship instituted by the old Law in the representative of the Church for a nation entirely external, should be succeeded in the Christian Church by a worship whose internal should be the principal, which could be accomplished only by a new Law. I will also remind you that in His Word God always has regard to circumstances of time and place, and especially to the state of civilization and the character of the people to whom

He addresses it; that is, the celestial and spiritual things that are transmitted to them are clothed with representatives and significatives which are always conformable to the times and places, to their state of civilization, and to their character; and this is so, in order that the Word may be more easily received. Thus the Word of the Old Testament, being addressed to the Jews, partakes of the ferocious and implacable character of that people; and that of the New Testament, being destined for nations whose manners were become somewhat softened by reason of the new period upon which they were entering, is stamped with sentiments of benevolence and universal brotherhood. Moreover, I will add that the abrogation of that worship does not affect at all the sanctity of the entire Word of the Old Testament; for the external of the old law which is found to be abrogated by the new law, remains not the less, on that account, the Word of the Lord; inasmuch as that external contains within it celestial and spiritual things which will exist forever.

The institution of the Christian Church was therefore the point of departure of humanity in its ascending period; but this Church, as is clearly announced in the Evangelists and in the Apocalypse, was itself to fall and to be replaced by a New Christian Church, designated by the emblematical name of the New Jerusalem. This great event is being accomplished at the present day without the knowledge of a large majority of Christians.

This new fall, however, at a period announced as an ascending one, seems to imply a contradiction, and must therefore be explained.

When the Lord instituted the first Christian Church, he was obliged to take men just as they were, since he never forces their free-will; now, when he gave the Word of the New Testament, they were corporeal-sensual, as I have said; if he had unfolded to them its internal sense, either they would not have admitted it, or they would have profaned it; and, in either case, they would have rejected the Word, and there would have been no Christian Church. Thus, although this Word was more clear than that of the Old Testament, it must, in order to be received, remain sealed, as well as that of the Old Testament, until the internals contained within them could be comprehended and accepted by men. It is true, that in this manner the Christian Church has fallen into the gravest heresies, and has gradually approached an entire state of devastation; but its existence and its fall have nevertheless been an advance, since the humanity of the present day is found capable of comprehending and of admitting a manifestation of the internals of the Word, or of the celestial and spiritual things contained in it, as is sufficiently proved by the existence of societies of the New Jerusalem in a large part of the kingdoms of Europe, and in North America. Thus, in consequence of the state of things, and of the free-will of which man cannot be deprived, the Lord could only found a Christian Church that must necessarily perish, as He Himself announced, but which was at the same time to conduct Humanity to another church, the crown of the whole edifice, which should exist forever, because it would be able to comprehend and receive celestial and spiritual things.

In support of the assertion, that there would have been no Christian Church, or that it would not have lasted out its time, if the Lord had revealed the internal sense of the Word, I will cite this fundamental truth of the New Church, viz.: that the Lord Jesus Christ is God Himself, and that there is no other God than He. If the Lord had said *openly* to the Jews that He was Jehovah, no one would have believed in His Word, and He would have had no disciples; or even if after His Ascension He had announced *clearly* in the Evangelist that He was Jehovah, His disciples would have made few proselytes, and Christianity would not have been sustained, as is evident from the discussions that have arisen upon the person of Jesus Christ in the Councils, and especially in the Council of Nice, where, in order to save Christianity, and prevent it from falling into Arianism, they were obliged to admit three persons into the Trinity.

It now remains for me to inform you briefly how the celestial and spiritual things contained in the Word of the Old and New Testaments have been revealed to men by the Lord for the establishment of the New Jerusalem, His New Church. The Lord has followed in this, as in all other things, the laws of His Divine Order, from which He never deviates. As He opened the spiritual man of the Prophets, in order to transmit His Word, so He opened the spiritual man of a modest and pious Savant in order to reveal the internal sense of this Word. There is, however, this difference, that the Prophets were blind instruments, inasmuch as they did not comprehend what they announced, or understood only the letter of it, whilst the Revelator of the internal sense of the Word was to be put in a state to comprehend that sense, in order that he might develope it rationally. It is for this reason that the Lord chose a Savant versed in all human sciences, in order that he might show the relations of the sciences with celestial and spiritual things; and it is also for this reason that Swedenborg, before commencing the publication of his writings, was initiated into the knowledge of spiritual things by a daily communication of many years with spirits and angels.

Accept, &c.

LETTER III.

In my last letter I gave you an historical exposé, so to speak, of the Word, by showing you first the Word in its principle; then, the Word engraven interiorly in the depth of the heart of the men of the Most Ancient Church; afterwards, the Word given to the men of the Ancient Church, in a compilation written according to the correspondences between natural things and spiritual things; and finally, a new Word written also according to these correspondences, viz.: our Bible containing the Old and New Testament; and you have seen that in these various phases, the Word [*La Parole*] has never ceased to be the Word [*Le Verbe*] or Divine Wisdom. Now, to neglect no means of confirming in you this important truth, I am going to attempt to complete this expose by some considerations drawn from analogy.

Man having been created in the image of God, everything that exists in him, so far as he remains in the order of his creation, must be the image of something that exists in God; thus, there must be a kind of analogy between the Word of man and the Word of God. Let us see, then, if this analogy confirms what has been said of the Word of God.

We have said that the Word in its principle, or first cause, created the Universe, that is, everything that God has made. Is the case similar in regard to the Word of man relatively to everything that man makes?

By the Word creating the universe, we have understood the Divine Wisdom or understanding of God, acting from the Divine Love or from the Will of God. With man the word analagous to the Word is therefore the understanding acting from the will, or, what is the same thing, the thought acting from the affection. Now, it is very evident that everything that man does is done by his thought from his affection; every work of man is therefore done by his word. Thus considered, the word of man is not merely what he expresses, whether by sounds and articulations, or by the expression of the countenance and by gestures, but also everything that is produced by him; so that this word of man is man himself, as the Word is God Himself, for the will and thought are man, as Love itself and Wisdom itself are God.

We have said that with the men of the Most Ancient Church this Word was engraven upon the bottom of the heart. Is there anything in this analogous to the word of man, or, in other terms, to what man says and does?

The analogy was complete in relation to the men of the Most Ancient Church who remained in the order of creation, and it would likewise be complete in reference to the man of the present day, should he live conformably to the laws of order; for then, whatever he should say and do, would be the expression of his thought which is at the bottom of his heart; but if, when man remains in the order of his creation, everything that exists in him is the image of something that exists in God, it is no longer so when he has perverted this order; whatever arises from the abuse of some one of his faculties is still, it is true, in relation with something that exists in God, but it is no longer as an image, it is as something opposite or contrary. Hence it happens that, at the present day, all that man says and does is not always the expression of his thought which is at the bottom of his heart.

As to the two written Words, namely, that of the Ancient Church and our Bible, there is also an analogy between them and the written word of man; but as the Word of the Ancient Church and the Bible were written according to the same principles, we shall speak only of the Bible.

We have said that the Bible or written Word is also the Divine Wisdom or Word [*Le Verbe*], and, consequently, God Himself. In regard to man, in the acceptation in which we have taken the word, there is a written word, when what he says is fixed by writing or by printing, and also when what he does is a work that has tangible existence, as, for example, a painting, a statue, a monument. Now, it is very evident that the man is found in this book or in this work, such as he was himself when he composed it or when he made it; that is to say, with the thought proceeding from the affection which he then had. Thus they say of a sincere author, that he is entirely in his writings; the painter is also in his pictures; the sculptor in his statues, the architect in his monuments, although each of these preserves his own personality separate from his works.

Is not the case similar with God? God is entirely in the Bible, that is to say, in his Divine Word, which becomes fixed by means of printing, since this Divine Word is the Divine Thought or Divine Wisdom proceeding from the Divine Affection or Divine Love; but he is in it as a sincere author is in his writings. Thus, although wholly in each copy of the Bible to him who seeks Him there with love and faith, God nevertheless preserves His Divine Personality without or separate from the entire universe which is his work, as an author preserves his own personality without or separate from his writings.

Let us still continue the analogy. Although the author of a book written with candor and sincerity is wholly in that book, he does not manifest himself in the same manner to all those who read it, or, rather, all his readers do not see him there in the same manner. The majority, far from seeking to see him there, do not even think of him while reading; others see him only superficially; some, on the contrary, endeavoring to seek him in each phrase, and even in each expression, succeed from day to day in knowing him better.

Is it not so with God in relation to the readers of the Bible? Those who do not seek God in the Bible, or who read it without thinking of God, cannot see him in it; those who desire to have no other knowledges of God than those which they have received by tradition, see him in it only superficially; those, on the contrary, who desire to have a more exact knowledge of God, with the intention of learning how to live a better life, see God in each phrase, and even in each expression of this Holy Book.

These considerations upon the analogy between the word of man and the Word of God, lead me to speak also of the difference that exists between the books of men and the Bible.

The book of man contains only that kind of truth that exists in the spirit of the author; but the Books of which the Bible is composed, having been written according to correspondences between natural and spiritual things, in order that they might be comprehended in this world by men, and at the same time in the other by spirits and angels, contain every kind of truth, from that which is adapted to the most imperfectly developed human understanding, to that which is suited to the most elevated angelic intelligence.

When you look at a work of man, whether a painting or a statue, after having seen the surface of it, you have seen all of it. It is not so with the works of God; whatever may be the exterior beauties of these works, dissection and the microscope would reveal to you interior beauties still more wonderful; and the *savant* who has pushed his researches to the last limits of science, still continues convinced that what he has discovered is very far below what remains unknown to him. Every one knows, it is true, that there is an immense difference between the works of God and the works of man; but a great number, regarding the Bible as only a human composition of great antiquity, it would be necessary, in order to lead them to consider it as a work of God, to prove to them that there is between it and an ordinary book the same difference as between the works of God and the works of man. Now, from what has just been said, you see that the difference between the works of God and the works of man consists principally in this, that the works of God, from the lowest degree on the scale of beings to the highest, have an interior organization beyond what appears in their exterior form. It is important, therefore, to prove that the Bible has also an interior organization, which does not appear in its exterior form, or in its letter; and that, like all the other works of God, although infinitely superior, since it is It which, in its quality of Word, has created all, it presents to the scalpel and the microscope of illustrated human intelligence interior beau ties, which become so much more wonderful as one penetrates deeply into it. This interior organization, which the Lord has Himself signalized, by saying that His words are Spirit and Life, is the internal sense enveloped in the external or literal sense of the Bible.

Farther on, when we shall together penetrate into the internal sense, you will acquire the entire conviction that this sense contains marvels more and more wonderful, and that thus the Bible, according to the expression itself of the Lord, is Spirit and Life.

Yet one observation before terminating this general exposé. From the fact that the Bible, as the Word of God, is God Himself manifesting his Divine Love by his Divine Wisdom, it follows that it contains the Infinite, and that, consequently, it is inexhaustible and impenetrable as to its inmost; inexhaustible, inasmuch as man and angel will be able continually and forever to draw new knowledges from this Divine Source without its ever being drained; impenetrable as to its inmost, inasmuch as man and angel will never be able to know all that it contains; but although impenetrable as to its inmost, it is not for that less adapted to all the spiritual and celestial wants of men and angels, by means of its spiritual and celestial senses which are successively accessible. It is even because that the Word is inexhaustible and impenetrable as to its inmost, that man can enjoy, as well as angels, a happiness which will continually increase during all eternity. In fact, angels as well as men live only by their affections and thoughts; now, whatever is the degree of love and of wisdom to which an angel has arrived, he will always be able to draw from the Word affections more and more filled with love, and thoughts more and more profound, without however ever being able to penetrate as far as the inmost. Suppose, on the contrary, the angel a perfect being in the strict acceptation of the word, having no more new affections or new thoughts to acquire, because that he would be in possession of all; what would become of his life? Would it be really living to be in view of eternity and without hope of ever obtaining any new affection or new thought? Would it not rather be only a state of *ennui*, produced by satiety, which would be entirely insupportable? I conceive that God is perfect, because that God is constantly delighted in his work, upon which he acts unceasingly in order that it may become more and more his image; but I cannot conceive of a single creature being perfect, because that then that creature would be God, and there can be only one God.

Such, my dear sir, is the Divine Word, the inexhaustible source of Love and Wisdom, the inestimable treasury from whence men can in this world, and will be able hereafter, in the future life, eternally to draw good affections and pure thoughts; and yet the Book that contains it is misunderstood by a majority of Christians; for the largest number among these have the greatest indifference for the Bible, others despise it, and those who have any respect for it, explain it in a manner so opposed to the Justice of God, that their commentaries often prevent the Divine Wisdom from being discovered in it.

We will soon study this Divine Book together according to your desire; and then the truths in it which have been adapted to the human understanding will become successively developed before your eyes, if you persevere, as I hope you will, in seeking them with love, that is with the firm desire of applying them to your life, in order to become a new man. But in order that this study of the Bible may become more easy for you, I must still remove certain prejudices, and cause certain obstacles to disappear which would retard our progress.

PREJUDICES.—There are particularly two prejudices, which it is important for me to remove immediately, because that Philosophy, having seized upon them as argument with which to combat the Bible, they may have left upon your mind a somewhat unfavorable impression.

FIRST PREJUDICE.—*The Jews considered as the People of God.*

The Theology of the Old Church, founding itself upon the letter of the Word without seeking the spirit of it, has diffused through all Christendom this false idea, that the Jews, before the coming of the Lord, were the only people of God, all the other nations of the earth having been rejected; in like manner, it also pretends, supporting itself by the letter of the New Testament, that, since the establishment of Christianity, Christians only can be saved.

Instead of combating this false idea, Philosophy has seized upon it as a pretext to attack the God of the Jews, supporting itself upon such attributes of the Divinity as no one can dispute; as for example, upon the Justice and Goodness of God. There is no one, in fact, who can dispute the first of these attributes; and whatever difference there may be between Divine Justice and human justice, it is always the case that true human justice is a reflection of Divine Justice, and that, consequently, that which is generally regarded as unjust by men, cannot belong to Divine Justice. Neither can any one dispute the second attribute; and notwithstanding the difference that exists between the goodness or love of God towards men, and the goodness or love of a father for his children, it is not less true that paternal goodness is a reflection of Divine goodness, and thus that that which is generally regarded as opposed to paternal goodness, can in no wise belong to the Divine goodness. Now, would not the father of a numerous family be generally considered as unjust and devoid of a goodness really paternal, if he should love and cherish for his heir only one of his children, to the exclusion of all the others; or, if all his children being obnoxious to him, he should save only one of them and condemn all the others to destruction? As this is incontestible, Philosophy concludes that God being Justice itself, and Goodness itself, the God of the Bible was not the true God, since he had condemned *en masse* all the nations of the earth to an eternal damnation, and had taken care only of the Jewish nation, which was as ferocious and as barbarous as other nations, and which even surpassed them often in the refinement of cruelty.

Philosophy was therefore combating the Bible, not indeed with the Bible, as it pretended, but with the false ideas disseminated by Theology; and the latter, far from seeking to rectify these ideas, intrenched itself behind the antiquity of the Bible and the respect with which it had been invested; or when it was necessary to answer reproaches made against the Jewish nation and its principal personages, it considered itself obliged to resort to all possible means for extenuating their actions, even though they were most clearly opposed to all the principles of justice, of morality, or of humanity. Thus, Theology, instead of again seizing the advantage over its adversary, furnished him by these very means, with new weapons against itself.

But the true Theology, which was given by the Lord in the writings of Swedenborg, could have nothing to fear from a contest with Philosophy, for this Theology is founded upon the principle that God is Love Itself, Justice Itself, and Mercy Itself; and none of its doctrines, as you will presently see, is contradictory to these Divine Attributes, which Philosophy cannot dispute. Thus the weapons which Philosophy used with so much success in the last century, and at the commencement of the present, would now be attended with no danger, since the true Theology explains in a most satisfactory manner, what is to be understood in the Bible by the People of God.

If the descendants of Jacob have been called the People of God, it is because they had been chosen to be a representative of the Church; and you have seen in my last letter, that if the Jews have been chosen rather than any other nation, it is not because they had been less corrupt. Now, as it is a general law of representation, that the thought is not occupied with the person or thing which represents, but that everything has relation to the thing represented, and that thus it matters little who or what the person is who represents, it follows that the

Jewish nation, however abominable it might be, was, in the sense of the letter, necessarily called the People of God, since it represented the Church of the Lord, which is composed of all those who acknowledge one God and live in good, whatever be their external mode of worship; and that Jewish personages were, also, in certain circumstances, necessarily called the elect of God, however blameable had been their conduct in other respects.

Far from seeking to extenuate the base and atrocious actions committed by the Jewish people, and by their principal personages, the true Theology leaves them in all their weight, just as they are related in the Bible: it by no means considers the Jews as the People of God in the sense of a privileged people, nor any of their chiefs, pontiffs, kings, or prophets, as the elect of God in the common acceptation of that word; for this would be to do injury to God, in whose view all men are equal; it is the life alone that makes a difference between men; thus, to appreciate the character of any one, we must consider his life, and not the function with which he is charged. Farther on, I shall often have occasion to speak to you of the Jewish nation, and to show it to you under its true aspect; it will be sufficient for the present to refer you to No. 433 of the Apocalypse Explained, where you will find interesting details upon the origin of the Jews, upon their character, and upon their faith.

SECOND PREJUDICE.—*The Pentateuch considered as the source whence all the nations of antiquity have derived their religious ideas.*

The old Theology founding itself upon this true principle, that without Revelation man could have known no spiritual truth, has hence concluded, and still pretends, that all the nations of antiquity have derived from the books of the Jews all their religious ideas which have any affinity with those that are contained in the Pentateuch.

Such a pretension had nothing in it very prejudicial to the

Bible, so long as Philosophy dared not enter into open contro versy; but it became very injurious from the commencement of that controversy, and especially since the theogonies and chronologies of ancient nations have been studied with more care; for it is no longer merely Philosophy that combats this pretension, it is science also, supported by all modern discoveries. In face of so many proofs, which at the present day attest the high antiquity of the nations of the East, in face of so many vestiges which prove the existence of a civilization far anterior to our historical times, how can any one dare still to pretend, that all the nations of the earth have drawn their religious notions from the books of the Jews, the most ancient of which do not go back, at farthest, more than three thousand and four or five hundred years? Is this not acting against the Bible, rather than in its defence?

The arguments which Dupuis has accumulated in his *Origin of all kinds of Worship*, are overwhelming against the old Theology; but what can they avail against the Bible and against the true Theology? Nothing; absolutely nothing. If Dupuis proves incontestably that the Orientals have borrowed nothing from a miserable people that lived in a retired corner of Asia, this proof is overwhelming only to the old Theology, which maintains the contrary; but it is without any force against the Bible, when the Bible is separated from its unwise defenders; it is also without any force against the true Theology, since the latter acknowledges that the Orientals have borrowed nothing from the Mosaic Word.

What is peculiar in this contest, is the fact that Philosophy and Theology are both in error; for Philosophy retorting against its adversary, maintains that the Jews have invented nothing and have copied everything; or, in other words, that the Pentateuch has been drawn from the theogonies of the Orientals.

Upon this point, as upon almost all others, it is only in the writings of Swedenborg that the truth can be found. You have seen by my last letter, that, anterior to the Word given to the descendants of Jacob, there had been in the Ancient Church a written Word; and that this Ancient Church, far from being confined to a small colony, extended over the largest part of the globe, and flourished principally in Syria, the Land of Canaan, Mesopotamia, Arabia, Chaldea, Assyria, Egypt, Nineveh, Tyre and Sidon. Now, Theologians of the old church cannot deny the existence of this Ancient Word, since the Bible contains some fragments of it, and gives us even the names of the two parts of which it was composed; and on the opposite side, philosophers and savants, who carry back the theogonies of the Orientals and of other ancient nations to an epoch anterior to Moses, when there existed upon our globe an advanced civilization, the vestiges of which they are collecting with avidity, have, consequently, no motive for denying the existence of this ancient Church. Now, therefore, difficulties vanish; if the ancient theogonies have all points of resemblance between them and our Bible, it is because they are all derived from the same source, the written Word of the Ancient Church; and if they differ, it is because this church having fallen, the science of correspondences, the only key of that Word, has been lost, and their worship having become idolatrous, each nation made for itself a particular theogony, founded however upon the original types of which they had no longer any knowledge. Thus all the systems of cosmogony and of worship of ancient times, were only adulterations more or less gross of the ante-Mosaic Word.

This explanation, as you see, leaves untouched the principle, that without revelation, man could have known no spiritual truth: and at the same time it protects the Bible against all attack, so far as it concerns the points of resemblance that it has with the theogonies of the ancient nations, for these points of resemblance arise from the fact, that the first seven chapters of

Genesis constituted a part of the Word of the Ancient Church, and have been extracted from it.

OBSTACLES.—These consist of a great number of charges and objections. For the present I shall examine only the three following points, which contain the most serious charges and objections.

I. *Jehovah in the Bible gives himself up to vengeance, anger, and other human passions.* This charge, which the old Theology is unable to answer, remains without force and falls to the ground as soon as it is known that the Word, being Written according to correspondences between spiritual and natural things, is expressed according to appearances and the fallacies of the senses. "Jehovah-God, or the Lord," says Swedenborg, "never curses any one, he is never angry with any one, he never leads any into temptation; he punishes none, much less does he curse any. Such things can never proceed from the source of mercy, of peace and goodness. If it is said in the Word that Jehovah-God not only turns away his face, is angry, punishes, tempts, but also that he kills, and even curses, it is in order that men may believe that the Lord governs and disposes all things in general and in particular, even evil itself, punishments and temptations; and after this most general idea has been received, that they may learn how he governs and disposes all things, and that he turns the evil of punishment and of temptation into good; it is from things most general that the order of teaching and of learning in the Word commences; hence the literal sense abounds in such most general things." A. C. n. 245. He further adds, "All these expressions have been used, in order that persuasions and lusts might not be broken, but bent; for to speak otherwise than according to man's comprehension,—and he comprehends only according to appearances, fallacies and persuasions, would have been to sow seed in the waters, and to say things that would be instantly rejected." A. C. n. 1874. Jehovah has therefore presented himself in this manner in the Bible, because of the barbarity and ferocity of the descendants of Jacob, who could not have conceived of God otherwise. But if God does not punish, who is it that punishes ? The true Theology replies: Evil itself punishes itself; that is, the wicked plunge themselves into the pain that corresponds to the evil that they have committed.

II. *Facts and expressions that offend against morality.* One of the gravest charges which Philosophy makes against the Bible, is that it presents pictures of manners which could be tolerated only in an uninspired book.

The best answer given by the old Theology is this; that every thing is impure to him whose heart is impure, but that every thing is pure to him whose heart is pure. This is very true, and it is for this reason that there is no danger in putting the Bible into the hands of a person of a pure heart. But as this answer is far from satisfying philosophers, since it gives no indication why such pictures are found in the Bible, I am going to present you with the additions which true Theology has made to it.

The Bible gives us, it is true, the history of the Jewish nation, but that which constitutes the principal subject of the Bible, since it is the Word of God, is not properly the history of the Jewish nation, it is the relation of certain historical facts, which by their correspondence, represent the spiritual states which the Lord wished to present in his Word. In fact, of what consequence to all the nations of the earth, and to all future ages could be a history of this little people written like that of other nations ? Not any, assuredly; but the case is not so in regard to the historical facts which the Bible contains concerning the Jewish people, they are of very great importance to us; and that, because they have been transmitted as representatives, and have been expressed by words, all of which, even to the least iota, are significative; for it is this only that imprints upon any written composition the character of the Word of God. Thus, when the history of a patriarch, of a judge, of a king, or of any other personage is treated of, there are given of his entire life only those facts, whether general or particular, which are adapted to represent in a series, the spiritual states which God thus enveloped in a literal sense, in order to fix them so that they might serve for a communication of the spiritual world with the natural world; whereas, in relation to all other facts, no mention is made of them; and this explains the reason why there appear to be gaps in the Bible, when it is considered merely as a history of the Jews.

If we now inquire what the facts are that were to be more particularly collected together in the Bible, we shall see that they are precisely those whose relation most offends the ears of our philosophers. In fact, the Word in its internal sense treats only of the Lord, of the church, and of men considered as a church; in every part of it the celestial marriage is treated of, that is, the marriage of the Lord with the church, which is the marriage of good with truth; and in the opposite sense, the infernal marriage, which is the marriage of evil with the false. Thus whenever the church was to be treated of as in evil and the false, and consequently perverted, this state was to be represented, and was represented in the historical books, by whatever constitutes the infernal marriage, that is, by facts of adultery, of prostitution, and even of incest, and in the prophetical books by expressions which describe infamous acts of debauchery.

III. *Indifferent assertions quite unworthy of the attention of God; contradictions in historical circumstances; contradictory propositions.* These objections which the old Theology has been entirely unable to remove, you may easily render void by means of the knowledge which you now have of the Bible.

You know that the Bible was written according to correspondences that exist between spiritual things and natural things; you know that its end is the regeneration of man by means of the knowledge of important truths of the spiritual sense; you know, in fine, that the literal sense was destined to serve as an envelope to this spiritual sense, and not to perfect man in natural knowledge. Thus when you find in the Bible passages which seem to relate exclusively to things that are indifferent and unworthy of the attention of God, you will be convinced that there are concealed other things much more interesting. When you shall find any contradiction in historical circumstances, you will come to the conclusion that it was necessary for the letter to bend in some respects under the weight of important matters that are contained in its interiors, and that, to express these more fully, some slight deviation must necessarily be made in the literal narrative; for every composition should be judged according as it is appropriate to the end of the author, and in the Bible God's end was the spiritual rather than the natural. Finally, when you meet with two contradictory propositions, such as the following: "*God repents*,"—Gen. vi. 6,—and "*God does not repent*," Numb. xx. 19—how can the two assertions be true in the same sense, and yet as they must be true *in a certain sense*, since they are both in the Bible, you will conclude that one is a truth entirely naked, and that the other is covered under the veil of a simple appearance formed in human ideas; thus that one is a *real* truth in connection with the spiritual sense, and the other an *apparent* truth, which, to become real, must be rectified by the spiritual sense.

I shall terminate my letter by this question which has been often put to me.

Since the true theology has nothing to fear from philosophy, why did not the Lord make it known sooner, in order to enlighten men, and prevent his Word from being outraged?

I shall first remark that the principles upon which this theology is founded are not new, and they are all plainly expressed in the literal sense of the Bible, although not united in a body; but I must add, that as soon as the Apostolic Doctrine, which renders faith subordinate to charity, had begun to be no longer regarded as the sole and only doctrine, Christianity became a prey to heresies, which multiplied to infinity; that hence sects arose; that each sect always found in the Bible certain passages to support its own doctrine, and that then it regarded these passages as the summary of the law, and passed over all those that could not be made to agree with their doctrine; that each sect thus made for itself a doctrine of its own, and was no longer able to see the principles of the true theology in the Bible, although these principles were nevertheless expressed there in very explicit terms. Hence, it is evident that Christians can have no occasion to complain of having been left in the dark, since they have always had at their disposal true spiritual principles; if they saw them not, or rather if they would not see them, it is because that love of self and of the world reigned in them; but the simple of heart, who lived conformably to the precepts of the Decalogue, have always seen them, in spite of the theological errors that had been inculcated upon them.

In regard to the true Theology itself, that is, as developed in a doctrinal body, and given by the Lord in the writings of Swedenborg, it could not have been presented sooner to mankind; if that had been possible, the Lord, who is Love Itself and Mercy Itself, would not have waited so long before making it known; but the impossibility existed, because the Lord, conformably to the laws of Divine Order, never forces any one, and, consequently, this doctrine could not have been received by any person. In fact, before Philosophy had attacked Theology with so much vigor, the latter was ruling with absolute sovereignty both in Catholicism and in Protestantism; woe to him who then dared to attack it, for it had recourse even to secular force, and the fagot was kindled. How can it be supposed that from that time it would have received, or permitted to be received, a doctrine which clearly shows that all the dogmas of Christianity have been falsified? Would it not rather have stifled it from its very first appearance? In order that the New Doctrine might be able to be brought to light, without being immediately annihilated, it was necessary that a breach should first be made upon the old Theology itself by Philosophy, and that it should thus lose a great part of the ascendancy which it had taken both over governments and people. Besides, that which clearly proves that the New Doctrine, if it had been given before, would have been received by no one, is the fact that at its appearance it was adopted by but a very small number of men; and although Swedenborg had sent gratuitously the works containing it to prelates of various Christian denominations, to Universities and to the principal public libraries, the theology which might have drawn thence arguments against its adversary, proudly disdained that anchor of safety which the Lord offered it; and after the example of the synagogue, it preferred darkness to light.

The Lord therefore could not have prevented his Divine Word from being outraged. Yet you are not to suppose that the greatest outrages that the Word of the Lord has had to bear, have proceeded from Philosophy; the scoffs that Philosophy hurled against the Bible, the sarcasms that it lavished upon it, the contempt with which it regarded it, all this was but little, compared with the outrages which it received on the part of Theology. Philosophy, it is true, attacked the Bible with fury, but it did not profane it, because it did not acknowledge it as the Word of God; and besides, in its blindness it had some correct notions of God, for it represented him as just, good, and loving all men, and it was indignant at the bare idea, that the evil passions of man should be attributed to Him. Theology, on the contrary, acknowledged the Bible as the Word of God, and yet ceased not to commit outrages against It, blaspheming It, even when it appeared to defend it with the most favor. And, in fact, is there a greater outrage against God, than to attribute to Him the worst of human passions, partiality, injustice, jealousy, vengeance and cruelty? Are not these passions so entirely in opposition to the attributes of Divinity, tacitly comprised in the dogmas of the old Theology ? These are the greatest blasphemies against God, and it is by dogmas thus falsified that the Divine Word is most basely outraged.

This is, moreover, confirmed by facts which transpired at the time of the first coming of the Lord. There were then in Judea many sects; that of the Pharisees, which was the principal, had acquired a reputation for its rigidity; it had added to the Law oral tradition, and thus had made itself the interpleader of the Law, which procured it much veneration. The sect of the Pharisees taught the resurrection, whilst that of the Sadducees denied it; well, it was not the Sadducees whom the Lord blames most, for when they came scoffingly to ask Him a question, He merely told them that they erred,—Matth. xxii.;—but He acted quite differently towards the Pharisees, those rigid observers of tradition and the law as interpreted by them; He treated them with the greatest rigor, He called them hypocrites, fools, blind, whitened sepulchres, serpents, a generation of vipers,—Matth. xxiii. In the relation of the Passion of the Lord, the Evangelists say nothing of the Sadducees, but they show us that the High-Priests and the Scribes were all set against Him; and it is even said in Matthew, that the Pharisees called him an impostor,—xxvii. 62, 63. The greatest enemies of the Lord, therefore, whilst He lived in the world, were not the Philosophers or Sadducees, but the High-Priests, Scribes and Pharisees; these are they who crucified Him; Him the incarnate Word, the Divine Word; and as similar things always take place at the end of each church, this same Word has received again like outrages on the part of the Pharisees of Christianity.

From these facts, which show so clearly that the Sadducees were less culpable than the Pharisees, it seems well established, that modern Philosophy has also been less culpable than Theology; and even at the present time, it is not so much Philosophy as the old Theology that will place itself in opposition to the establishment of the New Church, which the Lord is now instituting. Philosophy dreads the spiritual principle, only because it always has in view the horrors that have been committed for more than three thousand years in the name of that principle; it is not surprising, therefore, that it manifests much reserve and even distrust; but it will not always be hostile, and it will surrender itself to evidence. The old Theology, on the contrary, always thinks of the power which it formerly had; it mourns over its loss, and despairs not of again coming in possession of it, at least in part; it will, consequently, make constant efforts to extinguish the spiritual light of the New Church. Moreover, true Theology is not incompatible with true Philosophy; Philosophy, therefore, has no occasion for fearing destruction; it will only be modified, and will preserve its distinguished rank, but as a subordinate, and without pretending to occupy the first place. False Theology, on the contrary, cannot exist in concurrence with true Theology, the triumph of the latter will be the annihilation of the former.

Accept, &c.

THE END.

www.ingramcontent.com/pod-product-compliance
Lightning Source LLC
LaVergne TN
LVHW010244110826
845151LV00004B/1382

* 9 7 8 1 4 2 5 5 2 3 7 1 8 *